Acknowledgments

For years I have been telling stories about events in my life to friends and acquaintances and they often say “You should write a book.” So I did. I don’t much care for computers but I didn’t see how I could do it easily without one so I have been dragged kicking and screaming into the computer age. Perhaps the best way to put together your autobiography is to isolate yourself from all distractions. I spent the entire summer of ‘99 doing just that. If it had not been for my logbook I wouldn’t have been able to recall some of the events and date them. As it is I have only put in a small part of my experiences.

The author wishes to acknowledge the many people I have worked with over the years and the friends whose contributions helped to enrich this book. Since I was an only child (the Bock boys were as close to brothers as I ever had) and I didn’t have any siblings to draw information from, their reflections and perspectives were invaluable in helping me to recall events. Among them my cousins; Herb Bock, Bob Bock, Tom Bock, Robert Pope, and Madelaine Bader. Other help included

Paul Meyers, Conrad (Tiz) Lesh, Phil Calvert, Velma Harmon, Mary Danielli, Bill Smith, Rick Huff, and of course our children. Rey and Gloria Nelson were invaluable in designing and printing the dust cover. Betty was a tremendous help both recalling events and editing. The assistance Chuck Arnold gave me in the early days of my introduction to the computer was essential. The Plymouth Library, the Marshall County Historical Society, and the City office were also helpful.

The reason for writing "Palbykin" was to document and catalog events, dates, and pictures of the family and to help future generations understand how we lived and why we lived as we did. Betty's family has several family books, the Kimball family, the Sims family and the Perry families are the latest.

This book is in my words, which are not always the best phraseology because that's just the way I speak. I agonized for some time about the name for the book. Over my lifetime I have been called "The Hubcap," "Nature Boy," "Airpower," "The Judge," "The Don," "Nikyblap" (Palbykin spelled backwards) and some names that are not printable. For the most part everybody just seems to call me "Palbykin." I notice magazine articles and newspaper accounts just say "Palbykin" so I gave up on some of the more catchy titles.

Writing this book has been very enjoyable. Reminiscing about times gone by and events Betty and I have experienced have added to the nostalgia. Many thanks to the town of Plymouth, for providing the wonderful environment in which we raised our children. Betty and I expect to spend eternity here and have already put up our tombstone in the New Oak Hill Cemetery near other family members.

PALBYKIN

My Life As A Don

An Autobiography by

Donald J. Palbykin

PALBYKIN: an autobiography

Published by Pal Publishing Inc.

For information address:

Pal Publishing Inc.
310 N. Michigan St.
Plymouth, IN 46563

ISBN 0-9679577-1-0

PRINTED IN THE UNITED STATES OF AMERICA

To my wife Betty, the best co-pilot in the world.
And to my children,
Stephen, Alan, Martin, Julie,
Debra, Susan, Ann Marie,
"the best crew ever"
and to the Man in
the control tower
who guided
my life.

Contents

Foreword

It has been said that the true measure of happiness and contentment with one's life is directly proportionate to how close a person comes to achieving his maximum potential. Given the obstacles along the way if, as one approaches the shadows of the twilight of his life, he can reflect back with some sense of accomplishment upon the journey from its beginnings to the present day, he can be truly content with his efforts and achievements along the way; better still, if the journey was at least partially traversed outside the bounds and shackles of a routine life.

Piloting an aircraft as a career is the childhood dream of many young people; for most of them that dream must fade and die before the demands and realities of practical everyday life. The rewards of flying are largely esoteric; the awe of viewing the world from a lofty perspective; the escape, however temporary, from the cares and travails of everyday routine; the glorious spectacles of nature and the sheer joy of being able to "do a hundred things you have not dreamed of." In a practical sense, however, it is a career demanding much more time and patience and effort than a person could possibly be adequately compensated for, especially at the entry level; that level might last for many years.

The work which follows is not so much autobiographical as it is a narrative by a person who pursued his dream from entry level to managing and owning an aviation business and on to his own business success beyond aviation; this despite the early economic reality of having to provide for a large and growing family, and with no really clear-cut assurance of eventual success. Success came at all levels because of a total commitment to the work ethic, an unquenchable desire to learn and to advance and an enthusiastic approach to completing the tasks confronting him. These qualities, plus opportunity, spell "success" for anyone; some people call it "luck." The only "luck" involved was the incredibly good fortune in persuading Betty to share his life as wife, partner and helpmate. I suspect that she was instrumental in riding out the sparse times, in keeping faith that the future would be bright and promising and in instilling in their children the idea and the desire to learn, to work hard and to excel. The success of these children in their own lives is testimony to the quality of the parents and, for the parents, the ultimate confirmation of life objectives achieved.

This is a well deserved tribute to Don from a person who knew nothing of him prior to those entry-level days, but who admired and remembered the qualities, the effort and the attitude he brought to his everyday assignments. I am gratified that I was able, in a small way, early in his career, to help him "slip the surly bonds of earth."

Conrad "Tiz" Lesh

Red Lights

It was early on a clear March 27th morning in 1970 that I shaved, showered and dressed as quickly and quietly as possible so as not to wake my wife and family. I called the Weather Bureau at South Bend to check the weather for a trip to Nassau in the Bahamas. The weather was fine. I picked up some rolls and coffee for our VIP treatment of our best charter customers, drove to the Plymouth Municipal Airport less than a half a mile from my home and opened the office at Skystream with its white limestone face against the blue steel of the main hangar. My co-pilot John Eiff, a young pilot that had just recently gone to work for us arrived and we opened the huge hangar door, hooked up the tug, and pulled the gleaming white Lear jet from the hangar to the fueling facility.

After carefully topping off the tanks and doing a thorough pre-flight check we boarded, sealed the door, started the engine and initiated taxiing to the east end of the field for take off. We use only one engine for taxiing because a Lear Jet uses as much fuel taxiing as cruising at altitude. After the pre-flight checklist was completed, I pushed the thrust levers forward and we accelerated to take-off speed. I eased the wheel back and the Lear jet took off like a "homesick angel."

We only had to go about fifteen miles for our pickup so I quickly reduced the power and started our descent. After an uneventful landing, we taxied to the terminal and picked up Mr. Burton of Burton Plumbing and Heating. He was ready and eager to go. We could see why when we saw his home in Nassau.

In a very short time we took off for Nassau after receiving clearance from the Chicago center. We climbed direct to 41,000 feet. At that time in the history of aviation we were able to get clearances for such a climb because there was very little traffic at our altitude and even the jet airlines operated at a much lower altitude. The Lear jet flies above the weather actually in the stratosphere most of the time. Which is a big advantage because of lower fuel consumption. On this beautiful morning we could clearly see the curve of the earth with all of the clouds below us as we sipped our hot coffee and enjoyed the delicious rolls in the plush interior with perfect comfort. In those days there was always the threat of bombs or terrorists on the airlines. I always use to say to our customers that the nice thing about your own airplane or a charter aircraft is that if you didn't want a bomb or a terrorist you just didn't bring them along.

Within a short time we could see the ocean on our left and quickly passed over Jacksonville, Daytona Beach, Palm Beach, Miami and on down the peninsula of Florida. Everything was laid out so beautifully below us because at 41,000 feet everything looks really neat and orderly.

We started our descent well before leaving the tip of Florida since you could easily use more than 100 miles to get down to an approach altitude. Very soon we were landing at Nassau with its gorgeous beaches and coral lagoons as well as softly waving palm trees. Nassau has some of the bluest clear water anywhere in the world. So clear that you might feel that it was only a couple of feet deep when you may very well be in 50 feet or more of water. My logbook shows two hours and fifty-five minutes for the entire trip including the pickup.

Upon landing Mr. Burton asked us if we would like to come to his home and have brunch, and we eagerly accepted. When we arrived he was surprised to find that the cook and servants were gone. He personally prepared a meal for us in the commercial kitchen, all stainless steel and businesslike. Not at all the kind of kitchen you have in an ordinary house. We ate at a huge dining room table, approximately twenty-five feet long, and after the meal we were shown the rest of the spacious home. Each bedroom was a suite with private bath and many had terraces. We thanked the host for his hospitality and departed for the airport.

Upon arriving at the airport we realized that we would have quite a wait for fuel since there were several planes ahead of us. In those days buying fuel out of the USA required a special credit card called a Carnet card, which I had. It also required quite a lot of paperwork and time-consuming checks. We elected to go with the fuel we had since we had a very short flight to the tip of Florida and I knew that we could fuel in Miami when we went through customs without the hassle. After all it was just a short hop across the ocean to the tip of Florida, and we could go through customs at either Miami or Palm Beach.

After going through the pre-flight checklist, we contacted Nassau Tower for taxi clearance and taxied out on one engine. We were held on the ground for a considerable length of time behind several aircraft. Essex Wire out of Fort Wayne, Indiana, in a large business jet was ahead of us. As I said, every minute that we were held on the ground was one minute that we would not be able to fly. We were finally given clearance for take off. We started the run and with such a light aircraft it fairly leaped into the air. I turned on the igniters since I knew we would have a very steep departure and the possibility of a fuel void which could cause a flameout. We had no problem other than a slight buck and all went well.

Upon leveling off at approximately 20,000 feet we observed our DME (Distance Measuring Equipment) was showing that we were heading into a terrific head wind which slowed the ground speed considerably. Since it would take a lot more fuel to climb to a higher altitude where we could make it out of the headwind and save some fuel we decided that we would continue on as we were because we would probably use too much fuel climbing. We called Miami and found out that they were experiencing thunderstorm activity and we could expect a holding pattern while awaiting clearance to land.

Eerily the "Red lights" on the fuel indicators glowed brightly indicating that both tanks were extremely low. We found ourselves over the Devil's Triangle, where many aircraft have disappeared under unexplained circumstances. I called Palm Beach approach and found they too were experiencing thunderstorms but they were still making approaches in spite of the storm. They were giving sequences for approaches which meant some delay but we had to go on anyway because we had no alternative at that time. Realizing we were going to be extremely low on fuel I elected to pump all of the fuel over into the left wing and shut down the right engine. Now we had a single engine jet. It's better to have a single engine jet with enough fuel to feed one engine than to have a glider. At that point I was thinking, what a way to spend a beautiful Sunday morning. "Red lights" on over the Devil's Triangle with one engine shut down, low fuel, and thunderstorms at our destination. After sweating it out for a while we were given clearance to descend and to start our approach. You haven't lived until you have dived into thunderstorm activity even with the radar to help you around the largest cells. The roughness of the flight throws everything around inside the cockpit that is not fastened down. Even handling the radios and the pre-landing checklist was more of a chore. It was a rough approach and we gave a big sigh of relief when we saw the runway strobe lights at the threshold of the runway. As required we taxied to the customs office since we came into the country from outside the U.S.

I was embarrassed at the low fuel and when we called for the fueling trucks to come over, we elected not to fill it all of the way up because we didn't want anybody to know how low we really were. We probably didn't have enough fuel to go around for another approach. As we say in the flying business "one thing won't necessarily get you" it takes a series of mistakes. My first mistake was not fueling, that's obvious. My second mistake was not checking the weather. But since we had flown over just a few hours earlier and everything was clear. I assumed (never assume) that everything was fine on the tip of Florida. My third mistake was not getting the winds aloft analysis, which would have told me that at approximately 20,000 feet we would encounter severe headwinds. Now these are the kind of things that gang up on even an experienced pilot and put you in a serious situation on a Sunday morning with the "Red lights" on over the Devil's Triangle.

Grandfather

I was born, October 11, 1929, eighteen days before the big stock market crash, October 29, 1929. At that time things really got rough. My father was in the aircraft business and in those days being in the aircraft business was considered almost foolhardy. After all, the only people who had airplanes were the people who were playboys and many of them were severely hurt in the Stock Market Crash of 1929. So, when I was about one year old, my mother and I went to live with my Grandparents on their farm on the south side of Myers Lake in Plymouth, Indiana. It was a rather magical place that I still have many fond memories of.

Grandpa was born in Trenton, New Jersey in 1870 and christened John Valentine Keiper. He moved to Rensselaer, Indiana where he met and married Anna Donnelly. He and Grandma had four daughters, Martha (O'Neill), Agnes (Bock), Cecilia (Palbykin), and Mildred (Fox-Harris). In February 1901 they moved to Plymouth, having bought a farm on the south side of Myers Lake.

My Grandfather was a fabulous farmer. He was

one of the first farmers who ever used commercial fertilizer in Marshal Co. (He was a dealer for Globe Fertilizer). One of the first to ever hybridize his seed corn in this area. He was a great believer in Burbank and there were trees on our farm that had different fruit on each side of the tree. There were white blackberries, black blackberries, red raspberries, black raspberries, cherries, goose berries, sugar pears, Russet pears, regular pears, green gage plums, white peaches, regular peaches, all kinds of apples, Northern Spy, Transparent, Grimes Golden, Cortland, Maiden Blush, and Snow apples are some that I remember. We had strawberries, white grapes, Concord grapes, and quinces and every conceivable kind of fruit and vegetable. I remember a large cherry tree west of the house that I use to sit up in with those big beautiful yellow Queen Ann cherries with red blushes on them. They were just so good that you could go out there and get sick sitting up in the tree eating bunches of them. We also had watermelons, muskmelons, all kinds of squash, and pumpkins.

It was a great place to live and I am sure that since my Grandfather was getting up in years I was pretty much a thorn in his side, because I was a little devil. He treated me very well and I must say that we got along pretty darn good. It was a great place to be raised because of all of the things but it was also relatively primitive on the farm in those days. For example, there was no electricity, no running water, and no central heat. In the winter when you awoke in the morning and looked over on the window sill there would probably be some snow that had sifted under the window sitting there in the morning undisturbed by the coolness of the room. Downstairs, when you went to the bucket to get a drink of water there would be a little ice on the top of the bucket that you had to break to get a drink. So, it was not a perfect place to live. My Grandfather arose early in the morning to light the fires and slowly the house came to life. Grandfather went down to the barn to meet the hired hands and start the milking. Grandmother rose and went downstairs to start the breakfast.

Since it was a dairy farm we had to milk morning and evening. We had about 43 or 44 cows, which had to be milked by hand since there was no electricity. The barn was a kind of magical place too. When you entered the barn all of the smells of the animals and the heat of their bodies filled the air. The cats scurried from place to place and the cows chewed their cud. The hired hands hurried around feeding the animals, milking, and arranging the straw bedding for both the cows and horses. It was a very peaceful place to be and Grandfather insisted it be quiet so as not to disturb the animals. When the milking was done my Grandfather would put the milk on a cart and bring it up to the milk house, which was probably about 100 feet from the kitchen; Grandmother would observe him arriving there. He would have to stir the milk in the large metal cans which were placed in a cement water tank to get it down to a certain temperature as soon as possible since we sold to the Pure Milk Association. We also used a de la Ville cream separator and made our own butter and sold the rest of the cream to Schlosser Bros. (Cousin Herb remembers back when Grandpa sold to Wanzer Milk Co)

When he started for the house my Grandmother pulled the chair back and set breakfast on the table. Breakfast then wasn't just a big cup of steaming coffee. There were meat and potatoes at every meal on the farm. Homemade sausage and bacon cut real thick and eggs and milk and plenty of cream for your coffee and the butter we had made ourselves. There was a real wonderful atmosphere in the kitchen in the morning with the big old stove that we cooked on warming the kitchen with its reservoir of hot water to wash up with and wash the dishes.

There were a lot of things that weren't so wonderful. If you happened to wake in the middle of the night and had to go to the bathroom you were faced with two choices. You could use the chamber pot which was covered with a Good Housekeeping magazine and which you would have to wash out in the morning, or get your clothes on and go down the hill about 80 feet to the outhouse that was like an igloo. So, many times it was quite a decision whether you could hold out until morning or use the chamber pot, or just get up and get dressed and go outside to the outhouse. On one occasion I decided that the best thing to do was to open up the window and relieve myself out the window. Unfortunately, I didn't realize that you could not do that if there was a screen on the window. Therefore, the next morning, when people went outside to go down and use the outhouse, and looked up at the side of the house, there was a rather telltale yellow icicle for which I caught bloody blue hell. My grandmother was an extremely clean and very fastidious housekeeper. When you went to the outhouse, by the way, we took a kerosene lantern with us, because you had to put it between your legs to keep from freezing up. You weren't tempted to spend too much time down there.

Life on the farm was not all a bed of roses. For example I was told that children were to be seen not heard. I was not allowed to speak at the table. Later when I went out for freshman football my mother had to feed me down in a small house we had for extra hired hands because I did not get back from practice in time for supper and grandpa did not allow anyone to eat except at meal times. You also had to wash and comb your hair and be sure you had your shirt and shoes on before sitting down to a meal.

Since there was no central heat, there were a lot of places in the house day and night that were not very warm in the winter. There were a lot of places in the house that were extremely warm during the summer. The only place you could seek any relief was to go down in the old-fashioned cellar. The cellar doors opened up on the outside of the house. I would go down there and lie on the concrete floor and try to soak up the cool and since there was no light you either had to take a candle with you or just lie there in the dark. You could go over to the root cellar, which was a cellar off of the main part with dirt floors and dirt walls. That was where we kept all of the potatoes and canned foods. Another way to keep cool was with the old paper fans with the wooden handles that we used at home and in church. If you looked around in church all the women and some of the men were using fans. There were church fans and many fans had advertising for Coke, Pepsi, or shoes etc. on them. Fans were a big item at that time.

Dogs were a necessity on the farm and were used for herding, for chasing intruders, protection, and for sounding alarms. Grandpa always talked about how our dog Bounce had saved his life. Grandpa was down at the bullpen when the bull got loose. He had sent the dog back to the house for barking. He said he was just about to be gored when he felt Bounce's fur brush by him as he leaped up and tore one eye out of the bull. That took all the fight out of the bull. The dog that I spent most of my childhood with was named Fannie and she was my constant companion as long as Grandpa was in the house or away from the farm. She realized who was the boss. I would go up in the attic and get out the shotgun and she would hear it no matter where she was and start to bark.

Fannie loved to hunt and I was the only one that had time for such things. She could run a rabbit down if we could get it out in the open. Later when Grandpa died and we sold the farm we moved to town, she was still protective of our property and took the mailman for some long brisk runs. She also ran my friend Ed Pierce's Father two blocks down the alley to his home. When my Dad came home from WWII we moved to Chicago and we had to send Fannie to the farm of a friend of ours and I did not get over the loss for several years.

My Grandmother prepared canned food and everything she made was about the best that there was. I remember my mother and grandmother saying how could anybody possibly feed their family canned food that wasn't prepared by themselves. Who knew who prepared it or how it was prepared? They were shocked at the very idea of not preparing your own food. It gave you a good feeling to be living in that type of environment.

Everybody worked on the farm. I had my chores and so did everybody else. I took care of the chickens, gathered the eggs, and brought in the firewood. When it got dark it really got dark and we went to bed. There were no lights out there and there would be no light unless you had a moon, a bright bright moon. So, if you went outside you couldn't see your hand in front of your face. I suppose only a few people have experienced this when they went up north fishing or some place in the woods. When you get up in the middle of the night you realize that it is absolutely pitch black, and that is the way it was on the farm. And since there wasn't much to do, it wasn't too thrilling to watch a kerosene lamp, you went to bed.

I can remember a lot of stories about Grandpa. I remember a time when he had a large bull snake in the barn that was there to catch rats and mice and what have you. We had a new hired hand come to work and when he saw the snake he immediately ran a pitchfork through it. Grandpa fired him right on the spot. I remember another thing about Grandpa. We had an apple orchard, and in the fall Grandpa would go down to a sandy area down the hill from our house, and dig a big hole and line it with straw. He then gathered the apples and put them into this hole and threw more straw on top and covered it with sand. In the middle of the winter, when no one had fresh apples, Grandpa would open it up and in there were delicious apples, crunchy and sweet, just as they were when he had put them in there. So there were a lot of things that he knew that most people didn't know how to do or were too lazy to do.

I always thought of my Grandfather as an extremely intelligent man. He only went to the fifth or sixth grade because he was needed to help on the farm. In those times when you got big enough to work, school was regarded as a luxury. His writing looked like the Declaration of Independence, beautifully written. He was also a kind man in many ways. Here was a man who had only a few dollars and I can remember him during the depression putting the last of his money in the collection box at church on Sunday even though he was close to serious financial trouble himself.

He only went to town twice a week. We all went on Sunday to go to church. We all stayed home during the week except for Grandpa. He would get the essential things, coffee, sugar, salt, pepper, just the basics. We made our own butter. We made our flour by taking the grain to the mill to have it ground. Grandma made her own bread. You haven't lived until you have had Grandmothers hot bread fresh out of the oven with big gobs of home made butter on it. She also prepared every conceivable kind of food that you could think of. We had to buy the basics but most of our food was made right there on the farm. Grandma was an absolute expert. She was probably known as the best cook in the neighborhood. When we had thrashers, people who helped take the crops out of the field, we would ring the big dinner bell that could be heard clear on the back of the farm. The men would come in from the fields and wash up on the East Side of the windmill in metal dishpans with homemade lye soap. We never seemed to have trouble getting help because she was such a good cook and set such a good table. We were always envied, I think, for the food we had, especially in days like that in the middle of the depression. Grandma was also known for her sewing ability. She was an extremely talented woman. I always felt that even though Grandpa was a fabulous farmer, he couldn't have gotten along without Grandma. I think the women were the most important people on a farm. You could possibly get by with a shiftless farmer who would finally get the work done. You couldn't possibly get by without someone who knew how to prepare food and put it away so that you would have food in the winter. Who knew how to take care of the hams, chickens, and do all of things that were required for family life on the farm.

My grandfather was also a very kind man. There were times when I remember going to town with him on Wednesdays. He wasn't very happy with me going and would always tell me to sit back in the car so he could see because; I would be jumping around, and leaning forward. I didn't want to miss anything. He wasn't the greatest driver, by the way. After the Model T, he wasn't very happy with the new cars. He sold the Model T to the hired hand at a real good price and bought a Chevrolet. He wasn't feeling good about the Chevrolet so he would use the hired hand's Model T and would fill it full of gas. The hired hand felt good about that. Later on when the hired hand moved away Grandpa bought a brand new, 1941 Ford, 100-horse power. That car threw him constantly. His feeling was that if you drove it in a low gear it would be more controllable which was the exact opposite of what would happen. It was hard to drive it in second gear, and it was so jackrabbity that it would get away from him every once in awhile and he would run it into the chicken coop or the garage or something. It was a constant source of irritation for him and my mother usually did most of the driving. When he went to town on Wednesdays I would ask him for nickel for an ice cream cone. In those days he didn't have very much money but he never refused me and I never forgot his gift. That was a lot of money at that time. I use to mow the entire three acres around the house with a push lawnmower for twenty-five cents. Can you imagine Grandpa giving me a nickel for nothing? He was very strict but a kind and generous man.

The author at about 8 months.

At ease on my trusty horse.

At home on the farm in the front lawn by the arborvitae.

Fannie and me and some farm buildings in the background.

My class in front of St. Michaels Church in 1940.
I'm the fourth from the right side in the center row.

From the left Grandfather, Mother, Grandmother, and me. (Note model airplane engine in my hand)

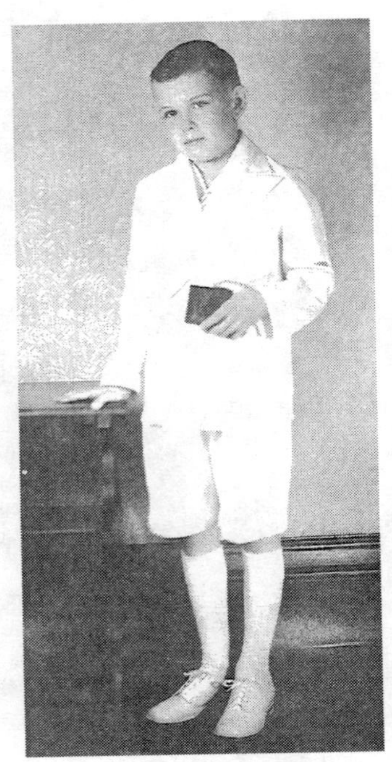

*First communion,
was I ever that innocent?*

*The bike dad bought me
(Note the knickers)*

*Will Beck, Grandpa, Herb Bock Sr. Father,
me, Bob Bock, Tom Bock and Dave Fox.*

Some of my model airplanes down at the house in the orchard that was used for hired hands.

Tom and me and Fannie.

Mother and me.

Grandmother

Catherine Anne Donnelly was born December 8 1870 in Rensselaer, Indiana. She was raised on a farm in Jasper Co. Grandma used to go from house to house before her marriage to Grandpa and sew for families. She would make dresses, pants, shirts, and undergarments for the entire family and then would move on. She got room and board and a little money, but not much. Grandma married John Keiper in 1895.

My Grandmother was good at just about anything you can think of. I remember she was really good with a shotgun. She use to move people down the road that didn't belong there, including some vagrants and Indians who were roaming around in that area. She use to go out and shoot blackbirds out of the treetops. In observing her doing that I thought that she took quite a shock, after all it was a 16-gauge shotgun. So when I tried it, I thought you were suppose to hold it away from you a little bit. Well of course, as you know, that isn't the thing to do because it will really knock you down and that's just what it did, right down on my back. I guess that's part of learning.

Life was pretty tough during the depression with everyone trying to get a job, and people walking through the countryside actually looking for a handout. It was a tough time for everyone and I can recall my grandmother who was an absolutely excellent cook handing out food to people if they came by there and looked like they deserved it in return for splitting a little wood or showing a desire to work for food. It wasn't that she wanted them to work she wanted a person who at least was willing to do something, and that's what she looked for.

We use to make maple syrup on the farm. When the sap began to flow we would drive bamboo tubes into the sugar maple trees and hang a bucket on them, usually a lard bucket, to catch the drippings. It comes out in a clear fluid that has to be boiled to condense it down to syrup. We also had sorghum that grew around the edges of the cornfield. Grandpa use to put about four rows all the way around the cornfield. The juice is squeezed out of the stem and then boiled down to syrup. I remember hired hands on the farm would put the sorghum on almost everything they ate because it was rare to have anything sweet.

Grandma's hams were one of the best things on the farm. My Grandmother use to smoke all of the hams and hang them in the smokehouse. She rubbed them with various sugars and spices. You haven't lived until you've eaten one of those hams. Fried chicken was a family favorite that Grandma made in an iron skillet. Her chicken would put Colonel Sanders to shame. We had reunions where Grandma took all kinds of foods and they were always well received.

She canned fruit of all kinds and vegetables of every type. She stuffed her own sausage using her recipe. First she took the intestines out of the animal and cleaned them thoroughly. She then put them on a machine and put the sausage into the machine turning the crank and feeding it into the sausage links. Grandma made jellies and jams out of the various fruit. We had honey in the wooden bee box with the wax comb inside. She also made her own sauerkraut. There was a big crock with a rock on the lid to hold the cabbage down in the brine. I remember her sitting out on the back porch with a big metal pan shelling peas, and breaking green beans. She grew all of these wonderful vegetables in her garden. She had an asparagus bed. She had a large rhubarb patch. She canned meats ready to be put in beef and noodles. She tended to the garden with loving care. I tried not to say that I didn't have anything to do or she would put me in the garden weeding. So I became very careful with what I said. She churned her own butter. Grandma had a summer kitchen with a separator in it. I would take the cream from the separator to her and she would put it in the churn and turn the crank until she had butter. She then took a flat wooden paddle and squeezed all of the buttermilk out of the butter and added salt and made them into large pats of butter. She baked the bread after Grandpa took the grain to the mill to have it ground into flour. Later on in life she bought bread but I remember her going through this process of baking her own bread. Fresh warm, baked bread with butter is a little bit of heaven.

Grandma was fastidious about her house. She would clean her floors and wax them and put down newspapers over the floor. I think that when people came into the house from the barn she was making sure that the dirt didn't get on her floor. She made donuts and put them in a brown crock in the summer kitchen. After about two or three days they became pretty darn hard and we called them sinkers. When I got a craving between meals I would steal a couple of them and just gnaw on them for the sweetness. The adults dipped them in the coffee to get them soft. She made pies and cakes but my Mother was better at baked items.

We had wild strawberries across the road that we picked like a bouquet of flowers. They were really tiny but good. We also had hazelnuts and black walnuts. We would take a piece of wood with a hole just big enough to drive the walnut through (you wore gloves so you wouldn't get stained hands from the dye) and hammered the walnut through peeling off the outer shell. You placed it in the bucket to dry out and then you smashed the hard shell to get the walnut out. We also had butternuts. I haven't seen them in years but we had them back then. Grandma also took care of the major things in the house. She always prepared the kerosene lamps by cleaning the glass mantels, replacing the wicks and filling the lamps. She always cleaned the windows, they had to be just right. I can remember mowing the lawn but I didn't want that job. I would get twenty-five cents for mowing the three-acre yard with a push mower. After that I would have to cut down the buckhorn. It wasn't unusual to see her trimming up after I was done, to suit herself. Grandma always had a saying she used a lot "this world the next and then the fireworks."

At Christmas time we had candles all over the tree. We kept a bucket of water next to the tree in case one fell over but the rule of the house was not to leave the room with the candles lit. Many homes burned down at Christmas because of tree fires. Once in the evening we would light them and sit and look at them but then put them out. It was a magical moment at that time. No one was allowed in the room during Christmas until Santa had arrived. Someone would be up on the roof tromping around to make it sound like Santa was up there but we always seem to miss seeing him when Grandma announced that "there he went." It was a big deal to get a present. I remember when I first got a football, and the first time I got a model airplane that my father made for me. I remember the time I was given a bicycle. We got English walnuts, an orange, candy and one present. Quite often the Bock family would come down and Tom and Bob and Herb would be there and it was a special time of the year and special time for family togetherness.

We had a telephone that had a crank on the side and hung on the wall. I don't remember a lot of talking on that phone unless it was an emergency. A long distance call was considered absolute panic. Especially when Aunt Martha died on Christmas Eve. After that Christmas Eve was always a little sad because everyone had Aunt Martha, the oldest daughter of the family, on their minds. Grandpa would get oysters for Grandma to make oyster stew, since we weren't suppose to eat meat at that time of the holiday.

Grandma was also almost against being too modern. She didn't think that the toilet belonged in the house. It belonged down the hill at the outhouse. In later years when she moved into town she got accustomed to having a bathroom inside. In those days she wasn't about to let Grandpa tear up the house making it modern. There was no central heat on the farm just stoves. As far as running water, she felt we had a good system as it was. We had a wooden windmill and later a steel one. This was a big advantage on the farm since all water came from the well. We also had a one-lung engine with the whole bottom open and you could see the crank and the rod, and all the innards were oiled by an adjustable drip system. It would pop and turn one or two turns then pop and turn a couple more. It was fascinating to me since anything mechanical was my cup of tea. It was used to operate the well when there was no wind to turn the windmill. It would pump into a large galvanized tank where we would get the water. The water in this tank was real cold so in the summer when we wanted to cool the watermelon and muskmelon, we put them in the water tank to cool. When the water overflowed from the windmill tank it would run down into the milk house. There was a couple of cement tubs that caught the water and Grandpa used those tubs to hold the metal cans of milk when he cooled it. When that tank ran over it ran down the hill to the horse tank. Sometimes in the winter we had to put a stove in the horse tank so that it wouldn't freeze up. It used coal for fuel and had to be fired each morning in the winter. When the horse tank ran over it ran into the pigpen. The overflow from the pig trough became mud and the pigs would lie in the mud to stay cool. You had to be careful around pigs. When the big sows had baby pigs they would come after you to protect their babies.

I recall one time my cousin Bob climbed up the ladder on the windmill and my Uncle Jim borrowed my BB gun to shoot at him but Bob hung on. Uncle Jim also sat me on the kitchen stove reservoir and burned my bottom. He was quite a joker but he never did anything to be mean just to pull a joke. There were some pretty tough and dangerous pranks pulled all the time and so you learned quickly to be observant. In the winter Uncle Jim would pull us behind his car on a sled. That was a lot of fun but he was a very fast driver and when he stopped we would have to turn quickly to keep from running under the car and breaking our head.

Monday morning on the farm was always wash day. I would be awakened in the morning by the sound of the washing machine and things were already going on. The galvanized tubs in the summer kitchen were full of water. One would have bluing in it to bleach the whites. Another one had soapy water and another had clear water. There was a good old Maytag washing machine with a gas engine with an exhaust pipe running out the side of the summer kitchen. The women would be bringing the water in from the well underneath the windmill to fill the tubs full of water. There was a kerosene heater turned on underneath one of the tubs to heat the water. There was a mechanical wringer to run the clothes through before drying on the clothesline. If it happened to be winter and it was too cold, ice would form on the clothes if they were hung outside, so Grandma would hang them in the summer kitchen and leave the kerosene heater on. We also had a lot of cleaning to do since it was a large house and there were no vacuum cleaners. In the spring you would take the rugs outside and hang them over the clothesline and take a rug beater and beat the living hell out of them. She kept everything in good condition.

She was also the official wallpaper hanger. This house had sand plaster. She would put the wallpaper on to keep the plaster on the wall. As I grew up I was always fascinated with plain walls in other houses that were painted. I associated wallpaper with covering up a bad wall.

She was in charge of the baby chickens. She would put on her bonnet and a big coat to keep warm and as the chickens hatched she would take care of them to make sure they went under the brooder heater.

After Betty and I were married and started having children we used to go to Mom and Gram's house after church on Sunday. When Betty became pregnant we would try to pick a good time to tell them about the upcoming new arrival. I remember telling Grandmother about Debra or Susan and she said Don "what's wrong with you" I said "absolutely nothing."

After I had learned to fly and had the Cessna 170 I talked Grandmother into coming to the airport to see my airplane. I opened the door and asked her to sit inside to see how comfortable it was. She got in and I fastened the seat belt, shut the door, and went around to the pilot's side and got in. Grandma looked at me and said, "I told everybody that I would never go up in an airplane." We took off and flew out over the old farm with me pointing out the farm and the lakes and other points of interest, neighbor's homes and all the roads. After considerable time we returned to the airport and landed very smoothly. After shutting the engine off she turned to me and said "Why there is nothing to that." She told all her friends about her flight and seemed genuinely pleased at having gone flying, and talked about all the things that she had seen.

Mom, Grandma, Grandpa, and the model T Ford.

How's that for corn! You don't see that today.

From the left Grandma, Jim Fox, Dad holding Ronnie, Ruth and Carl Kroger, Mom, Grandpa, and me crouched down in front.

Grandpa, Grandma, Herb Bock Sr. and Fannie.
(Note windmill on the right and barn in background)

Tom, Bob, and me with Dave Fox in the foreground
(Note farmhouse on left and wood shed on right)

Grandpa on the planter.

The thrashing machine.

The only vacation I ever knew Grandpa and Grandma to take. Grandpa, Jack O'Neill, and Grandma.

Grandma, me, Tom, Grandpa.
(My Knickers, Tom's long pants)

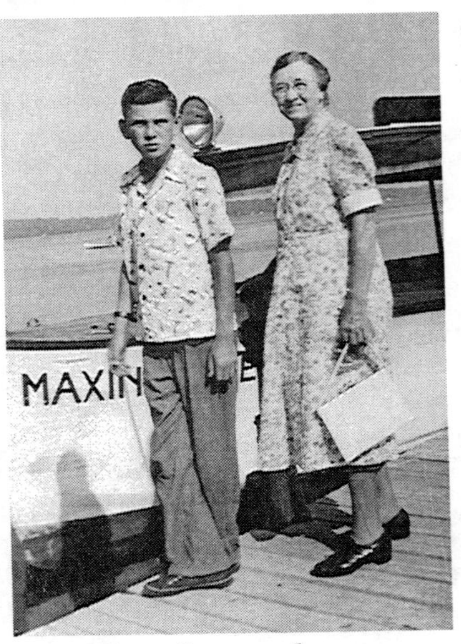

Grandma and me.
(Finally long pants)

John and Anna Keiper

Life On The Farm

One of my responsibilities on the farm was to take care of the chickens. I hate chickens. In my mind, chickens are one of the most difficult things to handle. They don't seem to have any manners and have terrible toilet habits. When I was a small boy they use to fly at me and I was told they were to trying to peck my eyes out which was probably the truth. Chickens were a real problem for me. One of things that I had to do after I got home from school was to gather the eggs and feed the chickens. I would go down with a bucket of water in a little wagon and pour it into the semi-solid buttermilk that was in a barrel in the feed shed. We had wheat, corn, and oats ground up and we kept it in the shed. I would take a bucket of this mixture and pour it into the trough. I would then take the semi-solid buttermilk and pour it on the top and try to stir it into a mash for their feed. They never waited until I got done. They stepped right up when you poured the meal into the trough and when the buttermilk was poured in their heads were in it already. In an attempt to teach them a little bit of manners, I would take the flat side of the paddle I was using to stir the mash with and wait until they were all lined up. I would run down the line hitting every one of them in the head and send them all spinning. It was the same thing every day. They never seamed to learn and I became convinced that they either had no brains or that they were the most stubborn "critters" on earth.

Later, I was told by Grandpa that if we had any setting hens I was to put them in a coop outside and keep them there for a couple of weeks until they were done setting. A setting hen is a hen that thinks she ought to be a mother and sits on top of the eggs. You reach inside to get the eggs and she would peck you. I tried cooping them and they came right back as soon as I let them out. This was in the later days on the farm and I had gone out for freshman football. I thought the thing to do was teach them my own way. I would grab them by the neck, take them out to the door and drop kick them. These were white leghorns and they could fly a long way. It looked like you really made a field goal. One night as I launched one into the air Grandpa caught me. The inside of the chicken house was painted with whitewash, which was ground lime and water. It would not stick well to the walls but it kept things clean. He took a hold of my head and pounded it on the side of the interior of the chicken coop and the whitewash fell all over me and I thought I wasn't long for this world; but he got his point across. I didn't drop kick any more chickens.

Along about fall we would try to get the chickens into the coop so they wouldn't freeze to death. A lot of the white leghorns would roost out in the apple orchard in the trees. We would wait until it got pretty cold and then lock up the hen house to keep them in there. We would go out to gather up the rest of them that were roosting in the trees. We would take fishing poles and try to knock them out of the trees. I remembered my Grandfather putting a corncob on the end of a pole, dipping it into kerosene, lighting it and burning the bag worms out of the trees. A bagworm nest is like a spider web in the tree but full of caterpillars. We burned them out so they wouldn't destroy the tree. So I thought that if I used that method the chickens would be motivated to move out of the trees. I would light the corncob and put it under the chicken and as it spread its wings to fly I would singe off some of the feathers and ruin its airfoil and it would flop out of the tree. When it landed on the ground Fanny could run it down with ease. I bet if my Grandfather would have found out he would have worked on my head a little more for using that method.

One time my cousin Tom was down from Chicago and we were gathering the eggs. We got a big basket full of them and we decided we would make a bull's-eye on the henhouse with one of those soft yellow sand stones and throw just a couple of eggs. Soon we had emptied the basket of eggs on the bull's-eye and we needed a good excuse so I went to the house and said that the chickens just didn't lay today. Of course, that went over like a lead balloon. They knew something was wrong but they didn't know what. It wasn't too long before they discovered that the backside of the chicken house was covered with broken eggs. When that happened I got all of the whippings and my cousin Tom went to the bedroom and back to Chicago the next day.

When I went to Chicago to visit with Tom we were sent to the store each day to buy Marvel cigarettes for his dad. They only cost ten cents so we got a pack for ourselves and sat out in the vacant lot smoking them. We devised a method for hiding the cigarettes by tying a string on them and dropping them down a grate in the sidewalk. Later Tom went home to brush his teeth in the middle of the day to take away his tobacco breath. This was very suspicious and again we got caught. I was sent to my room and Tom got the whipping this time so it all came out even in the long run.

We did a lot of things on the farm that caused great consternation. We had great big crockery jugs that the hired hands would carry water in. They had a leather strap around them and we would fill it full of water and leave it in the water tank under the windmill until it was nice and cold. Then hook the strap on the horse's harness so that you'd would have cool water to drink as you were plowing, or harrowing, or putting in crops. Of course, Tom and I got a hold of a couple of jugs and dropped them out of the trees breaking them and we were in trouble again. Whatever we did we were always in trouble. Just life on the farm.

On one occasion Tom was down from Chicago on a trip with his parents. We decided to make some gunpowder to blow things up with. I went to the library and checked up on how to make it. We had some success but it was not as powerful as we had hoped. We decided to make nitro glycerin and were well on our way when Tom's father found out and put an end to our explosive manufacturing.

I can remember attempting to ride cows. We would get apples from the apple orchard and lure the cows over to the fence. Judiciously placing ourselves on top of the fence we would leap onto the cows and try to ride them. Since these cows were rather docile, fortunately we didn't get killed. Unfortunately, we would get dumped once in a while and cows didn't have very good toilet habits either. Quite often you would land right in the middle of a fresh cow flop.

My Aunt Mildred and Uncle Jim's son David used to come out to the farm and spend time with me. They lived in town with electric lights and central heating as well as running water, hot and cold. I thought it was just wonderful to wake up in the morning and be warm and not have to go outside to go to the toilet. I can only remember a couple of times that I got the chance to stay at Aunt Millies. Dave was a couple years younger than I was. His brother Ronnie was younger yet so we didn't spend as much time together. Dave would come out and spend a couple of days quite often and we would always look foreword to playing at my little house behind the sand cherries. Later after Jim Fox died Millie married Ross Harris and David and Ronnie were adopted and changed they're last name to Harris.

We also had Belgian Draft Horses. As a small child, I thought that Grandpa's horses made the Budweiser Clydesdale horses look small. These horses were not for riding. If you sat on them they were so broad across the back and we were so small that you couldn't wrap your legs around the horse. They were placid plow horses and they just stomped along, but it was still very difficult to try to stay on them.

We were Catholic and because of that we were not really allowed to ride on the school buses. My mother had called the bus driver and asked if it would be okay if I rode. He said it would be okay for me to ride but he could not take me directly to the school. Only two Catholic kids rode the bus at that time a guy by the name of Dick McLochlin and me. They would drop us off at what was called Lauer's corner, about five blocks from the school. This was when I was five years old and in the first grade. In the winter by the time we got to school we were pretty well frozen. We went into the downstairs bathroom at St. Michael's Academy and tried to warm up while the other kids were in church.

We had a Priest by the name of Father Eberle and

everybody was scared to death of him. If he wore a German helmet with the spear on top he would have made a perfect villain in any movie. Students went to church each morning but we stayed downstairs until our fingers were thawed out and waited for the others to come back.

There was a big outside door on the north side of the school that led to the boy's bathroom and some of the kids got to fighting up there and tore the door right off of the hinges. It fell on the floor and everybody looked at each other in amazement. These guys got a hold of the door and stuck it into place but it was just hanging there by a thread. Along came a real good kid, one of those that did everything right, and leaned on the door and it went clattering to the bottom of the stairs, but guess who got blamed? We did. It was obvious to the nuns that that kid didn't knock the door off, but he sure looked pretty pathetic at the time.

When I was in the first grade I was one of the star students, even though I was about a year young starting out. My first nun was Sister Veronica a great teacher. But, in the second grade Sister Veronica wasn't there any more and I was given a nun who wasn't too happy with life. She was on me regularly. Nuns seemed to think girls were angels and boys were devils and they were probably right. The more she would get on my back the less I tried to do anything to please her. I remember one time she was so incensed with me that she said I had to stay after school. Now Grandpa only came to town twice in a week and when she made me stay after school, I sat there crying my eyes out knowing what deep trouble I was in. One of the girls, Marceline Helms, came over to me and put her arm around me and told me not to worry, that everything would be all right. Of course, everything wasn't all right. When they called and got a hold of my mother she was furious. She came to town in the car and picked me up and I was in deep trouble, but I don't remember many days that I didn't get a whipping anyway. I was careful not to get myself in that position again.

I remember when she would take me to the barbershop. They use to put a board across the armrests for children to set on. I didn't care for barbers clipping around my ears. I would put up such a fight the barber would say that he wouldn't cut my hair. I squirmed around so bad that my mother took me out of there and took me over to my Aunt Mildred's house in town. When we got there my mother got out the wooden spoon, dragged me out from under the bed and persuaded me that I better sit still when she took me back to the barbershop. She carefully wrapped the wooden spoon in a piece of paper and back to the barber shop we went and I sat there like an angel because I knew she had that wooden spoon in the folded newspaper on her lap.

In those days there wasn't such a thing as being too hard on your kids. They probably would have taken kids away from their parents if the laws were like today. You simply did what you were supposed to do and I think the world was better for it. Today it is incredible to me some of the things that children get away with. I think back to that time and look at today and see such a difference. I am extremely proud of all seven of my children who were raised in a less permissive society. They are all self-sufficient, good citizens, who know right from wrong, pay their bills, take care of their families and pull their own weight in this world.

My mother was a disciplinarian also. She would have me go out into the orchard and cut the switch for myself. If I cut it too small I would have to go back and get a bigger one. If I cut it too big, like a club, I would have to go back and get something smaller. She wanted one about the size of your thumb on one end and nothing on the other end. Her idea of getting you to dance was to use the switch on the back of the legs and boy it hurt. I don't remember very many days in my life when I didn't get a switching for something. I just wasn't the greatest kid in the world. I always thought that Dennis the Menace was a good kid. He never did anything as bad as my friends, cousins, and I did.

One time when my cousin Tom was down from Chicago we decided to set the woodpile on fire. The hired hands would split wood and stack it out by the wood shed. It was stacked about twenty feet from the summer kitchen portion of the house. These were nice rows of stacked wood, which were used during the winter to heat the house and to cook with. Tom and I decided to go down where the kerosene barrel was, (we called it coal oil) and fill up a couple of cans, take it up to the wood pile, and dump it all over the wood. We lit it and it started slowly so we put more kerosene on. We had a fire twenty feet high in a few minutes. The paint started to blister on the side of the house, Grandma was alone and when she saw the fire she started to throw water on the side of the house. Fortunately help arrived and they were able to put the fire out.

It wasn't long after the woodpile incident that Grandpa offered to pay the tuition if mother would send me to a boy's school just to get rid of me. Fortunately Mother would not accept the charity. In later years Grandpa and I became very close and I remember him waiting for me to get home from school so I could tell him what all happened that day at school.

We had a grove of sand cherries. Not a real good cherry but a type of shrubbery, down the hill from the house. There was an area back there where I decided I would build a house. After all I was alone all day each day and I had to have something to do. When you are a small child and have no one to play with you need a challenge. I remember being jealous of my cousins in Chicago because they had neighborhood children to play with. I made a little square house three feet by three feet, out of old boards, with a door on it. Just a place to go. I would go there and work on it every day. My main passion in life was to make it chicken proof. Of course the original house was chicken proof, no problem at all. But, then I added on to it with lean-tos'. If I remember right I built two more rooms and then four lean-tos', two on each side. Later on we got some sort of a large appliance in a wooden crate and I dragged the box down there and mounted it on top for an upstairs. I tried to make a basement but the dirt floor fell in so I dug the basement beside the house and covered it with burlap bags and sprinkled dirt on top. Once when I had appropriated some of Grandpas fence staples he came looking for them while the hired hands waited to make fence, and he fell into my basement and had quite a time getting out. I had electric lights long before they had them at the house. They gave me an old battery and I hooked up a small six volt light, so I had light long before anyone else. The battery soon wore out so I appropriated the battery from our tractor exchanging it in such a way that no one knew, by putting dust all over the old battery so it looked like the rest of the tractor. As I recall Grandpa and at least one of the hired hands spent the better part of a morning trying to figure out what was wrong with the tractor.

We had in the later days what was called Aladdin lamps. These were gas lamps that used white gasoline, with a mantel and had to be pumped up. Much like the camping lanterns we have today. They made a pretty good light but they were a lot of trouble. We didn't use them very much because after all what were we going to do, sit there and look at the light?

Along about the time I was in the sixth grade rural electrification came into being, REMC. My Uncle Jack O'Neil came down from Chicago and wired the house for electricity. In those days they didn't put receptacles everywhere. He used me to pull the wire through the inaccessible places. We might put in one receptacle a ceiling light and one switch in each room. I just could not resist experimenting with the receptacle in my room and many times blew all the fuses in the house. In the dining room we had an electric refrigerator from Sears, what a wonderful appliance that was. I can remember coming home from school and turning the light switch on and off, on and off. The idea that at night we could have lights and a radio was just phenomenal. Not only could we see, but we had entertainment.

After electricity came things got a lot better. Grandpa had a radio with a speaker on it. (Before rural electrification Grandfather had a radio with headphones that was run by a battery.) We would sit there and listen to the Lone Ranger, Captain Midnight, the Shadow and all of the various radio programs, Grandpa puffing on his pipe and me lying on the floor. He was about as fascinated with those programs as I was. It was a great thing to have the radio. In those days we never thought of going to movies. I think the first movie I ever saw was Snow White and the Seven Dwarfs.

On one of Tom's trips we went down to the gravel pit. We played down there quite a bit but didn't tell anyone. Gravel was easy to dig in so we dug a hole back into the side of the gravel pit. We would pretend it was a cave. Sure enough, after a while the thing caved in on us and we barely got out. We did not report that to anyone either. We could have easily been buried for life and I don't think anyone would have known where we were. That's just life on the farm.

As I grew up Dad bought me a two-wheel bicycle. This was a big deal. I would ride it into town with some of my friends and go to movies. Maybe we would go to the movies twice a year. First of all we didn't have the money to go often, and secondly we would not be allowed to go. Later when I built my little Maytag powered car I drove it to town a couple of times but it was more of a novelty than a dependable vehicle.

The back of our farm was on Myers Lake. It was a long walk to get back there, a good mile. We had about 360 acres, with the two farms together. We would go back and spend the day, being bitten by mosquitoes, fishing over the banks, putting in fishing outlines, sometimes making a camp, building a fire, taking a lunch with us and toasting marshmallows, just the things that kids did. We would take our BB guns along and see if we could terrorized anyone or anything.

I once bought a boat for fifty cents that had a rotten bottom. I repaired it as best I could. I then got some hard roof tar put it in a large metal can and heated it over a campfire until it was boiling. I was working in my bathing suit. I put a paintbrush in the tar and the brush curled up and sprayed tar all over my chest so I dove in the lake and the tar hardened. When I tried to take it off skin and all came with it. After a lot of work I finally had the boat waterproof and I had it tied up at the pier when a friend of mine, George Emenaker jumped in and went through the bottom. If I could have caught him I would have killed him. There are some things that would be worth going to jail for.

One time George Emenaker and my cousin Tom

and I were out on Myers Lake in a boat. I was in the center when they got into a fight. They stood up in the boat and started swinging and as I stood up one of them hit me and knocked me into the water but my feet were still hooked over the edge of the boat. Since the boat held my legs out of the water I was taking on water at a rapid rate and literally drowning. George saw my plight, which gave Tom the opening, he was looking for and he knocked George out of the boat. I finally got my feet in the water so I could swim and was beginning to recover, choking and spitting out water when they decided to save me. Then things really got bad and I had to fight them both to keep them away from me. Boy that was close, since we were in the center of the lake and no one knew how deep it was.

Airplanes always fascinated me since my Father was in the business so I decided that I would build my own airplane. I had a wooden crate about a foot and a half wide and maybe three or four feet long. That became the cockpit. I built a tail on the back. I built some wings and covered them with real thin wood from the basket factory. We had a basket factory in Plymouth and Grandpa would bring some wood home to use as kindling to start fires with. The wood was real thin, maybe 1/16 of an inch thick. I nailed it over the top of the wings and made some ribs so that I was sure it would fly. I had built it on top of the hill behind our house. I had a pair of wagon wheels nailed to the underside of it and I was going to soar into the stratosphere. Of course, needless to say, I started down the hill and nothing happened. Finally the tail came around; the wings hit the ground and tore them off. That was my first experience with flying.

We used to go fishing down by the Yellow River about a mile and half away. Once I had crawled out on a tree trunk that grew out over the water so I could reach further out to fish. A snake crawled down the trunk and as I looked up he was about four inches from my nose. It scarred me so bad that I fell in the river. I never did like snakes that surprised me. If I knew they were there it wasn't as bad. It did seem that they always sneaked up on me.

Farmers are a vanishing breed in America because of the economic reality of having to make a living. Not very long ago there were many more small farms and farmers. Many of them were working in factories and other non-farm related jobs in order to support their farm, actually subsidizing the operation.

A farmer is a very special person and has a much greater knowledge about a large number of professions than almost any other person. He must be a specialist in animal husbandry, a mechanic, a carpenter, fence maker, agronomist, a business specialist, a money manger, an accountant, a market analyst, and must be a self starter with a large amount of energy and excellent health as well as dogged determination.

If I had to pick one professional to take with me to a desert island it would be without question a farmer. No one else has the basic intelligence and knowledge of how to survive and get the job done.

My Grandfather Keiper worked his entire life on his farm and to the best of my recollection took only one vacation in his life. He and Grandma went on a fishing trip for one week with Uncle Jack. They so loved the farm that they were quite content to spend their whole life farming. Many of today's farmers feel that same love of farming and will be denied that independent way of life in our present society.

Aunt Agnes and Mother bringing in the apples.

Grandpa and me with a prize Guernsey cow.

Michigan street, Plymouth Indiana in the thirties.

Fannie and me.

A fierce Indian.

Mom, me, Aunt Mildred, and Jim Fox at the point on Myers lake for a picnic (Only sand beach on lake).

How's that for a big horse?

Dave, Ronnie, Fannie and me.

Fannie and me and the dog house I built for her.

Mother and me in the front yard.

That's me on the right for a school piano recital.

In front of the wood shed with my favorite toy.

The model airplanes were getting bigger and better.

The house on the farm that I lived in until Grandpa died.

St. Michael's Academy where I went to school 8 years.

Lincoln High School Plymouth, Ind. I attended Freshman and Sophomore years at this school.

Lane Technical High School Chicago, Ill. I finished my junior and senior years and graduated from Lane.

Elizabeth

Betty was born in Oak Park, Illinois, July 30, 1929, in West Suburban Hospital. I was born October 11, 1929 in the Oak Park Hospital. Little did we realize that our lives would be so entwined because neither family knew each other at the time. Elizabeth Mae Perry is a descendent of a long line of Kings and Queens and can trace her ancestry back to Roman Times 488, in England and to Charlemagne, in France in the 700's, some 46 generations back. Betty's paternal grandmother was named Elizabeth Sims Perry, her ancestors being Sims. They came over at a very early time in 1634 on the ship "Elizabeth."

James Perry, Betty's father, used to always tease his mother that her ancestors weren't on the "first boat" and she would retaliate with, "but they made the second one." Her Grandmother was extremely proud of her heritage. There is a book about the Sims as well as book about the Perrys, tracing these generational lines. James Perry, Betty's father, worked for U. S. Gypsum Company forty-three years starting right after College as a chemical engineer. During the Depression he was forced to take a cut in pay to retain his job. As things got worse during the Depression, Jim, Lillian, and Elizabeth moved to Port Clinton, Ohio and set up housekeeping there with Betty's Grandmother, Grandfather, and Uncle Paul. Jim Perry was the only breadwinner in the entire family and as such literally supported his family, his parents and brother (five adults and two children) during this difficult time. Shortly after moving to Port Clinton, Ohio, Lillian and Jim had a second daughter, Gloria Gae Perry who was born August 23, 1931.

During the Depression in Port Clinton, neighbors shared produce and fruit. They had a neighbor who was a commercial fisherman who brought them fish from time to time. It was very difficult to get even enough to eat in those days, especially if you didn't farm. They had a garden which Betty's father and uncle tended with loving care. Betty's grandmother did the cooking and her mother, Lillian, took care of the house and laundry. This was of course, not a good situation. I find it difficult to imagine my mother, or anyone in my family, who would have put up with a situation like that. It was as if you invited someone into your home and then they dominated the household as Grandma Perry did. She was a very authoritative person and used to giving orders and I think Betty's grandfather was used to taking them. When they moved in together she took command of the household. To the end of Betty's mother's life, she talked about how miserable those years were.

Betty tells about an incident that happened in Port Clinton, Ohio, between her mother, Lillian, and her father, James. It seems that Lillian wanted to have a dinner party and was wrestling with the table to get it apart to put in a leaf. She called several times for Jim to come and help her but Jim was lying on the sofa lost in a book, which was his usual occupation when off work.

She finally got so exasperated with him that she whipped the table on its back and tore a solid oak leg off of it. She came into the living room with it but Jim escaped out the front door. She was so infuriated. After recovering a day or so later they called a carpenter friend to come over to fix the table and he looked at the it and said, "I just don't see how that leg could come off with those six big screws in it." When Lillian got upset she was really scary.

In those days a driver's license wasn't required and therefore Lillian tried to drive. Betty and her little sister Gloria use to huddle in the back seat on the floor and howl in terror. Believe me, Lillian was not a good driver and never did get a drivers license!

Betty's mother always talked about how difficult it was to keep clothes on Betty. Lillian scolded her about going out without clothes. In an incident later on she found her outside with only her hat on. Betty felt the hat was clothing and that she was dressed.

Betty was in the first grade in Port Clinton when she drew a picture of a tree with many branches and many different colored leaves and foliage on it. The teacher was struck with Betty's artistic ability, since it was not a lollipop tree typical of first graders. That ability continues to this day. Betty has been an artist for years and belongs to Heartland Artists in Plymouth and several Artists groups in Las Vegas producing many of the excellent paintings in our home.

In 1935 Jim and Lillian Perry and the two children moved back to Chicago. Jim continued to send money to his parents until his Mother died and at that time his Father moved to Chicago and lived with Jim and Lillian until his death. They did a wonderful thing by taking care of his parents right up to the end.

Betty and her sister Gloria were educated in the Chicago Public School System and went to Steinmetz High School where Betty met my cousin, Tom Bock. To this day, Betty says that she had an excellent education with very fine teachers at Steinmetz High School. My cousin, Tom, and Betty became good friends at Steinmetz since they shared the same division class.

Tom was very interested in Betty's Irish friend, Mary Malloy. One day Tom asked Betty to get him a date with Mary and he would get her a date with Don. She assumed that he meant Don Lundell, a blond, good-looking president of the class so she immediately agreed. Then, Tom pulled out his wallet and said, "Have you ever seen a picture of my cousin, Don?" So she was really snookered into a "Blind date" with me. It was in the winter and Tom took his brother, Herb's "Little Junior" Model A Ford and picked up the two girls. I waited at his home on McVicker Street since the car could barely hold the two girls and Tom. When they came through the door Betty was wearing a dark blue Navy pea jacket and her beauty and her friendly smile immediately struck me. This was the first time Tom had ever gotten me a date that was pretty. Most of the dates that he had arranged for me were pretty sorry. As soon as I saw the two girls, I knew which one was mine.

Betty turned out to be a very intelligent girl and was a member of the National Honor Society. This meant that she was in the top five percent of her class. I on the other hand, was interested only in getting "Out" of school, and therefore a passing grade was sufficient as far as I was concerned. I was a little bit reluctant to let her know of my disinterest in achieving high grades. We spent the evening playing pool on a small pool table in the basement of Tom's house. We also spent quite a bit of time talking and getting acquainted. It was a very satisfying date and as I remember I decided I would call her for another. Betty later told me that she was impressed with my blue eyes and the way I dressed. She was not very impressed with the fact that I smoked a pipe. But after all, Hugh Heffner smoked a pipe in those days and got all the girls why couldn't I? Hugh Heffner went to Steinmetz, the same school that Betty attended.

Betty told me later that she wrote one of her duty letters to her Grandmother Perry in Port Clinton, Ohio. In order to fill the letter a little she mentioned the fact that my father was born in France and that I also had an Irish English grandmother, and a German grandfather. By return mail, her grandmother wrote her a letter in a very stern language that said, "It's too bad that you can't go with a nice American boy."

After meeting Betty, I pretty well zeroed in on her. She finally agreed to go out on a date. Tom, Mary Malloy, Betty, and I arranged to go to the Aragon Ballroom, which happened to be within about four blocks of where I lived uptown. We went by public transportation, the Lawrence Avenue streetcar. The Aragon Ballroom was a romantic place. This ballroom was known worldwide for its fabulous interior. The ceiling had clouds and stars that twinkled and moved. The bands were the best of the Big Band Era and they had the greatest singers. Betty and I saw Lena Horn perform at the Aragon. There were always big name bands and well-known singers at the Aragon. You'll see a picture of Betty and me taken at the Aragon Ballroom with my arm around Betty because the photographer placed it there. That was the first time I ever put my arm around Betty. We were just kids, sixteen years of age or so. From that day, Betty and I started to go steady. When we went to the Aragon for my prom Harry James played for us. When we went to Betty's prom Dick Jergens played for us at the Stevens Hotel (later the Hilton) in the Gold Room in downtown Chicago.

I used to call her every evening and spend the better part of an hour in the telephone booth with the embossed metal walls at the drugstore talking to her. It became like a home away from home. I think her mother was pretty aggravated with her about these long conversations. Of course, we didn't have a private telephone in our apartment.

I tried to take Betty on dates that were really nice. We went to such exotic places as Shangri-La a fabulous Cantonese restaurant set in a lush tropical atmosphere. We went to Rickets, a popular restaurant at the Watertower, which had superb food. When we went to the movies, she loved to go to Andy's Candies afterward and have a banana split; their atmosphere and the good ice cream always charmed Betty. I realized at that time that this was going to be one expensive girl. Shortly thereafter, I got an automobile, a 1933 Buick. That made dating her considerably better because it was extremely difficult to get back to my home by my ten p.m. curfew. I would pick Betty up early and we would go to the early show and then perhaps out for something light to eat. Then I would have to drive like a manic to get back home by ten. My Father imposed this curfew and he believed in it. That is all there was to it. You were either home by ten or you were locked out.

On one of our dates, Betty informed me that I was a nice boy but we could never seriously consider marriage because of my Catholic religion. She was a Methodist Sunday school teacher and firmly believed that Catholics worshiped idols and statutes and felt that this was totally unacceptable to her. If anything, this made me more determined to court her.

I remember at least a couple of times after I got the car when we skipped school and drove out to the forest preserve and had a picnic. My 1933 Buick didn't have a radio and for my birthday, Betty bought me a portable radio, which we also used for our park excursions. In those days, this was a tremendous gift, which probably cost about thirty dollars or so. We picked up cherry tarts at the bakery and went out to the woods and parked there. We had a blanket and the portable radio and laid out there spending the afternoon looking at the sky, and maybe smooching a little bit.

I used to try to buy her good jewelry as a gift. A gold locket, a gold pin, or some quality jewelry and I was always horrified when she would go to the dime store and pick out some jewelry which obviously looked cheap, and be so pleased with it. Had I known how fond she would become of quality jewelry I might not have bought her such good stuff. After we were married for some time and had some discretionary money we became amateur gemology buffs. We took several courses at the University in South Bend. We met John Marshall who was teaching the course. He is called Diamond John in the South Bend area and has an upscale jewelry business. We bought several rings and other fine items from John and became good friends with him.

One Christmas he showed me some large diamonds that were light brown in color. Some of them were seven or more carats in size He said they were not good investments, but he would sell them to me for one thousand dollars per carat. Betty was taken with a seven-carat coffee colored VVS-1 stone that had a beautiful marquis cut and wanted to buy it, but we talked her out of it. About ten years later in an interview, Liz Taylor was talking about her favorite diamond a seven carat coffee colored marquis cut just like the one we had talked Betty out of. To this day Betty tells me that Liz Taylor has her diamond. Some time after the interview I was talking to John Marshall and mentioned that those stones were a good buy. He said we were both crazy for not realizing the value of them since they are now worth at least ten times as much as he offered them to me for. Some colored diamonds have become "Fancies" and are much more valuable than white diamonds today.

Betty had a good job at Belmont Radio, which later became Motorola. She worked as a solderer and was extremely proud of the solder joints that she could accomplish. She made quite a bit of money about twenty dollars per week, at $1.02 per hour. I made about the same at Transo Envelope Company. I made $1.00 an hour but I worked as many hours as I could so I had a better per week income. I had a car to support, which got about five miles per gallon. I had to have insurance and constant maintenance and had to pay for the dates. When we went out on a date I had to save my money judiciously in order to pay for the banana splits, the movies and everything else.

On Betty's sixteenth birthday her parents gave her tickets for a boat trip to Benton Harbor, Michigan Silver Beach Amusement Park. There were two tickets. One for Betty and one for me. We were so excited when we boarded the ship in downtown Chicago and set sail for Benton Harbor. It just so happened to be one of the roughest days that they ever had for such travel on this tourist boat. We were hardly out of port when the entire ship was ill. Everybody was seasick. I recall Betty going into the ladies room so I went up on top to get away from the smell. The Captain came out and talked to me at some length while I was hanging onto the sides of the ship and he said, "Yeah, this is a real rough one." Even when we got to Benton Harbor it was a mess.

Everyone was sick or feeling terrible. As soon as we got on shore and good old terra firma, Betty started to feel better. It took us so long to get there we didn't have a lot of time to look around and we sure didn't need roller coasters. I thought seriously about sending Betty home by train because she was in such a terrible state after that trip. She elected to stay and come home with me. Even on the way home, the people who were suppose to play in the band, were sick. I'm not subject to seasickness or I would never have been able to instruct the Air Force Primary so I was OK. It was a lousy day to say the least.

When we arrived back in Chicago and got to feeling better, we were able to pick up some Chicago hot dogs. For those of you who don't know what a Chicago hot dog is, I will explain. In Chicago at that time there were little wagons on the street corners and they had hot dogs with steamed buns and they put tomatoes, onions, catsup, mustard, pickle relish and a little salt and pepper. They were so good after our ordeal that day.

We went out every weekend on a date and Mr. and Mrs. Perry felt sorry for me because I was such a string bean. I was a real thin, tall, lanky person. Mrs. Perry kept trying to feed me. Lillian was never noted for her cooking, and having been raised in a family where my mother and grandmother were excellent cooks and having a grandmother on my father's side who was an even better cook, with a son who ran a cooking school, I could tell the difference. I recall going over there for a chicken dinner one Sunday and being appalled at this poor little burnt chicken along with gravy so lumpy that you had trouble getting it down. I remember saying to Betty; "maybe it would be better for you to go to a cooking school." Betty was going to go to Rene's school of dress designing at the time and it probably turned out better in the long run. When things were really tough for us financially, which was most of our early married life, she made clothes for the kids that made them look band box fresh.

Betty always wanted singing lessons but her mother felt that it was important to have a piano background. Betty took lessons for a couple of years and hated them. At about that time her sister, Gloria, started taking piano lesson and became very adept at the piano and was playing many classic pieces from sight. At about that time Lillian realized that Betty was not cut out for the piano and let Betty take voice lessons.

Betty developed quite a nice voice and sang at a couple of different operas in downtown Chicago. I really never cared for that type of singing but I remember attending one of the performances and she did as good a job as anyone did. I was really proud of her and her accomplishments. She still sings today with the choir at the St. Michael's Church in Plymouth, Indiana, and at St. Elizabeth Ann Seaton in LaVegas, Nevada. (It's funny how the name Elizabeth keeps coming up).

If it wasn't for Betty I doubt that I would have gone back for my graduation and diploma at Lane Tech. She said that I earned it and should go and get it so I did with seven hundred other boys. After graduation at seventeen it was very difficult for me to adhere to the ten p.m. curfew because I wanted to go to events in the evening where we could stay out longer. I remember going home one evening about 10:20 and finding the door bolted. That was it. So, I rented a sleeping room across the street from Tom's house at 4325 McVicker's Avenue. This just added to my cost of living. I now had room rent to pay and food to buy, as well as the car and the dates, insurance and gasoline. I used to buy those little red peanuts at the dime store so that if I ran short at the end of the week I would have something to eat. At that time I decided to leave the Chicago area and go back to Plymouth, Indiana where it was a more leisurely way of life. I told Betty that I was going back to Indiana and she said that she was coming with me. Betty told her parents that we were going to Indiana and get married. I think it was her parent's finest hour. They suggested that maybe I should go back to Indiana and get a job first and maybe an apartment and then we could get married. It didn't sound too bad to me and Betty was amenable so that's what we did.

I moved to Plymouth and got a sleeping room to live in. Studebaker in South Bend was hiring and I was able to secure a temporary job on the extra board. After a few months I managed to get pretty well established. Studebaker was growing at that time. They had some new models out after the war and it wasn't too long before I had a permanent job and had arranged to ride back and forth with other workers. After about ten months Betty and I were married.

We were married Saturday 5/29/48 in Plymouth at St. Michael's Rectory. We had the wedding pictures taken in Argos and then rushed back to a lunch at Baldwins on route 17 which was held in their home as was the custom in those days. It was two days before Memorial Day so we could have the long week end for our honeymoon, since I didn't have to be back to work until Tuesday. I had to get permission from Mom to get married at eighteen; because a male had to be twenty-one in the State of Indiana to get married without parental approval.

Mom and Gram went with us a couple of weeks before the wedding to reserve the log cabin at the tourist camp where we stayed for our honeymoon at Niles, Michigan. It was approximately thirty-five miles North of Plymouth. Mom let us use the 41 Ford so we ventured up into Michigan during the day but we came back to Niles each evening. We had some pretty good meals and saw some of Michigan but we couldn't afford a fancy honeymoon. We couldn't wait to get home to our little apartment at 317 Monroe Street in Plymouth Indiana.

At that time we could not be married in the church, since Betty was not Catholic. Father Cross, the assistant Pastor who had been a chaplain in the service, who was a very nice man, married us in the rectory. One day shortly after we were married I was working on our 38 Ford convertible and had my head so far under the hood only my tail feathers showed, Father Cross came up behind me. We lived just across the street from the Catholic rectory and he was out for a walk. I was embarrassed because of the language I had been using. I said, "Why don't you do something useful. Go in the apartment and convert Betty." He did just that, in about a half an hour she was ready to take instruction to become a Catholic. We had always been amazed at the similarity between her religion and the Catholic faith. Father Cross was just the right catalyst to help Betty to understand our faith and to answer all of her many questions. She became a much better Catholic than I am. That's one of the reasons we have seven children.

Betty does have a devilish sense of humor and uses it quite often. She loves to shop, in fact our children consider her the Queen Mother of all shoppers. About twice a month on a shopping day she will depart for South Bend armed with her Visa card and make a day of it. I am always worried when she is out on a shopping trip and it gets dark. A few years ago I got her a cellular phone with the idea that she could call me if she was running late or in trouble. She never used it and I was paying monthly charges so I was becoming exasperated. She would arrive late and never have called. One day we both went down on the elevator at the same time to go out to dinner. I stopped in the office to talk to Charles Arnold, the man that manages our properties for a moment or so, which turned into five or more minutes. The phone rang and Betty was on the line calling from less than thirty feet away in the garage. Needless to say I dropped the cellular phone service.

I never met a woman before or since with Betty's intelligence, beauty and honesty. All who know her love her and I don't think she has an enemy in the world. She raised our seven children, many times virtually single-handed when I was out trying to make a living. Her artistic abilities, painting, singing, and all of the many things she has created in her lifetime to make our home a peaceful and beautiful place to live are exceptional accomplishments.

Lillian Kertson *James Sims Perry*

Lillian and Jim on their fiftieth wedding anniversary.

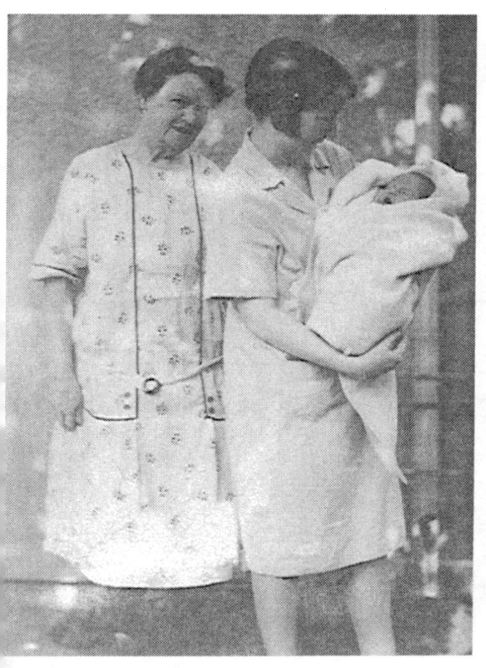

Gr. Grandmother Tiefenthal and Lillian, holding Betty.

Betty July 13, 1931 at ease in her chair.

Betty, Mother Lillian, and her sister Gloria.

Betty with one of her beloved kittens.

Betty doing a little gardening.

Betty in her curtsey cute stage.

Gloria and Betty (with kitten) on the front steps in 1933.

The Perry family 5/31/37
Jim, Betty, Lillian, Gloria.

Grandfather Perry, Uncle Paul, and Grandmother. (Elizabeth)

Would you believe Betty making model airplanes!

Betty with camera in hand. (A perfect picture)

Betty and Don when we were going together.

Dressed for our first prom

Betty working in tailor shop.

The first time my arms were ever around Betty.

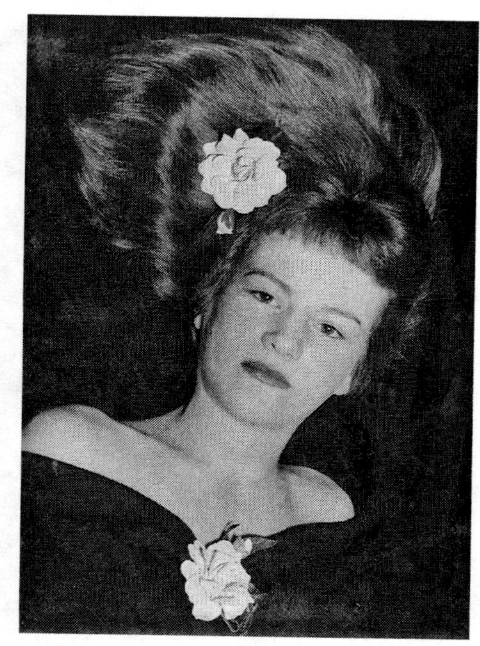

The glamorous and beautiful "Elizabeth Mae Perry"

Me with the infamous pipe.

The courtship begins.

*Don Lundell, Betty, Tom,
Randie Hozian, Marge Kopfer.*

*Two skeletons get married
at St. Michael's rectory.*

*From the left Tom Bock, Edmund Pierce, Delores Lawdenski,
Gloria, and a couple of freshly married children, Don and Betty.*

Mr. and Mrs. Donald J. Palbykin 5/29/48

The Good Old Days

During my life I have had many different jobs and many different experiences. The first job I had was mowing the grass at Grandpa's farm. I really didn't want it but I had no choice. I got a quarter for each mowing with a push mower and it was about three acres.

I had a lot of jobs on the farm that I didn't get paid for that were called chores; taking care of the chickens, gathering the eggs, weeding the garden, and bringing in the wood and coal. None of these were any fun.

Clyde Marks, our neighbor was clearing the land east of our farm and I would go over to help because he would sometimes let me drive the tractor. I worked with him each evening and I think he was pleased with my help because he gave me a half a dollar at the end of the summer. I really liked that summer job because of the tractor and the way Mr. Marks worked with me and best of all it was fun.

One time in the later years when I was a little older I was riding on the fender of our tractor plowing with the hired hand. He told me to get in the seat and drive. I did and was having a lot of fun steering when he asked me

“Did you ever plow?” I said “No I haven’t” and with that he said “You’ll never learn any younger” and he jumped off. I soon got the hang of it and he could sit in the shade and watch me. About that time it dawned on me that it would be good to have a business where you had other people working for you. Little did I know at that time how much of a job it is to be the so-called boss.

The next job I had was working at Lemert’s sale barn on the north edge of Plymouth on sale night. Several of us young boys were used to bring the livestock in to the sale arena where they were auctioned off and then return them to the stalls. If I remember right George Emenaker got the job for me. We were paid real money (between one and two dollars) for an evening’s work. Eva Lemert a very beautiful lady paid us in cash.

During the war I worked with Ed Pierce at the Pilot newspaper mailing newspapers to the GI’s and doing other odd jobs in the printing room.

I didn’t start my freshman year in school on time because I was working at the canning company canning corn. They needed help because most of the men were in the service and the crops had to be processed or they would be lost. One of the first jobs I had was upstairs putting the empty cans on the conveyer that fed the downstairs canning machine. We picked them up and put them on the rack and they went through the floor to feed the canning machine. One girl put a can with a dead mouse in it on the conveyer and I always wondered who got the can of corn with the dead mouse in it. I haven’t felt good about canned goods ever since and always check before putting anything canned in my food. I later ran the big canning machine downstairs that put the corn mixture in the cans and put the lid on.

During the time I was in Chicago, I worked for a small company called Transo Envelope Company. They made an envelope that had a green ring around the window and they used a process to oil the paper and make the paper translucent so that you could see through it and see the address. It was down the street from Lane Tech where I was attending high school.

During the time I was working at Transo, the union people who set up the machines went on strike and there was no one to install the type on the machines. I was approached by the management and asked to try it. I became pretty adept at setting up and adjusting the printing machines. Emil the head pressman was called the “Big Wheel” and I was called “the Hubcap.”

When we completed a set up we had to take an envelope to the proofreader for her OK before turning the press over to the operator for the run. We had a very beautiful proofreader who was full of the devil. She would sit at her elevated desk and show off her legs and sometimes her skirt got hiked up pretty high. She was about twenty-five and I was only seventeen. She constantly teased me and was always making flirtatious remarks to me or about me. One day as she was going into the ladies room on the opposite side of the hall from the mens she crooked her finger at me daring me to come in, so I did. All we did was stand inside the door and laugh. After about 30 seconds I opened the door to leave and there was the big boss. I was called into the office and told that there would be no more of that. We had a difficult time keeping a straight face working together after that.

After graduating from high school I was able to work long hours. I recall making as much as eighty dollars a week, which meant I was putting in more than eighty hours a week. It was a very good job even though it only paid about $1.00 an hour. Not very many people made more than that in those days. A good job paid about $35.00 or $40.00 per week.

After coming to Plymouth I got a job at the Studebaker Corporation in South Bend, about twenty-five miles north of Plymouth. I had a sleeping room at 310 N. Plum Street in a house that had several borders. It was difficult waking up in the morning and since work started at seven in South Bend I decided that I would put the alarm clock in a metal dishpan so it would make more noise. Well, this woke everybody else up in the house but me. I finally became a very light sleeper at that time. (This would not last). I would get up at four a.m. in the morning and go down to the Indiana Motorbus and ride to South Bend. I was on the extra board at Studebaker and since it was a union shop everything went according to seniority. When I arrived I stood in line according to seniority and as people were absent from work they would call each of the workers in line and assign you to a job. Joe isn't here this morning so you go over there, or Bill isn't here so you take his place. From day to day, you never knew if you were going to have a job or not. More often than not, I wouldn't have a job because I was low seniority, having just been hired.

I was working at the Chippewa plant on Ireland road and it seemed I was always getting the worst jobs at the plant. For quite a while I was assigned to putting wheels on trucks. I worked with several large black men and soon began speaking just like them. The tires were mounted on the wheels on the other side of the assembly line and we had to call for the wheels to be brought over by crane. I would say "Aw right rubba."

I finally got a job nobody wanted hooking up the battery and the two-speed transmissions. There were several men working in the pit area under the assembly line and they would cut my shoestrings with their side cutters. This was great sport for them. I retaliated by pouring body black frame paint down their coverall sleeves. Many of the men working in the pits were ex GI's and at that time I weighed only about 135 pounds wringing wet. They didn't take very kindly to cleaning body black out of their armpits and threatened to take me apart. One of them did pull a bad prank on me. He put a pair of ladies panties in our Ford convertible while Betty and I were at the movies. He then sent several letters to me that were saturated with perfume professing undying love for me, and crying about "our child." Fortunately Betty saw through the prank or I might have been sleeping outside.

When I was working in the truck plant putting in cardboard headliners we had a young man by the name of Toby that was always pulling cute tricks. We also had a Serbian by the name of Ted that although he was small in stature was a force to be reckoned with. Ted's lunch came up missing and Toby seemed very pleased with himself. No one knew for sure who took the lunch but we all suspected Toby. Ted was cool and did not show any emotion. A day or so later Ted's lunch came up missing again and again Ted was cool. A couple of hours later Toby turned green and couldn't get off the john. He had to leave work with a homemade diaper and did not return for several days. Ted had put a very strong laxative in a can of peaches and chocolate coated two donuts with Ex Lax. I don't think Toby ever bothered Ted's lunch again.

We had all kinds of ethnic people working at Studebaker and I remember some incidents that really stayed with me. One of my Hungarian friends had a habit of eating raw horseradish just like we eat cole slaw and the stuff was so powerful that my eyes burned when I was near him. Later I got a job in the upholstery department putting in headliners spitting tacks. In spitting tacks you dip a magnetized tack hammer in a box of tacks and put the tacks in your mouth and then put the tack hammer to your lips and put one tack on the magnetized end and drive it with a single blow. We got so good at it that I think we could beat any new stapler of today. There were several men working there that loved hot peppers. They would eat peppers that were so hot they would burn blisters on your lips. One of their favorite pranks was when you weren't looking they put the magnetized end of your tack hammer into a hot pepper and twisted it until the juice covered the hammer. When you dipped it into the tacks and put it in your mouth you would burn blisters on your lips.

While we were working in the upholstery department we used to put our soda pop outside the window in the winter to keep it cool. Several bottles came up missing and we finally found out what was happening. The workers on the floor above made lassos and dropped them over our pop and just pulled them up. By the time we ran upstairs nobody knew anything and they were just whistling. One of the men poured out about half of the pop and filled it with urine and put the cap back on and set it outside the window. Sure enough the little lasso came down and the bottle went up. News of this circulated throughout the plant and no more soda pop came up missing.

Many incidents happened on our carpool trips to work. One of the fellows had a big old Buick with a bad case of cancer (rusted out) and he was a motor mouth. He talked constantly while all the passengers just slept. One morning as we arrived in South Bend we were stopped by several stoplights and the car behind us playfully tapped our bumper at each of them. Drag never stopped talking but we were all awakened by the bumps.

At the next light we were tapped again and Drag pulled forward about ten feet and put the car in reverse and floored it. We hit the car behind so hard that it knocked the bumper off, crushed the radiator, and broke both headlights. Drag just put the car in gear and drove off, still talking. I looked back and people were gathered around the damaged car in amazement.

I got a good job in the paint department and we had a leader by the name of Steve Toth, a big lovable Hungarian who gave me a used baby crib when one of our children arrived. Part of the joy of working at Studebaker's were the pranks that we played on each other. Steve used to like to take a nap at lunch time and was sound asleep at his desk when we threw a bucket of water on him and ran before he could find out who had done it. After about a half an hour we came back to his office and he was waiting for us with a big bucket of water. His desk was right beside the elevator shaft and as he threw the water I stepped aside and the water went down the elevator shaft. The elevator was an open cage covered with wire mesh like a fence. Men had thrown scrap food and every kind of garbage on the top of the elevator. It was a favorite place for cockroaches and just plane filth. The water washed all this crud down on the men on the elevator and boy! Were they mad!

Toward the end of my employment at Studebaker I got an excellent job on the doll-up line where the cars received their final clean up. There was an old man that smoked a large pipe and just fogged the whole area. We cut the little rubber sprouts off the new tires and when he wasn't looking we mixed them in his tobacco can. You couldn't see them in the tobacco but when he lit up you could see the fire sparking in his pipe and the smell was awful. He either didn't notice it or wouldn't let on about it so we finally had to buy him a new can of tobacco so we could stand to work there.

One time when I was laid off I applied for the manager's job at a new local gas station and got the job even though I was younger than they wanted. It was a short-term job since I was responsible for all losses and we had some thieves working there. They gave us lie detector tests and I was absolved of any blame for the small losses. They found out who the thief was but I didn't want to work in that kind of environment so I quit.

During one of Studebaker's lay offs I got a job with R.E.M.C. the local electric company, as a grunt, and the word is descriptive. They told me "We'll give you a job; let's see if you can keep it." I was so sore I was almost unable to go to work the next day but Betty helped me into the tub and I got through the day. I was young and strong and I got more fit each day. Soon I was giving them as hard a time as they were giving me.

One day Bud Wilson, my boss at REMC, told me to put an oil filled transformer on the truck. I didn't realize that it was almost impossible since it weighed about two hundred fifty or three hundred pounds so I worked it over to the fence and finally got it over and up against the truck and pushed it up into the truck. I remember thinking this job is getting tougher every day. A few days later we went to a dinner for lineman where the companies tried to sell the linemen on their products. I overheard Bud during a lot of laughter tell some friends "So I told him to put it on the truck and he DID!"

I asked Bud if I could climb, he said sure and gave me an old set of McClay's hooks and told me to run up a pole and tie in the wire. I climbed up there and Bud came up beside me. He said "Lean back in the belt," I did but unnoticed by me he had grabbed my belt and after I leaned back he released it, I thought I was gone!

I had just started to fly and was interested in aerobatics at that time. Bud went up with me one time and I got some revenge by doing some loops, snap rolls, and spins. Bud was a great guy and during the time I worked at R.E.M.C. he taught me a lot and kept me from accidentally killing myself.

I had numerous jobs in an attempt to make a living. Most of the jobs were part time or between lay offs. I worked for my next door neighbor Earl Lee, who was a cement contractor. It was back breaking work but there was a lot to be learned about concrete and it sure helped when we built additions to 710 Ferndale and built future buildings. I worked at the lumberyard for Bert Seip unloading freight cars of cement and lumber. Betty had to cook meat and potatoes for me three times a day.

One day a man came to our house trying to sell us an Electrolux vacuum cleaner. After talking with him for a little while he said he thought I would be good at selling Electrolux, so I went over to Michigan City, signed up and picked up my demonstrator. I sold several of them but it was difficult for me to sell such an expensive machine to people that obviously needed the money much more for their families so I quit. Sometimes I worked in my spare time as a carpenter closing in porches and other minor carpenter jobs. I also did a lot of carpentry work at the Plymouth Building for Lee O'Connell who had just bought it. Little did I know that we would some day purchase the building and spend so much of our life living and working in it.

Paul Meyers and Howard Bauman approached me about buying into the Plymouth Speedway, which was a quarter mile asphalt racetrack. They were willing to sell me a one third share. I think they wanted me to help repair the guardrail that was broken at each race. Betty sold the advertising space in the speedway programs to the local businesses and worked race nights selling the tickets. The children loved it since it was very exciting. We made very little money with the track but I did learn about depreciation, and the tax benefits of owning your own business. Howard Bauman and I were always working on the racetrack fixing guardrail and all the other many things involved in running the track. During one of the times I was laid off Howard was good enough to give me a job driving dump trucks, changing engines in them, and working on pinball machines. I once fell out of a dump truck while turning a corner to the right. The door popped open and because the seat was broken down I slid right out, landed with no injury to me since the truck was only going about five miles an hour. I ran after the truck and caught it just as it hit a post. Howard just laughed and said, "Fix it." Howard was very good to me and we always had a lot of fun working together.

In the later days of my eight plus years of employment at Studebaker I could see the handwriting on the wall and I knew the company was in trouble. I met Curtis Thews while working in the Studebaker foundry and started talking about cars with him. He had obtained the Volkswagen franchise for the South Bend area and was putting up a building on Western Avenue to sell and service the cars. He talked me into going to work for him as a mechanic and salesman. Since Studebaker was in trouble I decided to take the job. We went to Chicago to study the Volkswagen and I became quite enthused about the car and could quite literally take it apart and put it back together again. The car became a big hit and we sold all of them we could get and had people waiting as much as a year to get one. That's about the time Stockerts called me to go to work for them flying. Prior to that I had worked in the aviation business only part time or between lay offs.

Automobiles

When I was a child I was fascinated with cars; cars of any kind. I still love cars. But in those days about the only thing we could hope to play with were toy cars. They were little die-cast metal Tootsie toys of various cars and trucks. My cousin Tom would come down from Chicago to visit and we would go out in the front yard and peel up the sod and make little roads and use twigs to make miniature fences and houses. We were always bragging about the cars that we had and the estates that we had made. We assigned names to each other for these playtimes. I was Bill Stevenson and my cousin Tom was Jack Nelson. After a few days of playing these roads got to be very extensive. We peeled the sod back about 1 1/2" wide and made little roads that went hither and yon in the front yard. The buildings were made of sticks and we used our trucks to haul the sticks. We spent all day playing out in the front yard and had quite a lot of fun those summers.

As time went by I graduated from toy cars however; I never did get rid of them. In fact, I still have most of the toys that I used when I was a child in a display case in my office. I read about people building soapbox derby cars and I decided that I would build one. I dismantled a perfectly good wagon to get four wheels. Then I got a crate or a box and built a little platform and tried to rig up a way to steer the thing, with ropes to the front wheel and a pivot on the front axle. I nailed cans on the sides for lights and even put an old license plate on the front. I was thrilled with my machine. In looking back at the picture of it, it really wasn't much at all. But remember I didn't have any help building it and I was only about six at the time. I was the sole engineer laborer and builder. There was nobody to say there's a better way to do it. When you are on a farm most people are busy trying to make a living. They sure aren't able to help some child playing around trying to make a toy car.

When I was about twelve years old I decided that I would make a car that had an engine on it. I went down to a neighbor's, Mr. York, and I purchased a Maytag gasoline engine from him. It was kind of a put-put engine. It was a two-cycle engine that used an oil and gas mixture. It didn't fire regularly like a four-cycle; it just fired when it needed to. It had a pretty good size flywheel on it. I mounted this on the back of a wooden frame and took two wheels off a real nice scooter that my father had given me. These wheels had air tires and I am sure Dad would have murdered me if he had known about me taking them off my good scooter. I mounted them on the back and bolted a v-pulley on the side of one of the wheels. A belt ran from the engine down to the wheel and then forward to an idler pulley with a big spring to pull it tight. When I pulled on the handle up front it released that spring, kind of like a clutch. I let it go a little bit until it started moving and then a little more, until down the road I would go. This contraption was something else. It had an automobile steering wheel (About a 35 Ford.) It had a canvas cover over the front to make it look like a car and as you can see from the pictures, it was a racy outfit. By today's standards, it was terrible. It just had a pivot on the front axle for steering; a clothesline rope fastened to the front axle to turn it wrapped around a broomstick down inside the cowling. When you turned it one way the rope would pull on one side and release on the other side. When you turned it the other way, it would go in the opposite direction. It was crude to say the least, but it worked. I cherished that vehicle. It was something that I really thought the world of since I had made it myself.

There were no paved roads where we lived. I had to go quite a ways to get to a paved road. This car had a difficult time going through the gravel. I remember many times when I sheered the valve stem off of the tire by letting the belt tighten to quickly and it slipped the wheel in the tire and cut the valve stem right off. It was a constant source of maintenance to keep it running. In the picture section the photo shows me sitting on an anchor and I have the neighbor's son on the back. I had a fishing pole in my left hand and tackle in a lard can hung over the rearview mirror. In the boy's right hand he had a bucket full of fishing gear. Shortly after this picture was taken he fell off as I turned the corner. This was a primitive means of travel. A bicycle was by far superior, but to me, it was a car and a car meant an awful lot in those days.

My Grandfather bought a new 1941 Ford, super deluxe, with a 100 horse power engine. It was a four-door black gleaming beauty. I was always eyeballing it and forever asking someone to let me drive it. That didn't happen very much at all. They let me drive it on the farm if my father was there but he wasn't there very often. When I was about 14 years old one Good Friday we went to church for the three hour vigil service in the 41 Ford. My cousin and I took great pains to stay way back in the church so that our parents couldn't see us. At an appropriate moment, we sneaked out of church and stole the car for a joy ride. Now you must understand that this is really taking a chance. We were freshman in high school, with no license, no experience no brains. We went roaring around town to the various homes where girls lived that we knew. We didn't see anyone so we went out in the countryside to do some wild driving on the gravel roads. We spent about an hour or hour and a half having a good time. When we came back to the church, lo and behold the parking spot that we had was filled. We were in a panic because when our family came out of the church we had to have the car parked in the same place so that they wouldn't realize that we had been gone with it. After some time we finally found a parking spot when somebody moved, but it wasn't where we were parked before. Somewhat of a distance from where we were parked. After church when we came out Tom and I went right to the car and everyone followed us and luckily, nobody realized that it had been moved.

We were pretty accomplished at stealing cars. I remember one time Tom stole his Brother Bob's Chrysler. We weren't gone very long and no problems. I believe it was while we were building a road back to the cottage that Tom's father Uncle Herb had on the south side of Myers Lake. Bob, his buddy Mort O'Leary, Tom and I were working on it and we kind of slipped away for a little while.

I remember staying with Mort in one of Wilmas's cabins. Mort was older and big and very much in command. He made breakfast one morning and the eggs had gone bad, boy did they smell. He said, "eat" so we put catsup on them and choked them down. Mort drove us down to Culver that evening for hamburgers, I think he was feeling bad about the eggs. Being fourteen, we were looking to pick up some girls, and we did, one of them got a ring my father had made for me when he was on Attu in the Aleutian Islands. She used it as ransom to get us to come back the next night. I really felt bad about losing the ring but there was no way I was going back because she scared the hell out of me.

I remember three of us boys getting together and buying a Model T Ford. It cost $9.00, so each of us came up with $3.00. That was a lot of money for each of us. The problem was that I never got to drive the Model T because the darn thing wouldn't run very good unless I laid on the running board and adjusted the carburetor constantly. If we did go some place with the Model T with our painted-up license place, (an old license plate painted to look like a new one), I was laying on the running board adjusting the engine and someone else was driving it. So, I never got to drive the thing. It was an unsuccessful adventure for me.

I also remember a date I had when I first went to Chicago. After my father came home from the WWII we moved back to Chicago and my cousin Tom took it upon himself to arrange blind dates for me with various girls. In fact that's how I met Betty. She was the only good looking date he ever arranged for me. At the time I thought it was very big-hearted of him. In hindsight I realized that he would simply find someone he was interested in going out with and then ask a girlfriend of that person to fix him up with the girl he was interested in. When the two girls arrived I could usually tell which one was mine.

On one particular date we had borrowed his brother Herb's "Little Jr." Herb was still in the service. It was a

Model A Ford with a tiny script on the side that said "Little Jr." Kind of a worn out car but it had a rumble seat (or at least it looked like one). I think they had just turned the trunk lid around. I am not sure if it had upholstery back there but at least there were pillows. During our date we put fifty cents worth of gas into this car depleting our finances to the point of pennies. We felt we had to contribute to the gas because Herb Sr. Tom's father kept a close eye on the gas gauge. I was in the rumble seat and Tom was driving when we started out. Tom was very interested in Mary Malloy and she was in the front seat with him. She was a real nice looking Irish gal with beautiful legs. I was in the rumble seat and as near as I can remember it was with the kind of girl that gives dogs a bad name. She was definitely edging up to me, a very aggressive person. Finally I knocked on the window and asked Tom to let me drive for a while. I don't think I had a driver's license. I got out and got into the front seat and he got into the rumble seat with Mary Malloy. As I was driving along this gal continued to try to harass me. Being stupid and young, instead of being inspired by this type of activity, I was trying to stay away from her and my attention was distracted. I wasn't watching the road as well as I should have. I don't know just where we were (I think Elmhurst) but I remember that there was a policeman standing there directing traffic. As I drove along not looking where I was going I ran over his feet. I don't know how much of his feet I got but I remember looking into the rearview mirror and I saw him looking down at his feet. Needless to say, we departed from there rapidly. Not too rapidly in that thing, because it had a terrible shimmy. It would shake so bad that we would have to stop and start over again. That was our fifty-cent date.

My first real car was a 1933 Buick Century Coupe with a rumble seat. A really wonderful car in my eyes, but it had surely seen better days. As my dad would say it had lost the bloom of youth. My father had come across it at work where it had been towed with a broken drive shaft. It was for sale for $50.00 probably to pay for the towing. So, parting with all of my cash, I bought the car. I remember Dad saying to Mom, "don't worry about it, it's like a tank, he can't get hurt in it." That was the truth. It only got about five miles to the gallon but who cared (gas was only twenty cents a gallon). It had heavy steel fenders, spring steel bumpers, and a big straight eight in line engine.

The car was a problem child from the time I got it. A neighbor of Tom's by the name of Paul Green fixed the drive shaft by welding it and we hoped it would be OK. After it was fixed I went for a drive and in about a half an hour it was broken again so we dragged it back to his garage. I went down to a place in South Chicago called Worshowski's with the pinion gear and the drive shaft in my hand. I remember going down on the streetcar and getting off in a rough area and finding Worshowski's. They said that they could fix it up for me and in a couple of hours they had prepared a drive shift and had welded the pinion gear to it with a special welder. I later found out that the torsion bars that went from the center of the car out to each side of the rear axle to keep it from hopping around back there were missing. That was probably what was causing the trouble with the drive shaft but I didn't know that at the time. Ignorance is bliss. I went back and Paul put the drive shift in bless his heart, and after that time it never gave me any further trouble.

They called it the Buick Century. Dad was right, about it being a tank. When I drove it on the outer drive

Yellow Cabs would yell out of the window that they were coming over into my lane and I would yell back "come ahead." They would look at that big hunk of iron and have second thoughts; no body ever tried to push me over. I had a wreck one time with the Buick. I was on the streetcar tracks and it was raining and I slid into an intersection and hit a 41 Chevrolet. That car was crunched all the way up to the rear seat. The Buick was absolutely undamaged.

The least of my problems was that the paint wasn't very good. I saw an ad for wipe-on paint so I purchased a can of it in black, since the car was black. Betty and I went out to the lakefront to paint the car. We pulled it up in a parking spot next to other cars. You were suppose to wet a rag and then dip it in the paint and rub it around like you were polishing the car. After I finished, I looked at the car next to me. There was a little wind at the beach and I looked very closely and there were little tiny black specks on the car next to us. When I say tiny specks they were less than the size of the point of a pin. You couldn't see them unless you were looking for them. I told Betty to get in the car because we were getting out of here. She didn't realize why I was in such a hurry to leave. I'm sure they would come off but I wasn't going to stay around there to find out.

Then I had another major problem with the car. In Chicago the brakes had to be tested to be legal to drive it. This had a mechanical brake system that wasn't very good. One of the cables on the front brake had collapsed. No matter how tight you tightened the brake you couldn't get it to work properly. For the test you had to run it up on a ramp and slam on the brakes and the fluid would shoot up in four separate glass tubes, one for each wheel and they all had to be pretty much the same within certain limits. When I first took the brake test I failed miserably. I pulled around the corner and tightened the front brake up some more and went back and took the test again. By the time I got it to pass the test I could barely drive it. The front brake was on all of the time but the guy passed me and I got my little sticker. I couldn't drive the car that way because it would smoke the whole thing. As soon as I got my sticker I backed off on the brakes.

Another problem I had with the car was really something. I was going along one day and the car started backfiring. It blew the muffler clear off of the car, along with the tailpipe. I coasted over the curb and picked up the hot tailpipe and muffler and decided that this was the time to call Dad to see if he could help me with this problem. My Dad was a great mechanic, as good as there was in those days. When he was off work he was "off." He dressed really nice with nice trousers and shirt, a very dapper looking man. He had a 1940 Packard that was immaculate. There was not a blemish on that car. I called him to come out and see what he thought was wrong. He wasn't too thrilled with coming over on a Saturday. He parked and told me to open the hood. He then told me to get in the car and try the starter. It turned over no more than twice when he said, "stop." You come out here and I'll try the starter. So we switched places and as he turned the starter over and I looked under the hood I saw spark's ricocheting around the distributor from a loose wire. I immediately knew what the problem was. He didn't say a word but got in his car and drove off. Those are the times that you really learn. You don't just think you learned.

I recall one time when I had to go to school in the morning and I went out to fire up my Buick. It had bad valves and it was quite a sight to see and hear start, rattles and bangs with a lot of sputtering but finally, I would get it going after a lot of grinding on the starter. This one morning Dad went out and his Packard wouldn't start. I pulled up along side of his car and said, "Dad, would you like a lift to work?" He got in the car, I took him to work, and he didn't speak to me the entire trip. He was not happy but the old rattletrap got him there so that he didn't have to miss any work. That evening, within a short time after he had returned from work he had solved the problem with his car and everything was fine again.

The car had one other major problem. Well, several major problems, but this one was dangerous. The exhaust manifold was cracked. It would pump carbon monoxide into the cabin. If it was a day that the sun was shining, you could see the carbon monoxide coming into the car. You could probably drive it with the windows open and expect to survive, but when it was cold that wasn't an option. I tried several times to have the manifold welded. As they tried to weld the cast iron, the crack would creep ahead. I just couldn't get it fixed. One time in the winter when I was driving down a side street in a daze with the windows closed, to try to keep from freezing in the cold Chicago weather I heard this zink, zink, zink, zink. The next day I noticed that there was a little paint missing from the right side of my car, no dents, so no problem, I still had that can of wipe-on paint.

Another problem with the Buick was that I couldn't change the oil. The oil drain plug was in an insert in the oil pan and the insert was loose. No matter how you tried to grab hold of the insert you just couldn't get hold of it so you couldn't get the oil plug out. Needless to say, the same oil was in all of the time that I had the car and probably some time before that, the oil had never been changed. I finally went over to a place that handled antique cars and did some repairs. They had Deusenbergs that you could buy for five or six hundred dollars. They had old Rolls Royces that you could buy for about eight or nine hundred dollars. I wish I could have bought some of them but I didn't have any money. They chained the car down and turned it up on its side and welded that insert in a couple of places so that I could take the oil plug out. For the first time I was able to drain the oil and boy it came out like heavy molasses. The oil really wasn't in good shape after all those years.

I had always used the oil that my dad drained out of his car. I went down to Goldblatts, which was a department store in Chicago that sold things at pretty reasonable prices, and I bought two gallons of oil for eighty-nine cents. I kept that oil with me in the car. I could actually change the oil, and put fresh oil in the car. I hardly knew how to act; it was wonderful to have fresh oil and plenty of it in the car.

I remember one date with Betty, we were always looking for a place to park so that we could do a little hugging and kissing. That's about all we got to do in those days, there weren't the free sexual morals of today. Anyway, we would slide down in the seat and do a little smooching. I had parked the car in a regular neighborhood, because if I parked the car in front of Mrs. Perry's, she was very prone to come down and extradite her daughter from my clutches as soon as she would see us park. So, we parked a couple of blocks away and we were slouched down in the car and I heard this terrible clanking. The 33 Buick's had a beautiful hood ornament that was fastened to the radiator cap with a chain. My hood ornament was broken off, but I had bought a 1947 Studebaker Commander hood ornament at a junkyard and bolted it on top of the old cap. It looked pretty good, sort of like a torpedo on the front. When I heard the rattle of the chain, I sat up in the car and looked, there was a little kid who had hold of the thing and had his foot up on top of the car and was trying to pry the ornament off of the car. I couldn't think what to do so I blew the horn. I know he fell off of the front of the car and I know he hurt himself, I don't know how much. I know that at that time I hoped he had hurt himself badly but he was gone in a flash. I still had my hood ornament and the old Buick was still OK.

I tried to talk my Father into loaning me his car for my senior prom but he was reluctant to trust me with his pride and joy. He just said "what's the matter with yours." The Buick had been heating up pretty bad during the summer and when you shut it off it would boil over and steam came out from under the radiator and underneath the car. I knew this was going to happen so Betty and I parked and I had her get out and walk away. I quickly shut it off slammed the door and ran over to her side and we casually strolled along with the other kids remarking about the car with the fountain coming out of the radiator. I later found out that the radiator was full of mud and a good washing with a hose cured that problem.

When I decided to move to Indiana and prepare for marriage, I put my 33 Buick up for sale in Chicago and got a pretty darn good price for it. I had pulled the head and ground the valves and it started real good. It was a nice looking car with a rumble seat and it was a coupe. By that time most of the skull and crossbones had been removed. It moved forward with great vigor and Betty had sewed up some seat covers for it so the interior looked beautiful. It was the kind of car that a lot of people like to have, so I got a pretty good price for it.

After being in Indiana for quite a while and using the bus to go back and forth to South Bend to work, I decided that it was time to purchase another car. The 33

Plymouth wasn't the best looking car I ever had, but I got it for a very low price (I think about $35.00). It had broken windows that I had to replace with plastic. I also had quite a problem with the right-front door; it would not open at all. I remember going to Chicago in that car and picking up some stuff that Betty was going to bring to Indiana before we were married. We were coming home on a cold miserable New Year's Eve. We had just turned on Route 30 and we were going down a hill and the engine let out a terrible roar and quit. I coasted over to the side and parked. There was steam coming out from under the hood. I got the flashlight out to look underneath the hood and as I shined it at the engine I couldn't figure out what I was looking at. What I was looking at was asphalt. The entire side of the engine was gone. My light was shining through the steam and everything and going right down to the asphalt. Shortly a car stopped and a man who had been celebrating emerged and I do mean celebrating. He offered to tow us to Plymouth, about 60 miles or more. So he hooked us up and asked Betty if she wanted to ride in his car where it was warm but she declined and said that she wanted to stay back with me. As we started out we were amazed at the speed that we were going. I think we were going at least 60. The old Plymouth had never gone so fast. We were careening around behind his car with terrified looks on our faces. Of course my brakes weren't very good and I was afraid that if he stopped too quickly we wouldn't be able to stop and would run into him. I couldn't say anything since we were back there and he was up front so we hung on for dear life. We ended up in Plymouth and I thanked him for the tow. He was very nice and seamed pleased that he could help us. I offered him money, but he wouldn't take anything for it.

My problem then was to get the car repaired. I

talked to everybody and they said to buy an engine at the junkyard and Jo Blow down there at his garage would put it in. So I went down to talk to Jo Blow and then went to the junkyard and purchased an engine. He went out and got it and after a lot of time the engine was installed in the car. This engine turned out to be worse than the first engine. It was really in bad shape. It rattled and clattered so bad that I didn't know what to do with it. I went down to the local BearCat auto parts store and asked for a set of bearings for a 33 Plymouth. Of course they asked me what "size?" The correct procedure is to use a micrometer to measure the shaft and find out how much under size it is and then put in bearings that are made for that amount of wear. I had no idea about that at the time so I asked them to give me whatever is normal. The guy looked at me like I was crazy but he sold me a set of bearings. I've got to tell you, after I got the bearings in you couldn't move the car. I had to back them off a little bit. The way I did that was to unbolt the cap and slip a washer under one side. Now any mechanic will tell you that this won't work. I still couldn't move the car. I got a friend to pull me around the block a couple of times and got it started. I ran it with the oil pan off until the bearings kind of burned themselves in, put the pan back on it and put oil in it and I never had trouble with the bearings after that. I tell my mechanic sons about this and they always say that's impossible.

There was another incident with that car. Betty and I were going down towards Culver, out southwest of Plymouth on one of the curves, and I looked down and saw fire coming through the floorboards. I had neglected to release the parking brake and there was set of bands that went around the drive shaft mechanism that held the car in park position. These had heated up to red hot, set the wooden floorboards on fire, so we had a nice little fire between us. I pulled off to the side of the road in a very calm way and said, "Betty, you better get out of the car, we've got a fire. I opened my door, on the driver's side of the car since her door didn't work and so help me; she beat me out of the car through my door. She was very rapid when it came to fires.

After we were married, Betty claimed I married her for her money, I had used some of the money (about $200) that she had saved during our courtship, to purchase a 1938 Ford convertible. This car was not too bad, but it had quite a bit of cancer (a lot of rust) along the bottom, but it was quite a desirable car. It did have one major drawback. It didn't have a top. When I went to South Bend to work, if it was raining, you had to move right along in order to keep the rain from soaking you. So, that was a serious problem. I ended up making a wooden piece to go across the front where it clamps down to the car. I took it up to South Bend and had some guys put a new fabric top on for me. That car was a pretty solid car. I got some chrome and screwed it on the side where the rust was. We were moving up in the world and really proud of our nice looking car.

After I worked at Studebaker for one year I was eligible to purchase a new car at an employee's price. I purchased (for about $1,350) a 1948 Studebaker Champion Starlight coupe, painted dark leaf green with yellow wheels. I thought it was the sharpest car ever, even though a lot of people didn't like the color. It was a great car except for one thing. It seemed to bother the Chicago police to no end that anybody, as young as I was, about 19 years old, would have a new car so soon after the war. Post war cars were at a premium and young men just didn't have them. I went to Chicago with this car and my buddy Joe Harmon was with me. A

Chicago policeman stopped us. The policeman asked me, "What were you doing back there? You passed a streetcar on the wrong side, you were speeding, you ran a light." I really didn't think that I had done that much wrong. I may have been going a little too fast and I know I passed the streetcar on the right side, because I surely couldn't pass the streetcar on the left side, and when I came to the corner, maybe the light was yellow. But really there was no problem, I think he just wanted to see the registration. He said, "do you own this car." I told him yes but he didn't believe me. After checking the registration he could see it was my car. He pulled me out of the car and really gave me a talking to and he asked if I had any money. I told him no that I didn't have any money. It was obvious to me that he was looking for a bribe. He said, "well, if I catch you around here again I'll put you in the s . . t house for good. My court date only comes up every month or so and you'll be in there at least a month before you get a hearing." He proceeded to stalk off. It seemed that every time I went to Chicago after that the police stopped me.

I remember another time when I went up to Chicago with my buddy Joe Harmon. We borrowed a truck to pick up some furniture that Mr. and Mrs. Perry were giving away. It was a dining room set and Betty really wanted it. We drove up there, picked up the furniture and drove over to a Chinese restaurant near the Patio Theater because I told Joe that the food was great. I ate there when I lived alone in Chicago because it was a lot of food for the money. I really built this place up to Joe and after eating there we found out that it had changed owners. It was probably one of the worst meals I ever had in my life.

As we left there we were on a boulevard and I passed a cop who was standing on the curb. As I passed him he pointed to his feet. Joe said to me, "I think you better stop, he wants you to stop." I stopped and he came trotting across the intersection and leaned in the window and said, "what are you all doing with a truck on the boulevard? You can't drive a truck on a boulevard." I didn't realize that you couldn't and told him so. He said, "man what do you think I ought to do? Me and 6,999 other cops just doing our duty, now what do you think I ought to do?" He obviously wanted me to give him a bribe. He asked me if I had any money and I told him no. He said, "and I suppose yo buddy's broke." Joe said, "no, I have a couple of bucks." He said my next court date is over a month away, so I suggest you get together. Between us we rustled up about $3.00 and handed it to him. The cop said, "don't wave that money around." Joe said that his hands were resting on the windowsill and when he took hold of the money it went inside of his fist like a vacuum cleaner. It just disappeared. We went on a couple of blocks and there was another cop trying to shake us down, but that one let us go. So, I was really glad to get out of the city. It seemed that I always had a problem there.

We used to wash and wax our new cars every weekend. There was several of us who worked at Studebaker who would get together to wash and polish our cars. We kept them spotless to the point of not letting anyone in the car with wet feet.

I remember one time Betty and I drove out into the country and parked to watch the sunset. We pulled into a lane, probably to do a little legal necking, since we were married by then. Lo and behold, our beautiful car got stuck in the mud. After a while I walked down the road to a farmer's house and he came down with his tractor and pulled us out. That was the last time I took our car where I thought it could get stuck. I tell you it was really a job cleaning that thing up to get all of the mud off and get it back to perfection.

The first "second" car we owned was a 1937 Ford 60 HP for Betty. We paid $75.00 for it. A great looking little car with a peanut engine in it and it didn't cost us much in gas and we didn't have any trouble with it. It was owned by the preverbal little old couple who kept it housed in a garage. The only thing wrong was all four fenders were wrinkled a bit from going in and out of the garage. Betty was then free to go when I was at work. We really loved that car and kept it for several years. Three or four years later we realized that it was worth quite a bit. It was one of the first cars that had a solid roof on it without fabric inserted into the roof. You could crank the windshield out and there was a radio in it. Someone offered me too much money for it; maybe $350 or $400 and I sold it. I went to Thews Motors Volkswagen where I was working at the time and purchased an old Packard for about $35.00 that we had taken in on trade on a new Volkswagen. It had an overdrive that didn't work, so I just wired the overdrive out. I loved that car because you could drive it out into the woods and put scratches on it since we didn't have hardly any money in it we couldn't care less. I don't think Betty was initially too happy with it. Eventually she came to like it because she loves large cars.

I remember the 1948 Buick Roadmaster convertible that we purchased. The most beautiful car you ever laid eyes on. I took it home and Betty got in and couldn't turn the steering wheel. There wasn't any power steering in those days. She raised right up out of the seat trying to turn that car. I told her that she had to get it moving a little bit in order to get it to turn. She had such a time with that car that after about a month or so we decided to get rid of it. There were a lot of old style great cars, but easy to drive, they weren't. It had another novelty. It had the first power windows I had ever seen. They were hydraulic activated and there were a few leaks. So, when you got into the car there was an aroma of hydraulic fluid, but because of the smell you knew that there were power windows. Anyway, I decided I couldn't live with it and traded it in for a Ford. I had sold the Studebaker (you had to keep it one year) and used the money (about $2,400) to build a living room on the house at 710 Ferndale.

As time went on I was to realize that with seven children we needed a large vehicle. I went to a Ford dealer and discovered to my dismay that a Ford station wagon, even in those days was well over $3,500. I said that what we really needed was a limousine. Of course, everyone thought that I was crazy. One day I was in Grand Rapids at the airport for an autopilot repair on Wheel Horse's Cessna 310. I called the Cadillac dealer and he told me about a limousine that was for sale. I got a cab and went out to see it. It was a beautiful 55 black Cadillac limousine in mint condition. I asked the guy what he wanted for it and he said about $1,500. He said that he turned down $1,800 a couple of months ago from a funeral home but that they had already gotten one by now. So I said, "Well, I'll give you $1,200 for it". And the guy said, "OK." Immediately I realized that I might have bought it at a better price. I never made that mistake again. I assumed (never assume) that he wouldn't take less. I saved thousands of dollars from that lesson. Then he said to me, "There is one thing wrong with the car!" I thought here it comes, transmission, engine, brakes etc. He said, "The clock in the back doesn't work." I told him not to worry about it, that we would suffer. That car had everything. power steering, power windows, power brakes and all of the goodies that came with a modern car. It got fabulous gas mileage. I can remember trips where we would get 24 or 25 miles to a gallon. It was incredible that a car that big got such good mileage. I wonder why they don't get that kind of mileage today with limousines. It's probably because of government intervention. Anyway, that was a great car.

A lot of things happened with that car. Out at 2111 North Michigan where we were living at that time we had allowed the kids to raise 4 baby pigs for a 4-H project. I remember coming home the first night after we had bought them at the sale barn. The pigs were in the basement because it was mid winter and the house smelled like a pigpen. (Pigs are not the most aromatic things that you come across). I said that the pigs had to go, so we put them in an old unused chicken house. I built a little straw house inside the chicken coop and put them in it. When spring came they got out and rooted up the whole yard. We finally had to put an electric fence around the pigpen and the pigs got pretty smart about that fence. They wouldn't go near it because it kept biting them. It was a powerful fence called the Weed Chopper. One time our dog Bingo got straddle of that fence and the fire really flew. He never went near it again either. One of the incidents with the limousine was when Betty asked me to go pickup the hog feed. I went to the local elevator to get the feed and a man came out with this bag of feed and asked me where to put it. I told him to put it in the limousine and he said, "Oh, you're the one with the limousine. You'd be surprised at how few people pick up hog feed in a limousine."

I had a little Volkswagen Beetle that I drove at that time to save money. When I was up at Wheel Horse with this Volkswagen everyone use to kid me about my little car and I told them that I kept the big car at home. I remember one night we had a cocktail party at our house and after the party we were going out to the Country Club at Plymouth for dinner. I had cleaned the limousine up so that it was spotless. Part of cleaning process was using gasoline on the rugs so it left a terrible smell. I went inside the house and got the bathroom spray, (I believe it was lilac), and sprayed the interior of the car to mask the smell of gasoline. We had an engineer from Wheel Horse by the name of Bob Witt and as soon as he saw the car he said, "Oh that's a funeral car." I said, "No, this was a limousine not a funeral car. Funeral cars had leather seats in the front and a window to separate them. This was just a nine-passenger limousine with no window between the front and back and the same upholstery in the front as in the back." Well, he was kidding me about it being a funeral car and when he opened up the door and stepped in he came right back out and said, Don, "This **is** a funeral car I can still smell the flowers."

I was upstairs painting a large bedroom yellow (which I detest) when Steve ran in the house and up the stairs. He was out of breath and he said "Mom just ran the Limo into your Volkswagen but don't say anything to her I don't think she is feeling very good". The Limo had a pair of chrome falsies on the front bumper that had driven into my rear fender and the whole fender had to be replaced. That is when I found out that you are not insured if you run into your own car. This was not really anyone's fault the driveway was glare ice and as she turned into the parking place she put her brakes on and skidded into my car. It could happen to anyone.

When I bought the car it was absolutely immaculate. It even had the chauffeur's hat with it and I would wear it once in a while. I wanted to take real good car of it. Since it had hydraulic valve lifters I assumed (never assume) that it used detergent oil because everybody used detergent oil with hydraulic valve lifters. So I changed the oil and put detergent oil into it. What I didn't realize was that they had used regular oil that leaves a little bit of a carbon build-up. When you put detergent oil in it, it cleans out some of the carbon build-up and for a while it will use oil. After about six or eight months I went out to use the car and started it up and a big red light came on the dashboard and it was clattering something fierce. I immediately shut it off and went around to open the hood. A tiny wisp of smoke drifted up. I don't want you to think that I felt bad when I pulled out the dipstick and there was no oil on it, but I felt real bad when I pulled out the dipstick and the dipstick was dusty indicating that it had been some time without oil. Trying to be very careful, I went inside the house to speak with my wife about this. I said, "Betty, do you ever check the oil?" And she said, "No, do I have to take care of that now too?" You have to understand that she had been wrestling with all of these kids. Then I said, "Doesn't the man at the gas station ever ask you if you want him to check the oil?" And she said, "Yes, but I told him you take care of that." Well, to make a long story short, that car used oil for the rest of its life. It got to a point that the boys didn't want to be seen in it. They would get down on the floor in the back so that no one could see they were riding in it. We had "old smoky" for 6 or 7 years and my oldest daughter Julie was in tears when we sold it to the junkyard. The next day it went by the front of our house with a big load of people partying in it.

Strange incidents happened with that car. One day when I arrived home I saw that the right front mirror was broken off. The car was black and it was dusty and it had big chrome mirrors clear up front on the fenders. They were square mirrors so that you could see behind you real well by looking forward. One of these mirrors was broken off at the base. I walked around the car and none of the dust had been disturbed. It was just like as if somebody had plucked that thing off without touching the car. Trying to control myself I sat down at dinner that night and said, "Betty, did you notice that the right front mirror on the Cadillac is broken off?" She said, "No, I didn't notice that." I said, "Do you have any idea when that could have happened?" She says, "well, maybe it's when the train gate came down across the hood and I had to back up." I silently bit my lip and quietly stared at my plate. She is a really good driver and never has had any serious accidents in her life. She is really observant and very careful and an excellent driver. Probably better than I am at least the whole family thinks so. She is just prone to freak accidents, such as the train gate.

One day I looked at the car and saw that the rocker panel was caved in. Just like someone went up to the car took a sledgehammer and drove in the center of the rocker panel. So I asked Betty, "How could that possibly happen?" Betty said, "Maybe it was when I was out at the hospital." She was turning around in the grass parking lot where they were staking out the new hospital and evidently as she was turning sharply she encountered one of those steel stakes and drove the rocker panel in. Nothing serious but boy oh boy, it was always something.

We bought a 1932 Ford coupe that had a Pontiac engine in it and a racing hydromatic transmission and was painted candy apple red. It was a gorgeous automobile and had so much power that if you stepped on it hard the nose came up in the air. After we bought it we only drove it a couple of times. It was featured in one of the Rod and Custom automobile magazine. We also had a Maxi Taxi, which was a Volkswagen frame with a fiberglass body, and it was an eye stopper. We never seemed to enjoy these special cars as much as we thought we would, so we sold them in a relatively short time usually at a profit.

Another time, in later years before the second limousine I had bought Betty a white Cadillac. It had those stiletto rear fenders that stuck back and were pointed and had pointed taillights. That time she backed into a tree and speared it. It didn't hurt the car, but it didn't help the tree any.

One winter when I was gone Betty had gotten the Limo stuck in the snow and elected to use my Eldorado which was a front wheel drive car. The snowplow had plowed the driveway shut and there was a big mound out by the road. Betty decided to make a run at the road and launched the Eldorado so it landed on top of the large snow bank with the front wheels in the air, not even touching the snow. When I got back from my trip we didn't have any moving vehicles and all of our friends and everyone else that drove by thought it was so funny.

Another winter incident that was just hilarious happened one morning after a big snow over unfrozen ground. I awoke early to hear the sound of a lot of automobile engines. A friend of Stephen's had come over early and got stuck by the gate that goes into our pasture. Steve had taken his car out to try to pull him out and got it struck. He then got Betty's limo stuck trying to get his car out. I looked out and just saw a sea of lights in our pasture and Steve going for my Eldorado. I jumped out of bed and hollered "Stop three is enough."

My oldest son Stephen had borrowed Betty's Buick to go somewhere and he pulled up with the car to get his girlfriend and opened the door and there was a post there. As he opened the door the car rolled back and the door caught on the post and peeled the door back. It was not a good situation but I was getting used to it.

After starting the airport we put in a rental car agency. Skystream bought our own cars and had our own rental agency and in those days I used Chevrolets. We both used Chevrolets. Betty used a four-door. I would send Marty down to sit on the hood while it was being given an inspection to keep the mechanics from screwing up the carburetor. When we first got those cars they ran pretty good but as soon as you took it back to the shop for the first inspection the car never ran right after that. When you turned off the ignition the car would just keep running. I didn't like that and eventually we were glad we passed that era.

Next we bought another gray limousine. It was a very beautiful nine-passenger sedan and it was loaded, air conditioning included. It was a fabulous car that we had for years and years. Ever since I got rid of that car I constantly hear from Betty about cars not being big enough. I remember buying her a brand new Cadillac Fleetwood Brougham and she referred to it as the "little" car. Later on when we switched from Cadillac's to other vehicles I remember we bought a new Lincoln Town Car and she still said that it was a "little" car. By comparison it was. With a limousine you could open the doors, put 15 bags of groceries, as well as bicycles and kids in and slam the doors, it was like a side door van today. It was a great vehicle and just what we needed for our large family.

One of the strangest sights to be seen on Plymouth streets was Betty driving the big gray limousine with little Ann sitting on the armrest in the center of the back seat. It looked for all the world like Ann had a chauffeur. Those were the days before the government told everyone they had to wear seat belts. We never had a problem in all the years we hauled our children around. I have two sons that are alive today because they were not wearing a seat belt at the time of an accident. One of them was thrown out of the car before it went off a cliff and he would not have survived. The other was thrown out the side and the impact crunched the whole driver's side where he would have been sitting and he surely would have been killed. I am not against seat belts I put them in my 52 Studebaker long before they became mandatory since I was using them in my airplane. I am against politicians and bureaucrats telling us what we can and cannot do. As usual they try to play God.

I am not a hesitater when it comes to driving. Long after I had left Studebaker I met a man that had carpooled with me. We looked at each other and could not come up with each other's names. He said I don't know your name but "you are not a hesitater."

Another automobile experience that sticks in my mind occurred in Germany in 1987. Dick and Karen Delp, Everett and Jayne Colvin, and Betty and I took a three-week trip to Munich Germany for the Rotary Convention. We spent the first week on a guided tour of Salzburg, Vienna, Oberammergau, and Innsbruck. We had a wonderful time and then spent the next week in Munich at the Rotary convention, which is quite an experience. We decided to drive through the Rhineland area the third week using the autobahn, which is the famous high-speed highway in Germany. An "ugly American" had, not returned the van we had reserved for the trip, on time. We were forced to settle for two BMW's. Dick Delp drove one car and I drove the other. I asked Dick how fast he was going to drive and he said about 80 kilometers per hour. That's 50 miles per hour. We drove for a couple of hours and stopped at a rest place for some ice cream and to use the bathrooms. The right lane was used by the trucks that had to drive at 80 kilometers because of a recording device on their speedometers, that they were required to turn in to verify that they were complying with their regulations. Automobiles had no limits so we were eating all the diesel fumes driving in the truck lane. Very few, if any, cars drove in the right lane. I said to Dick "this is no good" and he said he would put the "petal to the metal." In order to keep up with the traffic we were required to go as fast as those little cars would go (160 kilometers, 100 miles per hour). That was not nearly fast enough since most of the cars were going 130 to 150 miles per hour. That's the only time I can remember Betty telling me I was going too "slow." You haven't lived until you are going 100 miles per hour and are passed by a little old lady with a loden green hat with a bristle brush, at 150 miles per hour. I would look back and see a car way back and pull out to pass and they would be on my back in seconds. I told Betty that if we ever go over there again I'm going to rent a Ferrari. Betty says she is taking the train.

I always wanted to have a prestige car. I was down in Palm Beach where there are a lot of Rolls Royces. It was the end of the year and I was talking to a dealer and noticed that one of the cars had a very low price by comparison to the others. Most of the Rolls were about $150,000 to $200,000. I asked him what the difference was between the cars and he said, "oh, that's a used car." It seems a man had bought the car for his wife and she had it for short time and decided she wanted a different color. Her husband traded this one in and got the new one for her. After talking to the salesman about the car and checking it out I couldn't find even a small flaw and it didn't have hardly any miles on it. I came back again on the last day of the year. The showroom floor was almost empty. I looked at the car I looked at earlier and the salesman said to make him an offer. I huddled with Betty and told her that I would make him a low-ball offer and if they took it OK and if not we would walk. We presented an offer and the salesman said, "why I could wholesale it for that." I said, "well fine, wholesale it to me." The salesman went to talk to the boss and came back about fifteen minutes later and told me that I had just bought it. They were trying to clean out their inventory at the end of the year. I told him that we had flown down there and I wanted him to keep it for me until I came back and I told him that I wanted a cover for it. He begrudgingly agreed. I was in my glory. Here was this beautiful dark maroon four-door Rolls. Betty didn't like the smell of the English leather but everyone else did. But in the years to come I was never as disappointed in a vehicle as I was with the Rolls. There were so many things about it that I would find later that were negatives. It's a relatively small car, meant to seat four people. The dealer kept it for me for a month or so until I went back to Florida to pick it up. On my trip back to Indiana I had to stop and put a quart of oil in it. I thought that wasn't too good. Upon arriving back in Indiana, I stopped at the Rolls dealer in Zionsville close to Indianapolis and the dealer there told me that they use oil. He said that's the bad part but the good part is that the valve stems never wear out because that is where the oil goes through. At the time I thought that was OK. I also purchased oil filters there. Regular Fram oil filters that you pay about $1.75 for in a parts store and they were $15.00 each because they had an English Whitworth thread. You couldn't put the others on the car because they had a special thread for a Rolls Royce. The man told me that the only US oil recommended by the book was Castrol. So I bought some and kept it in the car. I also kept those filters in there too. Later when we were down in Florida and I needed an oil change I went to the dealer and said that I had the oil and filters but I wanted someone to change the oil. They changed the oil for me using my oil and my filter and the bill was only $110. They also informed me that inspections should be kept up and entered in the logbook or it would greatly diminish the value of the car because it was all on computer. Every time there was an inspection you would have to take in into the dealer. I remember hearing that on the 20,000-mile inspection, they change all of the fluids in the car, including both hydraulic systems for the brakes. It has a double hydraulic system for the brakes. They also change all of the belts. The total bill would be over $15,000. That was one of the reasons I never got to the 20,000-mile mark. I put it up for sale and only had it on the bulletin board at our condo for a day or so and sold it to a man right there in our building. I came out really good on it; I only lost a couple of thousand dollars in a couple of years. It's a great vehicle as far as resale.

Rolls are not great to travel in. Whenever we traveled I would run the nose of the car into the bushes so that no one would know that it was a Rolls Royce and I certainly didn't want them to get their hands on the sterling silver emblem on the front of the car. There was no protection on the side of the car, no moldings, and it had many coats of paint and was very costly to have scratches repaired. Another thing is that you have to get used to is people giving you the finger. Some of them are so hostile as to roll down their window and swear at you. I never had a problem like that with an airplane and airplanes cost much more than a Rolls Royce. For many reasons, the Rolls Royce was not a good experience for us. I remember arriving back in Plymouth the first night.

I sneaked into town in the evening and put the car into the garage and put the cover over it and saw the Rolls Royce name on the cover in the front so I put a towel over that so no one would see it. The next morning when I went down to the restaurant to have a cup of coffee, I found that the entire town knew about it. They probably thought that here is this rich guy driving around in a Rolls Royce and charging these little old ladies high prices for his apartments. I had the best prices in town but that didn't matter. So a Rolls is not a good thing to have, as far as I am concerned it is a negative in many ways.

We were shopping in South Bend and we parked it and went inside the store. I had parked where I could watch it and I saw a bunch of people gathered around the car. There was one of the non-participating experts standing there expounding all about the car. So I stood beside him and when he gave out some of the specifications I would just say, "is that so, is that so." Finally, I just got in the car and drove off. People feel that you are somehow not a good person if you are successful and a Rolls is a very prominent symbol of success. In certain areas of the country, like Palm Beach, Phoenix or California, it's probably not a problem. But if you get out in the regular countryside, you don't want to be in a Rolls. I think that is the reason that many of the quality cars made today are non-descript looking. Like the Lexus, it looks just like any other Japanese automobile. It is a good small car. An excellent car. But it definitely has a non-descript face to it. I think that was a smart move.

Lately I have been less impressed with the automobiles produced today. I don't see any of the cars that I loved so dearly like the Cadillac and Lincoln's. They are all changed to sports sedans. Huge engines and they corner like a racer. They want tremendous acceleration and deceleration. In most of them you can drive over a dime and tell whether its heads or tails. None of them glide across the asphalt like the old big automobiles. They fit better and are rattle free as well as the fact that they will probably give trouble free service for many years. There is no question that the new cars are better engineered and have many features that the old cars did not have such as anti skid brakes and air bags and many other creature comforts, but "quality and styling they don't have." A lot of cheap chrome moldings that are a part of the plastic trim, and some fake gold trim. Most last only a few years and are consigned to the scrap heap in less than fifteen years. They are truly throwaway cars. Very few will be shown in any auto museum in the future such as the Imperial Palace here in Las Vegas where they have a huge display of vintage automobiles including over twenty Dusenbergs. They have Packards, Cadillacs, Lasalles, Lincoln Continentals, Chevrolet Corvettes, Ford Thunderbirds, Rolls Royces, Mercedes Gullwings, Chryslers, Buicks, Auburns, made in the twenties, thirties, and forties and many other classic automobiles built even before that. Where would today's cars fit in that museum?

In the last few years I have decided that I am not going to fight them any longer and we purchased the same type of car. I am pleased with the Dodge Mini-van I have; it rides and sits better than any of the cars. We picked the Chrysler Concord as a car that has good room inside and a large trunk and that is about all you can ask for now days. I don't classify any of today's cars as being in any way as luxurious or as nice or classy as the old cars that glided along with their beautiful interiors and gleaming exteriors. We used to call them "boats."

My first homemade car with Dave, and Ronnie, what class!

The Maytag powered car with my neighbor on the back.
I'm sitting on an anchor with a fishing pole in my left hand.

The 41 Ford with a happy driver .

Dad's immaculate Packard.

My first car, the 33 Buick.

Betty and me with Gloria.

The Plymouth with bad engines.

Our 38 Ford convertible.

37 Chevy just before the new Studebaker.

1st second car with the peanut engine. (Like new)

First new car a 48 Studebaker.

Betty and me (She is pregnant)

Our 50 Studebaker,
a black beauty.

Betty Steve and me in
front of dad's Packard.

The 48 Buick Roadmaster convertible (Wish I had it now).

55 Cadillac Limo (Hard to believe it got 25 miles to the gallon)

86 Rolls in front of our Admiral condo in Florida.

Definitely not the car to have back home in Indiana.

Learning To Fly

One Sunday afternoon, 9/5/54 I decided to go out to the airport and see what was going on. I had never gone to the airport before so it was something new for me. As I arrived there I noticed that there were men sitting around by the airplanes talking. One of them was Paul Meyers, an instructor. I talked to him for a little while and asked him what I would have to do to learn to fly. He informed me of the necessary procedures and he said that he could give me a lesson at that time. With little or no information we got into a J-3 Cub, N2185M with a 65 Continental engine and took off from the local Plymouth Airport which was a sod field. After thirty minutes of straight and level and turns we came back and landed. Then and there I decided that I was definitely going to learn how to fly. I scheduled another flight on 9/8/54 for thirty minutes and on 9/12/54 for thirty minutes more. It became painfully obvious to me after those three flights that the cost would be prohibitive for me. I decided that the best thing to do was to buy my own plane.

I heard about a Luscombe 8A for sale at the airport

and went to talk to Floyd Mattix, the gentleman that owned it. I made him an offer and within a very short time we agreed on a deal. It was a very low price, by today's standards, about $1,000. In order to get the money to buy the airplane I had to go to the bank and talk to them because we had a home and that was all. I went to the bank and they said the home was worth a lot more than I owed on it so they would be happy to loan me a $1,000. I purchased the Luscombe on 9/17/54 just twelve days after my first flight. I rarely missed a day of taking instruction after that. On 9/30/54 I soloed with a total time of 8 hours 30 minutes. It was a big day in my life because I remember thinking as I took off that if I could do this, maybe I could be a professional pilot. I was really thrilled. I continued taking instructions and building my solo time, in preparation for getting my private license.

I took my private flight test on 11/20/54 with 45 hours and 5 minutes total time. You need 40 hours to get a license. I had no difficulty with the flight test other than Russ Miller, the examiner, trying to shut the gas off with his foot a couple of times and trying to get me to do some dumb things. It was such a simple airplane it was very difficult to come up with much to cause trouble.

To show how stupid I was as a young pilot, on 4/5/55 I went to the airport took off and went up over the field and did a loop, and the engine quit. I was able to coax the airplane back to the airport by judicious use of the gas primer, and pumped some gas directly into the cylinders so that I could get back to the airfield. Upon taking the carburetor apart we found that there was sediment in the sediment bowl and I had shaken it up and plugged up the jets. Other than that there were no further problems, she was ready to go again.

I had promised Betty that upon the purchase of this

airplane that we would travel and see the world. So, on 4/19/55 we departed Plymouth, Indiana and went all the way, non-stop, to Sheridan, Indiana, a total of one hour and five minutes. This plane did not fly very fast, about 105 miles per hour. We filled the airplane up with fuel at Sheridan and departed for Bardstown, Kentucky. We flew to Bardstown, Kentucky and had the airplane refueled there. After leaving Bardstown we went towards Bowling Green and I observed that the gas gauge was going down rapidly. Since we had only one twelve-gallon tank this was serious. Betty looked out under the right wing and sure enough gas was spewing out the top. The attendant had put the gas cap on backwards. If you put it on backwards it sucks the gas out of the tank. I had assumed (never assume) that the attendant had put the cap on properly. I decided that the best thing we could do was to land before we ran out of gas. I selected a field and plopped the old Luscombe down into a field that was a little short. The landing was OK and there were no problems with the airplane. Everything was in good shape but we were in this really short field. Betty got out of the airplane and we removed all of the baggage and even the seats. There was a man there that told me that I would rise up out of there with no problem and that he would drive Betty to Bowling Green. I attempted to take off but I could see that I wasn't going to make it and plopped it back down on the ground and did a ground loop to keep from hitting the trees at the edge of the field. I caught the tip of the left wing doing a very small amount of damage, but it hurt my ego quite a bit. I went back to the other end of the field and I decided I was going to get that thing out of there this time. I started the engine and went crossways of the field turned right and careened around the corner with just enough speed to get a good running start and when I left the ground I missed those trees by just a few inches.

I landed in Bowling Green, Kentucky. Betty was already there and was glad to see me alive. The people there were so nice to us. Mr. and Mrs. Robinson loaned us their car and we went into Bowling Green and got a motel room. We thought we were in heaven, safe and sound. The next day I made a local flight and decided that everything was fine. We loaded up and stopped in Louisville then Sheridan and finally back home to Plymouth. This was the end of our great adventure.

Jim Perry, Betty's Father, wanted to go to Port Clinton, Ohio to see his aging parents. On 8/13/55 we took off in Luscombe N2160B and flew to Port Clinton arriving in three hours flying time. We found his parents in what I would consider hardly bearable conditions. They were eating graham crackers and milk and hadn't had a good meal in some time. I looked around the house and found milk, eggs, bread and not much else. I made French toast for them and they wolfed it down like they were starving. We went into town and bought a supply of food and got them set up for the time being. What they really needed was someone to look after them. I had been watching the weather and a large hurricane (Diane) was blowing in from the east. We had to leave as soon as possible so early the next day 8/14/55 we departed. We had a real hair raising flight back to Plymouth, right down on the deck, many times only a couple of hundred feet off the ground. What amazed me was how cool Jim took the flight; he seemed almost nonchalant about our low flying and the dodging of the clouds. Obviously a man at peace with the world and his place in it.

In the early days of aviation, pilots were a very close knit group. When anyone would land at the airport we went out to see if we could help. We would take the pilot to a motel or a restaurant or where ever they wanted to go. It was like an exclusive club only more personal. About the tenth month of 1955 I had been elected President of the Plymouth Aero Association, which shows you how hard up they were for people. When Ken (Whitey) and Dorothy Fry, the airport operators at Plymouth left, we had no fuel. The club was allowed to use the fuel tanks and the metering system. We bought fuel for the tank and everyone was on the honor system. When you fueled your airplane you marked it down and at the end of the month each club member paid his bill. We sold it to members at cost. We might have added one or two cents for shrinkage.

During that time we had quite a few adventures with the various people at the airport. I can think of one in particular who had an airplane in real bad shape and he probably had the record for the most forced landings. It was an Aeronca Chief, a side-by-side airplane. It was really a problem child. The airplanes we had then with few exceptions didn't have electrical systems or starters. The rule was that when you propped your airplane, you either had to have someone in the cockpit or you had to tie it down. I remember one day he was out there and he propped his plane and it wasn't tied down. He had cracked the throttle just a little bit too much, and he jumped off the side as it started. The airplane started forward at a rapid rate, he grabbed it by the wing strut and was standing in the middle and the airplane was going around and around him like a giant U control model airplane. If he let it loose it would have gone through the hangar or across the field. Finally he made a lunge for the door, drove his knee through the fabric behind the door, reached inside and pulled the throttle closed. He just sat there on the ground panting. It sure did drive home the fact that you didn't prop an airplane unless it was tied down or unless you had a man at the controls.

One cold winter day I took off for Michigan City and after flying for a little while I could not move the control stick, it was frozen, literally. I decided I'd better try to break it loose because I was going to die if I couldn't move the stick. I thought I was going to bend the metal stick but finally it came loose and I moved it around as much as I could until I landed. We found that the drain in the belly had plugged with oil and dirt and allowed the water around the stick to build up and freeze. If I had waited any longer it would have been impossible to move the control stick.

Now I was ready to buy an airplane that had a little more performance. I wanted an airplane that had a starter and an electrical system. Then you could have a radio and fly at night. A retractable landing gear would be nice to give me more experience. Those features weren't available in most airplanes that I could afford. The only airplane that I could find that I could afford was an 85 horsepower airplane made by Globe Swift. It was an airplane that had too much power to taxi but not near enough to fly. 85 horsepower wasn't enough to drag that little tub of iron around. In fact, I had been going to Valparaiso to Urschel field to talk with Willard Rusk who sold used airplanes. He told me an 85 horsepower Swift would not fly, and I said I saw it fly, and he said where? And I said Macomb, Ill. And he said "Oh I see that's why it flew; "They have thermals down there." Paul Meyers, Willard Rusk, and Bernie Rogers from Valpo told me not to buy it. But, that's what I bought anyway and I got all of the problems with it. My logbook shows that on 10/15/55 I flew Paul Meyers' Cessna 140 N76954 airplane to Macomb, Illinois. We went over there to take delivery of the Swift and of course Paul was going to fly it back since I had no retractable time and much less experience. He flew it back and I flew the Cessna 140 back. It was about a 2 hour and 15 minute flight. The Cessna 140 ran right along side the Swift indicating it wasn't very fast approximately 115 miles per hour. My first flight with the Swift N90318 was on 10/17/55, an hour and 15 minutes. It wasn't too bad with one person in it, but it wasn't good. I used to take off from Plymouth and I would quite often go by the hangar before I decided whether to go under the wires or over them. It was just that much of a ground lover. It also had a retractable gear that in this case was a big disadvantage. When the gear was down you had two great big bushel basket size holes under the wing that would catch air and slow you down. When you only have 85 horsepower you didn't need that. You would have to get the get the tail way up in the air so that the wheel holes in the wings didn't slow you down too much. Then at the last second pull back on the control wheel, lift it into the air and immediately put the wheels up there to plug up the holes. Quite often I would take off and I would get clear to Grovertown (about 6 miles) before I got enough altitude to make my turn to the left to exit the pattern. It was really a slow climbing airplane. It had a service ceiling of about 5,000 feet. That meant that if you landed in Denver it became a permanent monument. The airplane didn't go much higher than that. It was a very under powered airplane. Paul Meyers told me that when I purchased it. But where else could I find an airplane that had the equipment I felt I needed that I could buy.

I remember Paul taking me up in his Ryan PT22 and trying to do a loop with it. The airplane fell out of the loop at the top and everything got real quiet when the engine stopped. Paul hollered at me "Hey Don " and I hollered "Hey Paul." We fell upside down for a very long time but finally the nose fell through and we regained flying speed in a dive, the prop started to turn, and just as we came out of the dive the engine started. It was just in time to get a good close view of the hind end of a cow.

Paul said to me, "the first time you think about looping that Swift I want you to climb up as high as you can, then I want you to forget about it. Don't do it." I couldn't stand it. One afternoon I took it out and got it up as high as I could. I cranked the prop into low pitch and dove it and it went around so good that I went around twice. I enjoyed the heck out of that airplane. It didn't have much power but it was a pretty looking thing. It had a lot of pizzazz. As far as performance goes it was lousy. You had to be on your toes if you were going to survive. When they built those things, they all ran off of the end of the runway and crashed early. So, I had one of the few 85 horsepower Swifts left in the country.

On 3/22/56 my logbook shows that Paul Meyers and I took off for a night flight and flew up to South Bend. We called, and called them on the radio, and finally got an answer from them when we got right on top of them. We landed at a controlled airport. That was a big occasion for me. I thought, "now I can go anywhere". The truth of the matter was the airplane had a very inferior radio and you could just about holler as far as it would transmit.

The club had a balloon busting and spot landing contest at the Plymouth airport. I did real well at the spot landing contest because the Swift wouldn't float as many of the lighter planes would. I had sold the Luscombe and I believe broke even on it or made $100 or so when I bought the Swift. I had all of my money in this airplane and on 8/17/56 it was damaged by a tornado at the

Plymouth Airport. It was really bad. It pulled loose from the tie down, turned it over and dented in the front and broke the prop. A damaged airplane is the kind of item that the public thinks is public property and they will take parts or accessories feeling that it's fair game. In order to protect a damaged airplane, you must secure it. I elected to tow the airplane back to my front yard in town and park it where I could keep an eye on it. Of course it made a rather peculiar monument in the front yard but that is where it stayed until I sold it. I had quite a time trying to figure out what to do with it. I ended up selling it to a guy who came and got it. I think I got $800 for it because the engine was still real good. I don't know whether it was repaired or not but at least it passed from my hands.

My logbook shows that at about that time I went to work part time for Jim Hanley at Hanley Air Activities in Elkhart, Indiana. I show on 9/10/56 that I ferried a Piper PH22 from Elkhart to Independence, Missouri a flight of four hours and twenty-five minutes. It was a big flight for me delivering the airplane. It was the first time I ever rode in an airliner. I flew back in an airliner to South Bend and was picked up by one of Jim's men. In those days, if you rode on an airliner, you were treated like royalty. It wasn't like today, a cattle car. My son Marty says today, that when he flies on an airliner, he "moos" a lot. I asked what he meant by that and he said that he feels exactly like cattle must feel, herded here and there and put in a small cubicle.

On 10/4/56 Jim Hanley recommended me for a commercial flight test. I went to South Bend for my test and on 10/5/56 I satisfactorily completed my commercial flight test. There is quite a bit to learn before you take a test. You have to take a written exam and have to study to know what you can and can't do, how to navigate, and all the various regulations. To learn this, I would get into the bathtub and Betty would sit on the stool and she would ask me the various questions required on the test. She would then tell me when I was right and when I was wrong. Eventually I got it through my thick skull what was required and what wasn't and I passed the written and flight exam. It was the kind of studying that today probably would not happen. You would go to a flight school to get this information. I did pass the flight test and became a commercial pilot. That meant that I could take somebody with me and charge for it. At that time I was still pretty well out of the business. What do you charge? What do you do? What I needed to do was get an instructor's license. That's where you build your time, you don't build it as a commercial pilot. So I started studying for an instructors rating. I was doing some flying with a pilot by the name of Ev Tourjee in Elkhart, Indiana. He was a very nice young man who was the instructor for Jim Hanley. I had arranged to lease a Cessna 170B N2487D from Paul Meyers and he was gracious enough to give me a very good rate with the understanding that when I got my instrument rating I would sell it for him. I owe him a huge debt of gratitude for the opportunity he gave me. I felt that I could go ahead with this because this plane had the necessary equipment needed for an instrument rating. A flight instructor job was all I needed. I went back to South Bend after passing the written examination and on 1/8/57 in N2487D I passed my flight instructor's test. When I became a licensed flight instructor Jim Hanley started to use me on a part-time basis. I would go to Elkhart whenever he would call and give some dual instruction. Also, at various times, I would put a hood in the airplane and take instrument flight instruction. In those days, all you needed was for someone to ride with you so that you wouldn't run into somebody. Ev Tourjee would go along as a lookout for me. After I would fly awhile, I would turn it over to him and would tell him to try it. I'm sorry to say that he had flown enough that he didn't put full trust in the instruments. So, he was not very good when it came to instrument flying. Everett was killed in a flight from Meigs Field Chicago to Elkhart Ind. He crashed into Lake Michigan after turning east on take off on a rainy night with some people from a chair company from Elkhart and they were all killed. In fact, I was a pallbearer at his funeral. It was a very difficult time for me, as Everett was a good friend.

Shortly after Everett's death, I was called on by Jim Hanley to instruct full time. In those days, instructing was not just flying an airplane. You came in early in the morning, gassed up customer's airplanes, washed their windshields and got them on their way. Then, if there was instructing to do, you did that. If not, you took a can of gas and washed down the bellies of the airplanes to remove the oil. Most airplanes dripped oil, especially then. We also painted hangar doors or whatever was needed. In the evenings when customers came back with their planes, I would fill them up with gas and taxi them back to the hangars and put them away. It was a thrill just to taxi some of the nicer airplanes. When I finished with that I would go to the office and clean up, sweep the floor, and put everything away. This was a seven-day a week job. I made very little money only about forty dollars a week. Not because Jim wasn't paying me enough, he was paying me the going rate, but pilots didn't make much money. We had to borrow money from the bank to keep going because the family was still growing and I spent a lot of money going back and forth to Elkhart every day. I decided I would have to find another way to make a living so I had to quit.

In the early part of June 1957, shortly after I left Hanley Air Activities, I received a call from Homer Stockert in South Bend. This was Stockert Flying Service, the largest flying service in this part of the country. He had heard about me from Conrad Lesh (Tiz) who had been giving me some free instrument instruction. He asked me to come up and talk to him. He wondered if I was interested in going to work for him. I went up to talk to Homer and laid it on the line that I expected to fly; not just gas planes, or wash them or clean and paint. Not that I wouldn't do those kind of jobs but I wanted to primarily fly. He told me that I wouldn't have to do any of those things and I held him to it. I went up to Stockerts on June 2, 1957 and started instructing in an Aeronca Champ, and a Piper PA11 and I did some instructing in a Cessna 170. As time went on it became obvious to me that I was going to get a better education that I ever received before. It wasn't long before I was checked out in a Cessna 195 that had a 300 horsepower Jacobs radial engine on it. I went out and flew it around the field a couple of times and Homer said that I was all set, no one ever went with me to check me out. From that time on Homer called me "Air Power."

Within a relatively short length of time I was given the title of Chief Pilot. Not that I was much of a chief pilot since I was the "only" pilot but they needed somebody to fill out the papers. I spent a lot of time in the next few years flying all types of aircraft out of South Bend. The one thing missing in my life at that time was a multi-engine rating. No matter how much you flew and no matter how many people you taught to fly, if you didn't have a multi-engine rating you weren't considered to be much of a pilot. And much less of a pilot, for not having an instrument rating.

On 6/12/57 I flew the Bumble Bee, the big Cessna 195 with the 300 horse Jacobs engine from South Bend to French Lick with a motivational speaker in the South Bend area by the name of Herb True. I listened to his dissertation down there and was just fascinated by the fantastic presentation he gave. After that time I decided that I wanted to learn to speak, probably never as good as him, but at least good enough to get by.

I still had the use of the Cessna 170B N2487D with the instruments in it with which to get a license. One of the people on the field who became very instrumental in my future flying career was Conrad Lesch the man who had recommended me to Homer. Everyone called him Tiz. He flew a Twin Beech and was the consummate pilot, as good as they come in my book. Tiz gave me what you can't buy, the most strenuous and exacting personal instrument instruction I have ever known. He was by far the best as far as I was concerned at teaching people what they could and couldn't do.

I was instructing at the South Bend airport and since Notre Dame is in South Bend, Stockert's was chosen to teach the Air Force Primary at Notre Dame. I spent many days flying the students to prepare them to go into the Air Force. It was a very exacting syllabus for the flying program, spins included. Many days I flew 7 or 8 hours. Lots of days they would just hand me a sandwich and a drink and I didn't even get out of the airplane. Many times these green students were really green, especially after spins. You kind of got used to the vomit on the floor of the plane. I remember one of the students came back a year or so later and said, "Mr. Palbykin, are you still flying those little airplanes?" They were all flying larger and much more sophisticated aircraft than anything I had ever been in. It was really hard on your ego.

I remember an examiner telling me about a prospective instructor coming in for a test. He explained to the applicant that he would pretend to be a student. He said, "now I am a dumb SOB so tell me everything to do that you would tell a student." He said the first thing he did was to put me in the airplane and go around to prop it without giving me any instructions. As soon as the engine started the examiner pushed the throttle forward to teach the prospective instructor a lesson. He jumped away from the prop and came around to the door and yelled in "you are a dumb SOB." Another incident he told me about was in the early days an examiner would stand on the ground and watch the applicant. The procedure was for the student to fly around the pattern and make a couple of landings. Speed control was an important part of a landing. If you were too slow the aircraft would sink rapidly, and too fast caused it to float down the field past the designated spot. This student was going fast and slow and it looked like a stair step. The examiner asked the student "what was that." The student said "I was just pumping it down". The examiner said, well pump your ass out of here and "go learn to fly."

Bendix Corporation had a North American B25 N5548N based at South Bend in our hangars, and Homer Stockert was the pilot. Since he needed a co-pilot I was elected. He never went outside to find anyone if we had someone in the organization that could do it. On 7/8/57 we departed South Bend Airport in B25 N5548N to show off the Bendix anti-skid brake device as well as the torque link steering that they had developed. We flew into Hagerstown, Maryland for a demonstration to Fairchild. We flew into Beth Page and Peconic on Long Island and showed it to Grumann. While we were demonstrating the anti skid there was a General standing between the pilot and co-pilot seats. I told him he better brace himself and he glared at me indicating that I should mind my own business. Just before Homer put the brakes on I put my arm across to the back of the pilots seat and when we stopped the General was draped across my arm with a startled expression on his face.

The next day we flew down to Miami to show it to the airlines. I can remember one kind of peculiar incident there. We had two nose wheels, the normal one and the torque link steering. We had to use the normal gear for anti-skid demos so we would have sufficient prop clearance since the torque link nose wheel was too short. We had just taken off from Miami International when I told the tower that we were just going to drop the other nose gear and come right back and land. They called back in a panic asking what we were going to drop?

We flew into Washington D.C. and landed the B25 at the Washington National Airport. Homer was an excellent pilot but not up on radio manners. I was waiting for the tower to hesitate so I could call in. Homer grabbed the mike and started hollering "Hello Washington Tower." The tower got so mad with Homer butting in he told us to shut up and just get in line in the pattern. I was embarrassed, after all we were suppose to be professionals.

The B25 was quite an airplane with two 2600 horsepower Wright engines on it and it was a very noisy machine. Homer was the kind of guy who didn't believe much in gas but believed in oil. I remember him coming out to pour an extra quart of oil in an airplane that I was going fly and I knew that as the engine heated up it was going to expand and spill oil out all over the belly of the airplane. So I knew that there would be oil dripping off the belly when I landed. It didn't bother me if it didn't bother him since it was his oil. But as far as gas goes, he just didn't believe in putting gas into an airplane. As a result of that, he had several forced landings because of the lack of fuel. I was a little concerned about it since we were coming back from Florida, and as we passed over Indianapolis north bound a good 125 miles from South Bend I checked the tanks and couldn't get a reading on any of them. We just continued on and I kept telling him that we were about out of gas but it didn't bother him a bit. I tell you one thing, I had a parachute on and I checked the hatch overhead. It would have only taken one burp from that thing and I would have been out the top. We made it to South Bend with no problem, so he must have known something that I didn't know.

I kept slipping a little bit of instruction on instruments in every once in a while. I tried to learn everything that I could in order to prepare myself for my instrument rating. We were sitting in the office one day and Tiz said, "Don, why don't you go up and take the written instrument test?" He must have thought that I knew enough to pass the test and since we didn't have much business that day, I took the test and passed my instrument written.

The way we handled instruction at South Bend, because it was a controlled airport, was with light signals from the tower. They would give us a green light to land, a red light to go around, a flashing red/green light that indicated caution. We would indicate we had received the message by rocking the wings. I had a set of headphones on the student who rode in the front seat of the PA11 and I rode in the back seat. I had a microphone in my hand and could just drill my instructions into the student's head.

In the summer we flew the airplanes with the side window open. The top door would open up against the wing and the lower part would open down. The whole side of the airplane was open and it was nice and cool.

Since noise wasn't a factor we didn't pay too much attention to it. There were stories about some of the guys at South Bend who were wing walkers who sat out on the strut when they giving duel. I wasn't that brave. I wasn't going to get out on the strut with a student flying the airplane for anybody.

I was getting a little bored with flying over the mud flats which were located southwest of the airport and doing all of the turns around a point and the s-turns and other maneuvers over the same area. One Sunday morning I decided for the heck of it to go northeast. I flew over the northeast area and unbeknownst to me I flew over a nudist colony. I was back in the back, as the student was gliding along, and as I looked down I could see a bunch of people running around down there without any clothes on. A couple of them lying on cots waving their legs at me. I told the student to let me take over the controls and I flew over this area again and sure enough they were waiving at me again. When I got back to the airport, Dora Stockert was fit to be tied. Evidently she had received a couple of telephone calls that I was peeping over the nudist colony. The truth is that I didn't even know it was there. So after that, we stayed away from there. The student didn't even know what was going on.

I had a student one time that got scared and froze on the stick. He was absolutely terrified. I shouted at him to let go, but he just held on. I had to hit him in the head with the hand held radio that was pretty heavy because it had batteries inside it. He grabbed his head with both hands and that solved the problem. Part of the procedure in the landing sequence was to close the throttle and start a glide. I had a student one time that didn't close the throttle, he reached down and shut the switch off. He did a good job after that and landed in a small parking lot at

Bendix. Dora informed me I had better get over there and get it out before the news found out about it. I went over and fired it up and got it out of there pronto. I don't think the CAA (Civil Aeronautics Administration) even knew about it or they would have made a big deal out of it. Then we would have been filling out a lot of reports.

Homer Stockert was kind of a legend in the area. We always called him "Pappy." He had been a test pilot for Republic on Thunderbolts during the war. That was a big powerful airplane. We had a lot of respect for him. We called Dora Stockert "Mammy." She was the mother hen for everyone around there. As I look in my logbook I see all of her notations placed so neatly. She put all of the entries in my logbook at that time because I was so busy giving instruction. Of course, my flight time kept building up.

As time went on in South Bend we were building more and more hangars every year. We taught more people to fly and they would buy airplanes and we needed hangars. Business was growing by leaps and bounds and I remember being asked to attend a Cessna meeting where they berated us for not having modern airplanes. We were still instructing in the old Aeronca Champion and Piper PA11. They told Homer that they didn't have much hope for him since Dora already had more diamond rings than she had fingers. I remember one time going back into the hangar to see about the Aeronca that I was doing spins in for the Air Force Primary program. I asked how the wing fabric checked out on the inspection. One of the mechanics said that he couldn't tell me. I said, "what do you mean you can't tell me?" I looked up and I could see where he had put the patch on over the test area. The tester had gone clear through and there was a huge hole. They had a tester that you put against the wing and if it tested real good it wouldn't make a hole in the fabric. If it was pretty good it would make a small hole. This one had gone clear through. The fabric was completely rotten and he was afraid to tell Homer. I went to the office and said, "Homer, I'm not flying that airplane any more." He wanted to know why not. I said, "go back to look at that airplane and feel the fabric and look at that test." He went back there and mumbled around a lot but retired the airplane. It could have been made airworthy by recovering it, but Cessna was after us to buy a new Cessna 150 for instruction. When you do spins, you put quite a bit of stress on the fabric and you can pull all of the fabric off leaving nothing to keep you up.

Homer was against frivolous maintenance. That meant anything that was not absolutely necessary for the aircraft to fly. I remember Homer taking a trip in the Cessna 195. He had some hunting dogs that he would carry around in the back of his Chevrolet. He also had some blankets that he kept in the back seat that the dogs rested on. On this particular trip he put the passengers in the back seat and threw the hairy blankets over them. After Homer came back from the trip Chuck Post, our mechanic asked him how the heater worked, and Homer said just fine. I thought something was wrong so I asked Post about it. He told me he had the heater igniter in his pocket and the heater could not work without it.

Another peculiar incident happened to me on 10/19/57. I was asked to take a lady out over Lake Michigan so that she could scatter her husband's ashes over the lake. She had the ashes in an urn in the back seat. A Cessna has the ability to open the window part way about a foot or so, with a hinge at the top. I instructed her to get the urn outside of the airplane before taking the lid off because of the slipstream. It had started spitting a little rain at that time, and I opened the window but before I had a chance to stop her, she took the cap off and held it up and immediately we were enveloped in a cloud of ashes. The interior of the airplane was full of ashes. It was a mess to say the least. Everyone was embarrassed. When we got back to Stockerts, we pulled the airplane up on the ramp, got the garden hose and washed the rest of her husband down the drain. We also washed the airplane where the ashes had stuck to the tail because of the slight moisture from the rain. We then got a vacuum cleaner to clean out the airplane. It was a very unhappy situation to say the least.

Tiz was still giving me a little bit of instruction on instruments every time we got a chance. Towards the end of 1957 I had really improved. We worked on different things to get me ready to take the instrument examination. On the last day of the year we flew for about an hour and a half so we were getting to the point that we worked at it pretty hard. On 04/18/58 I successfully passed my instrument flight test at South Bend, Indiana. It was quite a test. The airplane had an eight ball horizon in it. It looked like a ball in the center and you weren't supposed to be able to "spill it." It was a nice instrument but it didn't work and you had to ignore it completely. Since I didn't have a horizon it was a lot more difficult to fly instruments. Tiz was getting me ready, and there was nothing that he could do to me in that airplane that I couldn't recover from. I used the air speed and needle and ball and could straighten it right up no matter what.

When I went up to take this test the examiner that gave me the test, Lester Cooling, said he didn't want me to take the test in that airplane because it didn't have a horizon and I would surely fail. I didn't have the couple of hundred dollars to fix it, I said I would take my chances and I wanted to take the test. Tiz talked to him and told him I could do it. Since Mr. Cooling was going to give me an instrument instructor rating at the same time Tiz wanted to know how he was going to handle that test. Mr. Cooling told him that he was going to put me in the right seat and have me instruct him. I think Tiz was elated that I passed the test without the horizon because he had prepared me well. So I also got my instrument instructor rating that day.

I now had the instrument rating but you don't do much instrument flying in a single engine airplane. So the next move was to try to get some time in a multi-engine aircraft which was very expensive. One person in Plymouth, Indiana, Bob Kirkley, had an Apache with small engines, 150-horse power. I think it was the only twin in Plymouth at that time. He was willing to lease it to me to get my multi-engine rating. I took some instruction in the Apache that we affectionately referred to as a Double Breasted Piper Cub. If you lost one engine, and you were full you're probably going to come down, but it was the only thing that I could afford. That's the way it was. On May 20, 1958, I took my multi-engine flight test and passed. I also got my multi-engine instructor rating. I now had an instrument rating, a commercial rating and an instructor's rating as well as my multi engine rating. That is about all there was to get, but I still didn't have a job flying the twin engine airplanes that the pro's flew. I remember when I first went to work at Stockerts I made about $80 a week. Good wages for a pilot. We worked every day. My day off consisted of when the weather was bad. After my multi-engine flight test I came in and a couple of the top professional were there, Jim Abrams and Cap Elliott who flew for Associates, Cap said, "what happened out there today?" On take-off Mr. Cooling had pulled one engine on me. That airplane was extremely critical.

You had to feather the dead engine immediately. You had to hold that wing about three degrees up and you had to maintain a speed at approximately 115 knots. That's what I did. When I took off and he pulled the engine, we disappeared over the treetops. Cap Elliott said, "Don, we give you up. We thought you were done for. We thought you had had it." I said, "well I wasn't too sure I hadn't had it either." But I said that the examiner was in there and cut the engine and what was I supposed to do? Cap said, "I would have broke his friggen arm!" There are more people killed practicing engine failures than are killed in actual failures in multi-engine aircraft.

During the time I was instructing at Stockerts I met Dick Kistler who became a close and good friend of ours. We sure didn't have much discretionary money at that time and Dick and his wife Fern would always ask us to go with them in their airplane on vacations. I think part of the reason at first was because I had an instrument rating and he knew we would be able to fly in weather where he would have to land and sit out the bad conditions. He loved flying and enjoyed the trips where we were flying instruments the most. We had some wonderful trips down south stopping here and there to visit caves and other attractions. One time we spent a week in New Orleans that was a memorable experience. We became close friends and in later years we toured with them in their motor homes. (They bought four new Blue Birds during the time we knew them).

There were several people that I taught to fly that I was very concerned about. One of the people that I taught was a very nice man, who owned a large drug company in South Bend. He passed his written examination with about a 98 that was unheard of, he knew everything. When it came to flying the airplane he left a little to be desired as far as his skills were concerned but he wanted to go all the way. When I started flying with him it took about 20 hours to solo him because he was just so slow picking up the skills connected with flying. When I took him cross- country I remember instances where he just didn't get the job done. We would be flying using pilotage with his finger on the map and I would ask where were we supposed to be. He would point to the line he had drawn. Then I would ask where are we now. He would show me and I would say, "why are we over here? Why aren't we over on the line?" Then he would just continue right on. I remember the first time I let him go on a solo cross-country. I was very worried but he said, "Don, don't' worry about a thing. I'm going to go north out of here until I get to Grand Rapids and if I get into trouble I'll turn left and run west until I run into the lake, I'll take the lake to Michigan City and the road until I get home." So, I let him go. One of the things that happened that he told me about later was when he got to Grand Rapids he said that he spotted the field and called them but they told him they didn't have him in sight yet. Then they said that they had him in sight now but he said that now he didn't have them in sight. After a while they got him worked around and he got in and out of the airport. Another time up in South Bend he was doing touch and go landings. He was in the pattern and was all set to land when they told him to go around. He said "too late now" and went ahead and landed. He was a character but he got the job done. Eventually he got an instrument rating.

Another guy that I taught to fly worked for a very large steel company that put round steel pipes under the railroads, Anco Steel, and he was the type of guy that would go hunting for bear with a club. He had no fear in him. We would go somewhere in an airplane and fly back into South Bend and if South Bend was instrument conditions I would call the tower and get a special instrument clearance into the control zone, then make an approach and land. When he was alone he would get out and get stuck somewhere and he would do the same thing. He didn't have the ratings and wasn't legally allowed to do so. I had an awful time getting him to turn around in such a situation but he finally agreed and did a fine job of flying. I later sold him a multi engine airplane, as I did many of the people I had taught to fly.

There was a time when I was giving instruction to a guy I just couldn't handle. I just didn't seem to get through to the guy how to fly. Usually these people were very wealthy and heads of companies. I didn't want to insult the man and went to Mammy and said, "Dora, I'm not going to get it done with this guy, he's just not going to make it. I want to bow out of this." She said, "that's okay I'll send Tiz out." Now Tiz didn't suffer fools lightly. He was a very good instructor. He went out with this guy and in about thirty minutes the guy comes in the door, red in the face, pays the bill and slams the door and departs. He never came back again. Tiz was over in the corner sanding on his model airplanes. I was just dying to find out what Tiz had done and finally I said, "Tiz, what happened?" "Well", said Tiz, "after we were up there for awhile I told him that only a jackass makes the same mistake twice and you've made it three times. Let's go back. You're wasting your money and my time." So I guess I wasn't too hard on him in the long run.

Students always tell me after a little instruction that they don't have any trouble with taking off but they are worried about getting down. I always tell them "Then you don't have a problem because we never left anyone up there yet, they always come down."

During the course of my instructing I taught a young girl by the name of Joan Garlanger to fly. Betty and I had decided to take a vacation down to New Orleans. We were looking for someone to share the cost of the fuel since we would be using the Cessna 170 N2487D. It would be a good deal for who ever we took since that's all they would have to pay. When Joan found out about the trip she asked to go. We agreed that she and her girl friend could make the trip with us. We met at my house on the morning of our departure 7/14/58. They arrived with two huge suitcases that were so heavy I had trouble getting them out of the car. I had assumed (never assume) that they would bring reasonable luggage. I said Joan they just won't fit. They took all the clothing out of one suitcase and put it all in the other. So we lost the bulk but very little of the weight. We took off from Plymouth early that morning and it was still cool. When we landed at Memphis for fuel it was boiling hot. I was concerned about getting the tired old Cessna 170 off the ground with such a heavy load. I think we used up most of the large runway before it started flying. It was the better part of an hour before we had climbed to cruising altitude. We had a wonderful time in New Orleans and the return trip was uneventful.

In April of 1959, Mr. Stockert sold a Piper Comanche to a Mr. Cecil Pond who was President of Wheel Horse Products in South Bend, Indiana. They built a small garden tractor and on April 14, 1959, I flew out to the Piper plant at Lock Haven Pa. with Mr. Pond to pick up his new Comanche. While we were there we had an opportunity to meet William Piper the man who introduced the Piper Cub, the first light airplane that ordinary people could afford. He was giving a tour of the plant and I asked him how many people worked at Piper? He turned around and said "About half of them."

He was quite a man and probably more than any other person was responsible for the growth in general aviation. I feel I owe him a lot because most of my life was involved with general aviation. Cecil and I flew the new Comanche back to South Bend from the factory. It was a 180 horsepower version, and that was the smallest engine for that airplane. I thought it was an excellent airplane and would do real well. I proceeded to teach Mr. Pond how to fly the airplane in the weeks to come. He was a good student and did a first class job of flying. He wanted to be absolutely perfect. I worked with him quite a while and got him soloed in the Comanche. He ended up getting a private license so that he could take trips in his airplane. Meanwhile, I flew quite a few trips with him in an attempt to get him started. So, for some time I acted as his pilot and flew him from place to place.

While working for Stockert Flying Service I met a man named Lee Fisher of Lee Fisher and Associates who was an airport designer. A gregarious, good-looking man who was like a huge teddy bear. He had a wonderful wife by the name of Nancy. I flew him in the Bumble Bee, the Cessna 195, N4378V to look at various spots for the new airport in Grand Rapids. He asked me where I thought he should put the airport. I told him where I thought it should be and at the meeting I attended with him he announced that after careful study and great consideration of the city's growth he decided to put the airport right where I had pointed out. He made a great name for himself and did a heck of a good job. He designed the Grand Rapids airport and the Indianapolis Airport as well as many more. We became friends and he asked me to teach his wife Nancy to fly.

Nancy was a wonderful girl but she wasn't red hot when it came to taking instructions. I would set her like a clock. I would tell her were going to take off and when we get in the air I want you to climb up to 600 feet. I want you to level off and I want you to look back to your left, turn and climb to pattern altitude. I want you to level off, look back and turn left again. You'll be on down wind leg and on the southwest end of the field opposite the end of the runway I want you to pull on the carburetor heat and call the tower and tell them that we are down wind for runway 9. Then I want you to fly to the southeast end opposite that end of the runway and reduce power for descent. As soon as you have established your glide I want to you turn on to the base leg and level off and clear the engine, make sure your speed is OK and turn final. I had to set her just like a clock but she got pretty good at it. Lee and I had a bet that I would never solo her. I called Lee one day and I told him that he better get out there pretty quick because she will be flying solo when you get here. Sure enough I soloed Nancy 5/30/59 and she did a fine job. I doubt that she ever flew again but it was a great accomplishment for her.

Mr. Pond and I had taken several trips in the single engine Comanche but there were times that we couldn't go because the weather was too bad. He decided that when he wanted to go he wanted to go. On 8/1/59 Mr. Pond of Wheel Horse Products purchased a brand new twin engine Cessna 310 N1855H. We flew the airplane back to South Bend Indiana. It was a fast and in the early days considered an unstable instrument airplane. I was a new multi engine pilot and I am sure many people wondered if I could handle it on instruments, me included. Tiz said no problem and proceeded to get me ready by giving me some instrument dual in it.

In the later part of 1959 a company named Fairbanks Whitney moved the base of their DC 3 from an airport in the Chicago area to South Bend Indiana.

Captain Jack was the head honcho but the steward was the guy that gave the orders as far as the aircraft went. I had given him some instruction and he seemed to like me, as most students like their instructor. They occupied the large hanger across the ramp that had been used by Studebaker. They had a Douglas DC 3 that was really a cream puff with the big engines and a fancy interior. They had a need from time to time for a co-pilot. They used to be gone all of the time. I was the only one with a multi-engine rating and instrument rating that was available so they asked Stockert to provide pilot service. So I was drafted to go. They called and said that they would pick me up at Lincoln, Nebraska. I took an airliner out there and while I was sitting in the terminal my name came over the loud speaker. They said that they couldn't meet me there but they would meet me in Denver. I got another flight to Denver and got the same call over the loud speaker that they would meet me in San Francisco and to come to the hotel. When I got to San Francisco I was a tired puppy after a whole day of chasing them. I was treated like royalty because these guys were big tippers. I was picked up at the airport in a limo and taken to the hotel. The steward was a real operator. He ordered the fuel, did the tipping, arranged for the hangar and pretty much took care of everything. He always ordered meals for everyone on the airplane. He had the best ones marked for the crew, the pilot, co-pilot and himself. He also was in the habit of having his laundry done on the road. Whenever we would get to a destination he would grab all of the laundry and send it out to the cleaners. For years my shorts had his name stenciled on them because he sent them all out. He was also quite an operator when it came to tipping and gratuities. I would keep a list of my expenses and he asked to see it. I was very careful with what I spent and

I showed it to him. He said, "Oh, this will never do." So he tore it up and threw it away. He said, "write down what I say. Put down $8.50 for breakfast and $2.00 in gratuities, $12.00 for lunch and $3.00 in gratuities and $25.00 for dinner and $5.00 for gratuities. Then he asked if I needed any shirts or anything. That is the way they handled it. They were a little concerned that I would submit a lesser amount in my expense report and thereby make problems for them. So, they dictated what I put down. The thing about the DC 3 is that when you were on it you lived there. The next day we went from San Francisco to Las Vegas and then from Las Vegas to Albuquerque and then to Midland, Texas. I remember we picked up Drew Pearson and some people for an overnight trip to New York. We loaded them up in their bathrobes and they went to sleep while we flew all night and watched the sun come up. That was a slow airplane.

I got along real well with the Fairbanks Whitney people and they offered me a job. I really considered it because I was use to making about $100 per week and they were talking about paying me $25,000 a year to start. I had to make a decision to either make a lot of money and possibly lose my family or continue working at Stockerts and just barely get by. They were buying a new airplane a Convair and it would have been a good career move but I turned the offer down with much regret. Being away from my family that much was more time than I was willing to give and in hindsight it was the right decision after all.

The proud owners of a Luscombe 8A.

My three sons, Betty, and my other love.

The Swift in all its glory with its proud aviator.

The Swift after the storm. It sold for about $800.

—OFFICIAL 1956 PROGRAM—

Plymouth Speedway

INC.

Sanctioned By

NORTHERN STOCK CAR RACING ASS'N., Inc.

CO-OWNERS

Howard Bauman - Paul Meyers - Don Palbykin

TIME TRIALS 7:30 P. M. — FIRST RACE 8:30 P. M.

RACING EVERY SUNDAY NIGHT

DON'S SPORTING GOODS

For Your

Johnson Motors — Fishing Tackle
Hunting Supplies — Photo Equipment
And Numerous Other Sporting Goods Items

"It Pays To Play"

DON'S SPORTING GOODS

Price 25c

Paul Meyers, his Plymouth Speedway car, and me.

Plymouth Speedway official 1956 program.

My three sons, and Betty, 710 Ferndale where we parked the Swift.

Betty and me taking possession of Cessna 170B N2487D.

Helen DePew, Betty and me about to fly back to Plymouth.

Stockert Flying Service where I really learned to fly.

Conrad (Tiz) Lesh's Twin Beech, yours truly in front.

Homer Stockert in the center with two Bendix technicians.

The author leaning against the B25 with one technician.

A young instructor with a Piper Tri-Pacer. (The flying milk stool)

Wheel Horse Products

I note that in my logbook my last entry for Stockert's was January 11, 1960. Previous to that time Mr. Pond had talked to me about going to work for him and I had accepted. Dora said a couple of weeks notice would be OK. I had been teaching one of our line techs, Joe Mrozek (Joe later became an airline pilot) to instruct and he was about ready to take over. I went to work for Wheel Horse Products the next week as their pilot. Mr. Pond had attempted to make a VFR, (Visual Flight Rules), flight to Stuart, Florida and wound up getting socked in at Atlanta. I think his wife Betty decided that she wanted no more trips like that, she wanted a professional pilot on board. I picked up the airplane in Atlanta on January 12, 1960 and flew to Stuart, Florida.

While working for Wheel Horse Products, when I wasn't flying for them, they used me in other capacities. When we got back to South Bend I remember going to the office where I had been told to report the next morning. I went in with the leather jacket on that I always wore at the airport. Everyone else was wearing a suit and it dawned on me that unless I put a suit or sport coat on and dressed up a little bit, I was always going to be "just the pilot."

I was asked by the American distributor to go to Paris to evaluate a new Potez aircraft. Shortly after going to work for Wheel Horse Betty and I flew to Paris and really enjoyed our first European vacation. We also met with the Wheel Horse dealer and they showed us the town. We visited the Louvre, Notre Dame, the Opera, and the Follies as well as many wonderful restaurants.

Cecil was a perfectionist and had gone to the airport to practice take off's and landings. I went out a couple of hours later and Dora was in the office. I said to her, "Is he still out there?" She said, "Yeah." I said, "Call the tower and have them send him in for tires." She did just that and he came in with a big grin on his face.

While working for Stockerts I had flown the Wheel Horse people to the New York Hardware Show. It was the first flight I had made in that congested area around New York City and as a single pilot you are as busy as a one-armed paperhanger especially in the Cessna 310. It went very well and I think that was a big factor in Mr. Pond hiring me to fly for him. He saw that we were lined up with the runway as we emerged from the clouds and I am sure he gave a sigh of relief. He didn't know it but I gave a similar sigh.

Now that I worked for Wheel Horse and had a mechanical background, Mr. Pond felt that it would be best to use me to take care of service problems. He made me Service Manager. Since there was no service department and they had just launched a new line of tractors, it was incumbent upon me to find out what this tractor was all about. I asked to check out one of the tractors and it was brought to me in a carton. I assembled it and found numerous things wrong. You couldn't get the wheels on the front because the axle was bent in such a way that it wouldn't allow the front wheels to go on. When you sat on the seat and bounced up and down the seat spring hit the battery and shorted it out. The throttle cable was bending if it were pushed forward. This was a brand new model. We had them all over the country ready to be delivered to customers. I brought this to their attention and was told to write a service bulletin about it. I had never written a service bulletin but I proceeded to write one, and got assistance from the printing company to make drawings and print the detailed information I had written.

We also had a starter that was very weak and had a set of bi-metal points in it that would pop open if it encountered any heavy lugging. As soon as you turned the starter key it turned over once or twice and popped the points and nothing happened. It was an American Bosch starter and it worked all right in the summer but it just didn't have enough power to turn the engine over in the winter. The battery was small and when it was cold it was not very efficient. Since we sold these tractors to push and blow snow it was imperative that we do something about this immediately.

Mr. Pond set up a meeting and we flew to the Tecumseh factory in Wisconsin and met with Mr. Cal Role, the Vice President of the company. He was a most impressive and dynamic gentleman. I asked Mr. Pond as we were flying up there what he wanted me to say to these people. I was really a novice and didn't know what to say. He said, "just tell them what is wrong with it." Mr. Role's office was beautiful, with a huge desk and electric powered drapes overlooking an artificial lake. We sat down; he pulled his chair forward, leaned his elbows on the huge thick glass desk and ask, "what can I do for you?" Since I didn't know what else to say I responded, "your damn starter is no good." Well, he scowled at me for a little bit but he knew that the starter had a problem. I am sure he did, because they were already developing a new one. Then a big smile came over his face and from that time on Cal Role and I got along extremely well. I eventually got him to send new starters out to everyone and we put stiffer springs on the seats and fixed the throttle control system and ground off the wheel bearings a bit so that the front wheels would fit on. The new Wheel Horses were off to a good start in spite of all the initial problems.

After preparing a couple of the service bulletins I became acquainted with the various people who were distributors around the country. Cecil and I would climb in the airplane and go from distributor to distributor. Many of these people had done millions of dollars of business with Wheel Horse and we had never met them. They would pick us up the airport, and we would go to their office, talk over their problems and then take them out to lunch. We would then go on to the next place that evening and do the same thing and wind up having dinner with the distributor. As time went on, I remember Mr. Pond would go to sleep on each flight that we took and catch 40 winks. I was up front doing the flying. He would always say to me, "how come you're tired? I'm not tired." As a result of this contact I became friendly with the distributors in the United States and Canada. As Service Manager, if they had a problem, they would call me and I would climb into the airplane and within two or three hours I would be landing at their airport to look over the problem. Therefore, I became a fairly useful part of Wheel Horse by taking care of the service problems.

Mr. Pond then decided to make me Assistant Sales Manager. As such I worked for Jack Nelson the Sales

Manager. He had worked in sales for Motor Wheel Co. and sold the very popular Reo mower and camping equipment. He thought that while I was going around to all of our distributors, I might as well be selling.

After I had started the Service Department they had asked me to write a warranty policy. Since I didn't know anything about warranties, I gathered copies of our competitors warranties, took what I thought was good out of them, made up a warranty policy and sent it to our attorneys to have them check it, and that's what we used.

At that time I was writing a lot of service letters. I recorded them on a Dictaphone and the secretary typed them for me. I am a notoriously bad speller and even to this day have to use a Franklin Language Master to help me with my spelling. I do like to use large words and elaborate on some explanations. We got a new secretary to take care of my correspondence and one day she came into my office to ask me how to spell a word. I said I don't have the vaguest idea how to spell it, "What do you think we hired you for?"

As far as parts were concerned, since we were such a small, growing, company, we had just shipped the dealer the unpainted parts at no charge. Well, I had to set up a place to store parts, have them painted, and ship them from so that when we had a problem we could take care of it properly. They assigned a small area in the plant for parts and we put a little fence around it. If we didn't, the production guys would find the parts there rather than looking for them in the plant, and we would come back to fill orders and the parts would be gone. So it became quite a battle for parts between production and service. In the long haul, production always won. There was no way that they would shut down the line; it had to keep going. Eventually we were able to work around it and developed a pretty good parts department.

I hired a guy by the name of Jack Walton to run the service end of it and he became Service Manager. Jack Walton, if anything did a better job than I did when he started in the service department, since all he had to worry about was service. He developed a lot of good information that went out to the dealers. Later yet I hired another man named John Ulbricht to run the parts department. I was still responsible for parts and service but I had capable people to take care of the everyday problems. At that time they had a big meeting and decided to change the names of everyone. Jack Nelson became the Director of Marketing and I became the Assistant Director of Marketing. Nothing changed but the name.

When I went to Wheel Horse I made $600 a month. That was a lot of money to me, not much for a pilot, but to me a lot of money. When you go from $100 a week, which is $430 a month, to $600 a month, you begin to think that you are doing "okay." I always like to tell people that I never asked for a raise in my life. I never thought that I should ask for a raise. If I was doing a good job I shouldn't have to ask for more money. Perhaps it would have been wise to do so. I could have said that I was worth more than that but I feel good about it to this day that I never did.

With a background in printing at Transo Envelope Company in Chicago I felt we could improve our ability to get brochures, parts lists and instruction sheets out on time. We were always fighting a battle to get those things printed. So I said that I wanted to put in our own printing press and do our own printing. I got approval to purchase a little A B Dick lithography machine and put it in. This was another new department. I took the pictures myself in most cases and started to develop a small specification sheet in two colors with a lot of information and pictures to get by until the new four-color brochures were available. With the new spec sheet we had a picture of the tractors, with a little blurb about them, before they were ever ready for delivery. These were very well received and were a big hit with the distributors, because they had them ahead of time when people were asking what the new line looked like. They were able to show spec sheets on all of the products. Before we did this the Biddle Company our advertising agency that prepared the four-color brochures usually didn't have them ready until well after the introduction of the new models. Another reason was that the four-color brochures cost us and the distributors and dealers a lot of money. The printing department got so big that I could not run the press and take the pictures and still take care of my other duties. I hired a man by the name of Harold McCartney to run it. I told him that we did not have enough to print then so he would have to work in the parts department when he was not printing. I was sure I could find enough for him to do soon since we had so much printing done outside. As soon as we started printing the manual for the tractors and the parts lists we were swamped. In fact we had to hire several people to help in the print room. Not only did we improve the availability of spec sheets, tractor manuals, and parts lists but also we saved over $ 200,000 per year according to Bob Hawkins the comptroller. Harold is still a friend and lives in Henderson, Nevada close to where I now live in Las Vegas, Nevada. We see each other for dinner from time to time, and still talk about the Wheel Horse days.

I had developed quite a relationship with a lot of our distributors by then and I remember a couple of exciting incidents. We had starter switches on the early models that were on top of the hood at a slight angle. It was easy to get water into that switch and cause it to short out. One of our distributors in Chicago told a story about a customer that purchased a tractor. We called the Wheel Horse tractors our adult toy department and the units were often the apple of the owner's eye, and were all waxed up and put in along side the cars. This guy was sleeping one night and heard the tractor starter grinding downstairs in his garage next to his car, like someone was trying to steal the tractor. He grabbed his shotgun and went down the basement and just about that time the tractor started again (from a short in the starter switch) and he blew a huge hole in the floor of his house.

I remember a dealer in Texas writing me a long letter about how he had Wheel Horses tied up at a rail in front of his store with rings attached from them to the tractor. We use to do a lot of gimmicks like that. The motto was "get a horse, a Wheel Horse of course." He said a rainstorm came up and two of them started up and left. He had parked them in gear. One year we built a larger tractor with the same transmission but a much bigger engine and frame and one started down the hill with a guy on it and no matter how hard he pushed on the brake he couldn't stop it and rode it right into a river. I heard about all of the problems and was constantly writing letters to distributors and in some cases customers trying to get them solved.

One year our advertising company, the Biddle Company, developed a stick horse. A little broomstick with a Wheel Horse head on it. The wheel with a horse symbol in a plastic covered soft emblem that fit on the head of it. The idea was that we were suppose to buy them for a certain amount of money and sell them to the distributors and they were supposed to sell them to our dealers, and the dealers were to give them to their customers. I've got news for you; most dealers don't want to have anything to do with giving away money. I don't care if we paid part and they paid part, they still didn't want to have anything to do with it. We couldn't give those damn things away. They were just taking up space in the plant. We made tractors and took them right out the door and put them in the truck and shipped them. We didn't have sufficient room for parts much less stick horses. We decided that we would ship some of them to the New York Hardware Show and give them away as an advertising promotion.

We had a display made where the stick horses were stuck in like a bunch of suckers broomstick handle first. That was at a time when other manufactures of lawn and garden equipment as well as farm equipment, were trying to get started in the garden tractor business. I remember Porter Cable was trying to get started and International Harvester and several others. People tore down our booth to get at the stick horses. I guess everyone wanted to take one home to their children or their grandchildren. Within a very short time they were all gone and we had to call South Bend to have them send a truck over night to get more to us. It was an unexpected phenomenal sales promotion. Later on that night we found out that the girls at the Copa Cabana were dancing around the stage with stick horses.

Our sales manager, Jack Nelson, was quite a guy to get things done like that and he was delighted at how things were going with this promotion. Cecil and I had gone out and had dinner early in the evening. We usually stayed together but this time I was sharing a room with Jack and had gone back to the room early that night to get a good nights rest. I took a shower and climbed into bed au natural. (I don't wear clothes in bed). I don't think that it's good for you. I think you could get bound up that way. I was sound asleep and the next thing I remember I look up, and here is Jack Nelson, and he had this gal with him and she was giggling and right behind her was the house detective. Now Jack had gone through the lobby with this gal and the house detective had followed them to our room. Jack came into the room, turned the lights on and whipped off my covers and said, "there he is. He's young go get him." This gal was giggling and squealing and the house detective was threatening to run us all in. What an embarrassing way to wake up.

Cecil really enjoyed kidding around with the waitresses and the bartenders. He had a small hydrometer that could tell if a martini was dry or had a lot of vermouth in it. It had a clip on it just like a pen and he kept it in his pocket at all times. He would very deliberately ask for a very dry martini and when it came he would pull out his hydrometer and with a big flourish check the drink. Almost without fail it would have too much vermouth and would not check out. When he complained the waitress would take the drink back and bring one that was pure gin. Cecil would thank them profusely after checking the drink and from then on we didn't get any watered drinks.

We were flying the Cessna 310, an excellent six passenger twin engine airplane that cruised at about 230 miles per hour. One night we were coming across from Buffalo, New York into Boston. Suddenly there was a terrible noise. It sounded as if someone had fired a shotgun in the cabin. I didn't realize it at the time but we had struck a large bird, and fortunately the windshield didn't break. When we landed we could see that it was a bird, or what was left of a bird.

Another time we were really high trying to get over some clouds and eventually we couldn't top them and I had to go down into the weather. That time we encountered the worst case of St. Elmo's Fire I had ever seen. This is a static electricity phenomenon. As we looked out of the windows we could see fire coming off of the tips of the props about one foot long. The flames just flew off of the tips. It's not a dangerous situation but it sure makes you feel uncomfortable. Jack Nelson was with me and he pointed to the props and sparks flew from the tips of his fingers to the windshield.

Each year when our new models came out I was the pitchman for them and Jack as the Director of Marketing introduced me to explain the new models. I would tell them what we had improved and explained how we had helped the salability of them. As I did this I got to thinking about how Herb True had done such a fantastic job of speaking. I followed some of his methods. I got to the point where I really enjoyed putting on those shows.

I remember one time Herb was demonstrating the difference between a good salesman and a mediocre salesman. He claimed that a good salesman would hand you his card and say, "My name is Joe Blow, what's yours?" And you were so taken aback, you might sing "Happy birthday to me" you were so confused you could hardly get your name out. He talked about how he went out to a dealership to see the new cars. The salesmen were lurking around the corner and ignoring him. He was wondering about all of the features on the new models, so why didn't someone come over? Finally a salesman came sauntering over and said, "Did you drive out to see the new cars?" I wanted to tell him "No I rode my bicycle out here" but I didn't. Then the salesman said, "What kind of a car do you have?" He said that he had a 1947 Dodge. And the salesman said, "Boy, that was a dog!" Needless to say he was so insulted that he left. He went to the other side of town and the salesman came right up to him and handed him his card and introduced himself. With that he asked him to come over and see the new cars. He opened the trunk and climbed in and jumped around to show him how roomy it was and how easy it was to get things in and out. He got in the front seat of the car and ran the seat back and forth to show him the power seats. He put the seat back and said this position is for you, then brought it up nice and close and said this is for your wife. The salesman went on and on and asked, "What kind of car do you have?" He said that he had a 1947 Dodge. The salesman said, "How much do you want for it?" I said I would like to have $500 for it. The guy said, "That speaks awfully well for the care you have given that car." And he said, "Let's go talk to the sales manager and see what "we" can get for it." We meaning the salesman and the customer that wanted to purchase the car. The purchaser said, "What do you mean, we?" The salesman said, "Oh, I'm on your side."

That is the kind of salesmanship I was trying to teach to our dealers, and the dealers were not the kind of people that normally sold anything; they were the people that repaired lawn mowers. The message we were trying to impart to the people selling our tractors was foreign to them. We were very successful in getting them to adopt some of our "sales techniques." Our sales were almost doubling each year.

When Mr. Pond was going to visit some part of the country and was going to be there a week or so, I immediately leased a car and drove around to spend time talking with our dealers trying to get their insight, as to what we could do to improve our product. I established a good relationship with them. We spent a lot of time in Florida. That was a great place to go and there was a lot of things to see and many good dealers in Florida. I found out down in Florida that you were a lot better off if you didn't wear a tie. You just came in like a "good old' boy."

In the first month of 1962, we took delivery of a new Cessna 310. It was a later model and it had the canted tip tanks and a de-icer system. It was a very good airplane N2905R. We had put so many hours on the other aircraft that we felt it was time to trade. We used the Cessna 310 and had nothing but good luck with that model. I don't remember any serious problems; maybe a radio squawk or chasing down a wiring harness that caused a little problem.

There were some minor things that happened. I am looking at a clipping with the headline:

"Plane lands after alarm"

A twin-engine private aircraft landed safely early last night at Hancock Airport despite indication the landing gear was not locked in place. Airport officer John Hannon alerted city police, fire units and sheriff departments in a Code Baker when the pilot radioed the tower that the landing gear trouble light flashed on. Pilot Don Palbykin of 515 West Ireland Road, South Bend, Indiana, said the light came on as he put the gear in place it was an apparent malfunction of the lighting circuit not the landing gear. Palbykin was accompanied by two men who were not immediately identified in his trip here."

You'll always have things like that happen but nothing drastic ever came of anything.

March 1, 1965, a local company, Associates Investments of South Bend had decided to sell their Twin Beech. They were buying a new jet aircraft, the North American Saberliner. We purchased their Twin Beech, an excellent machine with very little time on it, and immediately flew it to Stuart, Florida to check it out. The good thing about the Twin Beech was that it had a big roomy cabin, and there was a potty room in back, and a table to play cards on. There were cabinets where I kept nuts, crackers, cheese, miniature martinis, and all kinds of scotch as well as ice containers, and thermoses. It wasn't as fast as the 310 but it was so comfortable for the passengers in the back. I know that Mr. and Mrs. Pond really loved the airplane because it had such a big roomy cabin. I enjoyed flying it because I liked the radial engines. We took the airplane to Dayton, Ohio and had it refurbished. I had the engines overhauled, had it repainted, and the instrument panel done over and everything brought up to snuff. April 14, 1965, I went over to pick it up and brought it home. It was a great airplane as long as we had it and did a fine job for us.

When we had the refurbishing done we had the number changed to N215W for Wheel Horse. By December 3rd I was able to sell the old Cessna 310, N2905R to Schrade Batterson Company of Chicago which was owned by my cousin Bob Bock and his partner Bill Fournier. We delivered the airplane and I checked Bill out in it. A great airplane and Bob tells me they enjoyed the airplane as much as we had in the previous years.

One night a few months after we got the Twin Beech we had a meeting with one of our distributors that lasted into the wee hours of the morning. We were all dead tired and climbed into the Twin Beech and started for home. Within a few minutes after take off everyone was asleep. When we got back to South Bend the weather was bad and I had to make an instrument approach. After landing and taxing to the hanger I got out of the plane, the fresh air hit me and at that moment I didn't remember making the approach or the landing. I can't believe I was asleep but I didn't remember anything. My mind must have been on autopilot.

We never locked the doors at 2111 N. Michigan and one night I returned home and the door downstairs where I always entered the house was locked. I couldn't believe it so I hit it with the butt of my hand and broke several bones in my right hand. I had to go to my friend Dr. Coursey and he put a cast on the whole hand.

Most companies used two pilots on a Twin Beech but I can tell you that "It can be flown by one pilot with one hand" because I did it for several months. One of the problems with flying the Beech with one hand was landing because the right hand handles the throttles, mixture, fuel selectors, manifold heat, trim wheel, and all the other minor things such as radios and maps. Cecil liked to go to Homestead for golf each year, which had a small runway on top of a mountain that required a fair amount of skill to land on in a Twin Beech. You had to keep your speed up on approach to the mountain so as not to catch a down draft and yet you only had a short distance to stop in. On an approach like that you are busy with both hands. With only one hand it was a real feat because when I let loose of the control wheel to trim the airplane it would dive and as soon as you got on the ground I had to release the wheel to pull the throttles back. We made it but it was a wild ride!

After a few months of having a cast on my hand my Dad helped me cut it off early. My wrist felt like a wet noodle and had no strength at all. Dr. Coursey's wife Maxine came over just after Dad and I had removed the cast and I didn't want her to see it so when I stood in the doorway I leaned my right side against the frame so you couldn't see my right arm. Maxine asked me how my hand was and I said fine and she must have been suspicious cause she said, "let's see it." The jig was up and I am sure Doc knew about it that evening, and the worst part was the hand was good for nothing.

On February 12, 1966, we flew the Twin Beech to Tulsa, Oklahoma and on to Tucson, Arizona the next day. I thought that we were going to be there quite awhile and that we were going to stay with my Aunt Mildred and her husband Ross Harris. The next morning the 14th they called and Mrs. Dainelli, Cecil's secretary had called and we had to return to South Bend for an emergency. So on the 14th we left Tucson, Arizona. The Twin Beech had an oxygen system on board and being a radial engine I had the ability to lean on the cold side. You were able to lean all of the cylinders the same, where a flat engine you always had some discrepancies in how much fuel goes to the various cylinders because of the manifold and you run the risk of burning the valves on a cylinder that was too lean. In a radial engine the carburetor is in the center on the back of the engine and dispenses fuel to each of the cylinders equally. After getting it up about 14,000 or 15,000 feet, I pulled the mixture controls back until the engines about quit. I checked the cylinder head temperatures gauges, and I could see the fire was beginning to go out and that's where we stayed. By the time we got to Tulsa, Oklahoma we had to come down to a lower altitude for the rest of the flight because we ran out of oxygen. We went non-stop from Tucson, Arizona to South Bend, Indiana; we were in the air eight hours and five minutes. The manual says that you can't do that, but it can be done. When we landed in South Bend we had about thirty gallons of fuel left. I could have stayed up another hour and a half easily.

Cecil liked the Twin Beech well enough but he didn't like the speed. His wife loved it because of the roomy cabin. He was ready to buy something that was a little faster. When some new jet airplanes came out we began to talk to Don Duncan of Duncan Aviation in Lincoln, Nebraska about a Lear Jet. On April 20 we went to Lincoln, Nebraska and flew a Lear Jet to San Francisco. (I met Carl Rinstrum on that flight). We spent a little bit of time out there and then flew to Phoenix, Arizona and then to Omaha, and then on to St. Louis. I grew to like the airplane very much even though it was quite a controversial airplane. Quite a few of them had just fallen out of the sky, they were dropping like flies. I think that of the first hundred Lear Jets made over half of them crashed eventually. When we came back at the end of that trip I was asked what I thought of it, and I told Cecil that we should consider it.

He also wanted me to look at the Jet Commander. Since he was going to be in Phoenix, Arizona, I contacted the sales manager of the Jet Commander dealer in Indianapolis and they agreed to fly out to pick him up for a demonstration flight back to South Bend. So, I flew the Twin Beech down to Indianapolis and parked it and went in to meet with the salesman for Jet Commander. It is an impressive, well-built airplane, and is still being built today under a different name. He was a very nice man but a little ill at ease. When we went out to fly he went through the checklist in a very slow and fastidious way. I thought that he was going through the checklist slowly to show me how to do it, but he put me in the pilot's seat. We fired it up and got in the air and on our way to Oklahoma City where the Jet Commander is made. They gave me a tour of the plant and I saw how well it was built. I spent quite a bit of time talking with the people there and was very impressed with the airplane. It had a pretty good record. If you recall, this is the aircraft that Arthur Godfrey flew around the world.

When word got around about Godfrey trying to set a biz jet record Hank Beard, Lear's test pilot took off with very little planing and beat him to the punch. The Lear went faster with less fuel and with no special equipment. On the 29th we flew from Oklahoma City to Phoenix, Arizona. It was hotter than Hades at least 115 degrees. An airplane at high altitude is flying in very cold air, and when you land the same thing happens to an airplane that happens to your glasses. When you are outside in the winter and come inside they steam over. That was our situation in Phoenix. The Lear Jet has a defogger that puts hot bleed air on the windshield to help prevent fogging over. Even that won't help in extreme situations. The Jet Commander had an inferior system at that time and we fogged over completely. The next day we decided that we would fly back to South Bend. The Jet Commander salesman said that he didn't think we could make it because the weather was too bad. It didn't look that bad to me, especially since we could fly instruments. I said, "I'll tell you what. We'll just go up to the north of the weather and we will be okay." That should be an easy flight without having to refuel. But, it didn't happen that way. We put everything in the airplane. We were very short on baggage space; we had to actually take some belts and tie the golf clubs in the hellhole in the back of the airplane because we had very little room. That was one problem with the Jet Commander, it had very little luggage room. We got in the airplane and started through the checklist again in a slow deliberate matter. I said, "knock it off, It's so hot in here and we have no air conditioner." He just wouldn't speed it up he was bound and determined to go through the checklist slowly again. Just before take-off I looked back and Mr. Pond was just wet everywhere that he could be on his shirt. Maybe a little dry spot in the middle but everything else wringing wet. Mrs. Pond looked like she had been put through a wringer. It must have been 110 degrees in there and we were just wilted. We finally got in the air and stormed off towards South Bend. Of course, this airplane didn't fly as high as the Lear Jet. We finally got to our altitude and got the inside cooled down a little so that they could live back there. After a while he announced that we were not going to make it to South Bend. I looked at the fuel gauge and saw that we couldn't make it, so we landed in Des Moines. I put the airplane on the ground, right on the money and right on the speed. When we got to the end of the runway, the brakes were almost on fire. The thing had very limited brakes.

We went in the terminal, and the demo pilot was popping pills by that time and running around there like he was in shock. Betty and Cecil got a little something to drink or eat there and we got back into the airplane after fueling and flew back to South Bend with no trouble. I told him at that time, "Okay, now were going to fly to Indianapolis and that's where the weather is bad, why don't you hop over here and fly it." He answered, "no, no, no, you fly it." So it finally dawned on me that he was pretty scared of that airplane. Since it was my first trip in a Commander I wasn't keen on making the approach but I felt sorry for the demo pilot so I agreed to fly it. It was a difficult approach, but we were on the ground in about 30 minutes in Indianapolis.

We had the airplane pulled into the hangar without any scratches, but the brakes looked like they had been burned up. That was the end of the Jet Commander for us. It didn't have the luggage room, it didn't have legs, (long range) it wouldn't go very high and didn't have an air conditioner.

Within a month or so another Lear Jet had a fatal crash. I think it was the Rexall airplane that finally put a temporary end to Lear Jet sales. It crashed in Clarion, Texas. with no understanding of what happened. There were all kinds of stories out like maybe it was carbon monoxide problem in the airplane, and everyone had a tag on the dash that was suppose to turn color if there was carbon monoxide present. (What would you do if it did turn color?) They also believed that there was possibly an electrical failure and they lost their ability to maintain the gyros and therefore lost control and dove out of the sky. It dove straight into the ground. After that the market went to pot and they couldn't sell Lear Jets.

On June 8, 1966 we purchased Lear Jet N969B from Duncan Aviation. It think that it was the first Lear Jet aircraft purchased after the Clarion crash. I was seriously concerned about the aircraft, but it was such a good buy, a little over a half of million dollars. In the event it was an electrical failure we insisted that Duncan install a battery powered electric horizon. I went to the Lear Jet plant and started going through the ground school on the aircraft. As soon I got out there I also started flying to get ready for my type rating.

I wanted to complete both ground school and flight training at the same time if possible, because I was in the process of building Skystream, the new operation at Plymouth, Indiana. I worked at both school and flying pretty hard. The class had several very well known people. Sinatra's pilot was there, since they had a Lear

Jet, and he would stop in every once in awhile. Danny Kay was there, Sonny and Cher came by the classroom Robert Cummings was a good pilot and he came by, he loved the Lear. The guy sitting next to me was not familiar to me at the time. His name was George Peppard and he was in the movie Breakfast at Tiffany's, the CarpetBaggers, and many other films. At this particular time he had made a movie with Ursula Andress called "The Blue Max." On the side of a Lear Jet they had painted "Lear Jet flies the Blue Max." I didn't know who he was and I was interested in learning about the airplane, not anything else. Evidently he noticed that because everyone else was fawning all over him and when we were done with school he would say, "Come on Don, let's get the hell out of here" and away we'd go. In fact, that week end his new wife Elizabeth Ashley came out to Wichita. He was "quite a guy" a real nice no nonsense man. A pretty darn good pilot too. He always said that he would come to Plymouth some time to visit but he never did. I guess he was just too busy. We spent several evenings together and the women just mobbed him. I remember one night there were a couple of gals crawling all over him when I went back to the motel. The next morning I asked him how he made out and he said, "I couldn't split the two of them up and didn't figure I could take care of both of them so I went back to my room."

Bill Lear was a real character and there are many true stories about him. He named his daughter Crystal Shanda Lear for example. One day he was flying his converted Lockheed Lodestar (a Learstar) and had his young son with him when he wandered over a restricted airspace and the Airforce sent a couple of Jets up to check it out. Bill put his very small son in the pilot's seat and ducked down so no one could see him. Imagine those jet pilots surprise in finding a small boy flying the aircraft. The best story of all to me was when Bill went in for his Lear Jet rating. The examiner asks questions about performance and other technical questions. Bill answered as fast as he was asked. The examiner said I am sorry Mr. Lear but those figures are not the figures in the book. Bill shot back "Those are the figures that are going to be in the book."

The pilot that was assigned to teach me was a jet pilot who spent a lot of time in the service flying single-engine jets. There wasn't anybody who had any experience instructing in Lears. After all, this was a new breed of business jets and he was going to teach me to fly. Now here is the guy who was going to teach me to fly and he didn't have a multi-engine rating. He couldn't sign for any of his time because he wasn't an instructor. As a result it meant that I was going to go up for a type rating without a recommendation from an instructor. Those are rough odds. You like to have an instructor who sends you up there and says that this guys knows what he's doing and that leaves the examiner a little room if you don't do everything perfectly. He was a good pilot and taught me a lot about the airplane.

One day we flew up to Dodge City and landed and went through all of the attractions, the cemeteries, Boot Hill, and various places people had been shot, etc. Another time we flew over a small airport and he asked me if I could land there and I said "Well, I didn't know if we could or couldn't." He then wanted me to check it out and after checking I said that we could land there and he said "You're absolutely right" and we landed. Of course, I'm thinking immediately that if I could land here I could land in Plymouth. That was all part of the learning process. When I got done with Lear school I went to Lincoln, Nebraska to take the test and on 6/17/66 I was issued a Lear Jet type rating. I remember part of the flight test, I was obviously not that good after only a few hours of flying the Jet and a week and a half of ground school so he asked me a lot of questions. I remember the examiner asking me about the temperature on the gauges. He said, "What temperature is okay? And I said that as long as it is in the green it is okay. He then said, "Yeah, but what temperature is it?" I said, "I don't think that the green paint is going to fall off of the dial and I'm not going to clutter up my mind keeping such trivia in my memory, and if the green paint does fall of the dial, I'll have it repainted." I think he thought that it was a pretty sensible way to think and he approved my type rating in the Lear Jet.

I remember I wasn't overly proud of my approach because even though it was within limits I was all over the scope, up and down and around and about, I just wasn't doing my usual smooth job. In the prop aircraft you adjusted your altitude with the power. When you wanted to come down you reduced your power and when you wanted to gain altitude you would increase the power a little bit. I could take that old Twin Beech or 310 and glue the indicators to the glideslope just like they were painted on. The Lear Jet is a whole different animal. It was a while before I got the hang of it; you just aim the Lear and adjust the speed with power.

The Lear Jet had to have a co-pilot. You couldn't legally fly without one and your insurance was no good so my co-pilot was Cecil Pond. Since he was my boss at the plant and the company, I had to have an arrangement with him. So one day we had a talk and agreed that "When we're in the airplane I make the decisions and everywhere else you're the boss." He became a pretty darn good co-pilot. I used him all of the time wherever we flew. In essence, I flew the airplane, single pilot, except for take offs and landings because he was back in the airplane playing cards, chatting with the other passengers, or relaxing during flight. It was a very excellent situation for both of us.

I recall one time flying up to Kohler, Wisconsin for a meeting with Kohler Corporation, who made some of our engines. They built very excellent engines. As the pilot I couldn't drink during the course of that evening because I had to be ready to fly. I remember Elmer Pond, Cecil's Dad, the Chairman of the Board, grabbed me and said, "Don, take me home." I called Milwaukee for clearance and had to be off the ground at such a time and be at such an altitude by a given time. It was probably one in the morning. I took off and gave Milwaukee a call and by the time they gave me clearance I was leveling off at altitude and the man said, "That's either a Lear Jet or a Saturn rocket."

Jack Nelson, the Director of Marketing and I were on a sales trip and we wound up one night in New Orleans. Jack was known to toast a friend from time to time so we went out to see the town. We wandered by the Bunny Club. I said to him, "Boy I wish I had a key to get in there!" Jack said, "We can get in there." He went over to the door and announced that he wanted to get in. There were a couple of big bruisers waiting for us at the door and they asked him for his membership number (which was on a key). He started to look through his wallet for a card and I went over there to him and quietly told him that it wasn't a card it was a key. In a loud voice he said, "I know it's a key." Then they let us in and said that they would call Chicago to verify the number. After about fifteen minutes a bouncer came to us and said they couldn't find anything in Chicago under his name. Jack gave them a hard time about not being able to find his name so they said, just give us a check, and in case we don't find anything we'll be covered. Jack signed the check they furnished, not that you could read his scribbling. About ten minutes later the bouncer came back again. He couldn't read the name and we were thrown out of the Bunny Club in New Orleans.

If you had maintenance on a Lear Jet it was best to take it out to the Lear Jet factory itself. Since we had just bought the airplane and it had a few squawks I flew it out to Lear for them to fix it. I found out that someone had removed my Collins radios while it was in the maintenance hanger. The kinds of radios they had at that time were made by Wilcox or by Collins. I had opted for the Collins because they had a much better reputation. So, someone needed a set of Collins radios and they took them out. I was told you aren't going to be using them for a day or so and by that time we'll have a new set of Collins radios here for you. I said you better have some new Collins radios in here unless you are looking for some legal problems.

Bill Lear took a liking to me since his son was going to Culver Military Academy close to Plymouth and he wanted to know about this new airport we were building in Plymouth, Indiana. He would grab me every time I was at the Lear plant to talk to me. He told me that he would be using that airport as soon as we got it ready. He used it all right. While it still had the white x's (not legal to land on) on the runway he landed at Plymouth, so I never got to be the first one to land a Lear Jet at Plymouth. He had a couple of peculiarities. Whenever he wanted to go somewhere he went out on the flight line, and selected an airplane he liked, and took off because, he regarded all Lear Jets as his. People were pretty tolerant of him, but I don't know if I could have been that tolerant.

When Bill Lear came to Plymouth he got out of

the airplane and Hank Beard who was the test pilot for Lear and flew the first test flight was handing out the luggage. Hank was a friend of mine and use to kid me whenever I came to Lear for service, saying, "What have you done to our airplane now." Anyway I reached down to pick up the luggage and Bill pulled me away and put his arm around me and started walking to the terminal. He said, "I go Indian style." I looked back and here was Moya his wife struggling with the luggage. We had Lear Jet serial number 89; there were less than 100 Lears in the World at that time, a small elite group.

When Mr. Pond and I started Skystream in Plymouth we did so on a 50/50 basis. I had to put in half of the money and he had to put in half of the money. I mortgaged my home to the hilt and I imagine Cecil just reached into his pocket for small change. So many people said that this venture wouldn't work and I was risking everything. At that time the town was only 7,558 people. When I invested what money I had in the business it was "Do or die." We completed the negotiations with the City and agreed to build the buildings and put in a fuel system, maintain airplanes, have a flying school, and rent hangars, and do all of things that a fixed base operator does. We had to pay rent on the land since it belonged to the city. We did secure a twenty-year lease with a ten-year option and the stipulation that the hangers were ours to remove or sell at the end of the lease.

When we first got the Lear Jet, Cecil was very proud of it, and rightly so. It was the world's best space machine. I remember one night when Betty and I were getting ready for dinner; Cecil called to ask what we were doing. I said, "We're just going to dinner." He said "Well, come on to dinner with us. I'll meet you at the airport." I met him at the airport and he and his wife had another couple with them and we flew to Texas for dinner and came back by eleven o'clock. A flying carpet, quite an amazing machine. A few weeks later he said he was going to Florida for dinner, so we loaded up the airplane to go to Florida but Betty couldn't go that evening. After a lovely dinner at the Hawaiian Village in Tampa we got in the Lear for the return trip. As we were taxiing out to the runway the tower called and said that we were losing fuel. I returned to the ramp and sure enough it was gushing out of the back of the airplane. The Lear uses about 300 gallons an hour initially so it has a pumping capacity that will really put the fuel to the engine and any leak will pump a lot overboard. The tail pipes were right over the jet fuel and it's a wonder we didn't catch on fire. If we had been using JP4 fuel like we later used in the airliners we would have blown up for sure, it's so volatile. There is a clamp in the hellhole (large hole on the bottom to get into the rear fuselage) that holds the fuel line on. It was about midnight and I didn't know quite what to do so I called Lear Jet. They said that once I got the fuel pipe up there and got the engine started it would suck into place. They said it was the same type of clamp that trucks use. Well, I didn't want to fly with that thing loose so finally I got a guy to drive me over to a junk yard and went looking for a hose clamp like the broken one. I expected a large dog to chase us out of the junkyard at any moment. We wandered around the junkyard and finally found one. I put it on and put a fan in the hellhole to try to dry it out. I was seriously concerned about it since the battery and a lot of electrical devices were in there. I fired it up and we came home but I had a lot of misgivings about it.

About the last year that I was with Wheel Horse, I was made Assistant to the President. I was getting so busy supervising the service manager, the parts department, the printing department, and working as assistant director of marketing, I really didn't have much time to haul Mr. Pond around and he wasn't too happy with that. After all, his time was the most valuable time that Wheel Horse had. He then made me his assistant. There was a nice office, more prestige and I sat in on all of the meetings, and took notes for his consideration if he was not there from time to time. From my point of view it wasn't very good. He wanted me to keep an eye on everything and wanted me to report back to him about things that weren't going well. These people were all my friends and I didn't want to become the kind of guy that no one wanted around, especially if I went to Mr. Pond with some of the problems I saw. That is one of the reasons that Cecil and I went into negotiations with the City of Plymouth to build the Skystream facility. We planned to open the doors January 2, 1967. On New Year's Eve we had a big party at the airport with all of our friends to celebrate and on January 2nd we opened Skystream. My log shows that 1/3/67 I flew Senator Birch Bayh to Washington and back. We were popular with the Lear Jet.

om the left Joe Kennedy salesman, Jack Nelson Director of marketing, Cecil Pond President, and me at the Indianapolis 500.

The author at the lower right corner of the Wheel Horse Sign with one of our distributors at the New York hardware show.

The HITCHING POST

Formula for Selling: DEMONSTRATE!

W. A. Matheson, one of the country's top salesmen, suggested in his book, "The Selling Man": Sales are made directly in proportion to the number of times the salesman commands the attention of his prospect—tells his story in full—and makes a bid for the order.

How do you command the attention of your prospect? It has been proven time and time again, by dealers all over the country, the best way is to demonstrate your product—Wheel Horse, of course!

Outline a demonstration program right now. Set up a calendar for making demonstrations. Commit yourself to make so many demonstrations a day, so many a week. Then stick with it.

The number of sales you make will be in direct proportion to the number of times you demonstrate and tell the Wheel Horse story.

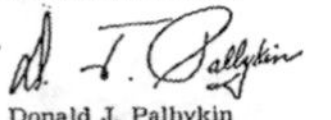

Donald J. Palbykin
Assistant Director of Marketing
Wheel Horse Products, Inc.

ABOUT THIS MONTH'S EDITORIALIST . . .
Don Palbykin is as much at home at the controls of the Wheel Horse company airplane, a twin engine Cessna, as he is behind a desk. Before joining Wheel Horse as Customer Relations Manager, he was chief pilot for a commercial flying service in South Bend. As Assistant Director of Marketing, Don travels a great deal attending trade shows, holding distributor meetings, and visiting with Wheel Horse dealers. His responsibilities at the factory include the Parts Department, the Service Department, and the Sales Literature Department. He and his wife, Betty, have six children and they live in Plymouth, Indiana.

An article I wrote for the hitching post in Wheeling & Dealing.

Cecil Pond, his son Gary, and me on a fishing trip.

Wheel Horse's first Cessna 310 N1855H, Green and white.

Betty and me in Paris at Notre Dame Cathedral on Potez trip.

The Potez 4 engine turboprop that I was invited to Paris to see.

The Wheel Horse Lear Jet N1968W ready to go with pilot.

Lear Jet ground school with George Peppard.

On the flight line with some pilots and instructors.
I'm the second from the right, George Peppard is the third.

Skystream's Early Days

When we opened Skystream on January 2, 1967, things were pretty quiet out there. I had enlisted two of my very best friends, Joe Harmon, who I had worked with at Studebaker for over eight years and his wife, Velma, to help me get things started. Many people brought their aircraft to Plymouth to base since there was a shortage of hangars at other airports and also since we had new hangers. Joe pumped the fuel and took care of the facilities; Velma took care of the front office and the unicom radio and became known as the "voice of Skystream." I did the flying. On January 12, 1967, I flew the Lear Jet from Miami, Florida to Plymouth, Indiana, and that was the first time I landed it at the Plymouth Airport.

One of the most difficult tasks that anyone has when starting a new company is to make people aware of you and your services. This was especially true of the aviation business because in the Plymouth community with only a single runway and very little else going for it, it was imperative to get our name out. I remember the

Yellow Page people coming to me to talk about running an ad. I had allocated very little advertising money, for the year. I think about $100. I looked at some ads and I thought we would pop for a pretty good size ad which ran about $40. I thought that was $40 for the year but it was $40 for the month. I was absolutely livid that they didn't tell me it was per month, and I was on the hook for the entire year. My entire advertising budget and more was shot on that one item.

I was approached by one of the fellows in town who ran a liquor store, Bob Snyder who had been involved in aviation in the service. He came out to see me and bought some flight instruction and said "I'm going to come out and get my license and teach flying." He sold his business, learned to fly, got his instructor rating, and taught for us. He was a good student and a good teacher. I am sure a large portion of what was imparted to the students at Skystream came directly from Bob.

I had gone to Chicago to Aviation Activities to see about becoming a dealer because they were the distributors of Cessna products in our zone. There I met a man by the name of Angelo Marasco and he was to work with me for years to come. A very nice gentleman and a competent businessman. We purchased a Cessna 150, a little two-passenger aircraft for our trainer, and a four passenger Cessna 172 shortly thereafter. We used the 172 as a demonstrator, and our first charter aircraft as soon as we got our charter FAA approved.

Many people from town found out that it was rather inexpensive to fly, $12 or $14 an hour. Most people could afford to take 30 or 40 minutes of instruction a couple times a week. It wasn't long before we had a bunch of people coming out to learn how to fly.

After they became pilots we were often able to sell them a new Cessna aircraft.

In looking at my logbook, I find there were several doctors learning to fly at that time. Dr. Coursey, Dr. Holm, Dr. Bauer, Dr. Reed, and even Dr. France took some lessons. There were a lot of businessmen in town that took instruction Schori, Weeks, Coplin, Towns, Young, and even Fred Morrow (President of the aviation board) and it wasn't very long before they wanted to own an aircraft. By the end of February we had delivered a couple of aircraft and each time we delivered one the sale of gasoline and maintenance and hangar rental boosted our income. Each one of these sales helped our small company. It wasn't very long before we became very busy at the airport. I would give four or five lessons each day. We applied for a charter license, received it, and began flying people all over the country. If I wasn't on a charter trip I was teaching or looking for new business. The company really grew by leaps and bounds.

Upon leaving Wheel Horse I was still in a position to do Wheel Horse a lot of good so they kept me on their books as a pilot so that I could retain my health insurance and profit sharing and still fly for them. If they called I had to fly, which happened quite a bit. Whenever I went somewhere we were out of business at Skystream as far as instruction went. That was when Bob Snyder began teaching and before long we were able to function very nicely without me constantly being there.

We embarked on a trip to Denver then on to San Francisco, where we stayed for almost a week. When we left Mr. Pond came out to the airport with another couple. They came in one cab and the baggage came in another cab. We're talking steamer trunks and even this airplane with its large baggage capacity was strained. I had to get in the airplane, pass the baggage down the aisle and fill the luggage compartment at the rear of the cabin. After doing this, I filled the airplane with the passengers and then proceeded to fill the aisles with the remainder of the luggage, closed the door and we departed. We flew from San Francisco to Tucson, Arizona put on a load of fuel, and took off for Acapulco. Having never been in Acapulco I didn't know what to look for. I knew that I would have trouble with the aircraft windshield fogging over because the air there is very moist. I put the defogs on early, which is a heating system to direct hot air on the windshield during the descent. We landed and tried to look out to see where to go, we taxied over to the edge of the runway and a man led us out onto a field to park. I shut the airplane down, opened the door and proceeded to unload the baggage. As I did so, someone greeted me and said, "I'll take care of the baggage," in broken English. I said that we could take care of it because I was afraid it would disappear. Sure enough, it was gone.

I went into the customs office and the customs officer wanted to see all of our passports. Mr. and Mrs. Pond had passports, the other couple had their passports, but I didn't have a passport with me because I had assumed (never assume) I would be told if we were going out of the country. I didn't know we were going to Mexico. There was a big hubbub for a while and they said they would have to call Mexico City and then the United States to confirm my passport. Actually, he wanted money for this, so I paid him, and I don't remember seeing him make any telephone calls to clear up the matter. But, everything suddenly was approved. We went out the front of the building and ordered a couple of cabs. We had discussed the fact that if you are in another country you should be very careful regarding offending the people of the country that you are in. Out of the woods came our luggage, every last piece of it. I tipped them generously. Mr. Pond and his guests got in the first cab and departed for the Pierre Marquette, which was one of the great hotels in Acapulco. I took another cab with the luggage. I'm the guy who paid the expenses since it was easy for me to put charges on my expense account and not be audited by the IRS. I didn't make enough to cause them to look. I was awestruck by the amount of the bill. I didn't want to argue, so I paid them and they grinned and drove off.

I got a cab to the airport the next morning to make sure the airplane was secured. It cost something like fifty cents. I realized that the night before I had been taken and taken well. I went to the office at the airport and asked them to fill the airplane with so much fuel on each side so that the airplane would sit evenly. If you get too much fuel in one side it will lean clear over and in some cases fall down on the tip tank on the heavy side. It was like talking to a wall. No one understood me. I said, "You don't speak English?" One of the men said, "You don't speak Spanish?" He was right, here I was in his country and I expected him to speak in my language. I got a couple of hundred dollar bills out of my pocket. Sure enough they understood that. I got one hundred dollars worth in one side and then one hundred dollars worth on the other side. Eventually I was able to get the aircraft fueled. I wanted to put some chocks under the wheels and found out that "si" meant maybe, someday, I might, if I happen to think about it. I wasn't about to leave until I saw chocks under the wheels. I went over and picked up a chock and waived it at the guys to indicate that I wanted the airplane chocked. They went into the hangar got chocks and put them under the wheels so it wouldn't blow away.

A close friend of mine from Plymouth, Dr. Coursey, who had delivered the last three of our children, indicated that if we went to Mexico we should beware of the water we drank. The bacteria in the water isn't the same type of bacteria we are use to here in the United States. He had given me a bottle of sulfa pills and instructed me to take a couple of these pills and then a couple more in an hour or so if I began to have trouble. Sure enough I had to take some of the pills. I had mentioned to Mr. and Mrs. Pond and his guests that I had this medication. In the middle of the night I was awaken by someone rattling my door. It was Mr. Pond who needed some of the medication. Within a day or so everyone recovered but we all had a pretty good case of dysentery.

I remember taking a bus from the Pierre Marquette to the Bay of Acapulco. The hotel was on the East Side of town and the Bay was about five miles west. They had a bus that went back and forth between the two. I got on the bus and went down town to spend the day looking around and to buy some jewelry for my wife. I picked some various rings up for her and was quite pleased with myself. Later in the evening I was at the stop where the bus was to pick me up when an enterprising young man rode up on a bicycle. On the luggage rack behind him was a box full of wallets. He tried to sell me a wallet. I have very definite thoughts about wallets. I do not want a wallet that has any stitching in it. The stitching gives way and the wallet becomes useless. I was fond of the one I had since it did not have any stitching and was put together in a very nice way and I had no intention of changing wallets. If I remember correctly, I think he started the price of these wallets at about ten dollars. Anybody knows that goes to Mexico that if you offer half the asking price you have bought it. Well, I didn't offer him anything and he came down to two and then down to one dollar. I kept telling him no, I didn't want any wallet so he deliberately folded it up, put it in the box on the back of his bicycle and said "You will never amount to anything, you can't make up your mind."

A few days later we flew to Mexico City that's a fabulous place to visit. I went out to the pyramids, and toured the city to see the various sites and museums. I remember a particular Anthropology Museum, that's the best I have ever seen. There was a model depicting the pyramids. As you looked at it you thought it was the most modern city you'd ever seen. Mexico City is rather high up and has a problem with land settling. Some of the buildings over the years have settled slowly into the ground as much as three or more feet.

I had an awful time getting out of the Mexico City airport. Since I was the captain, I was responsible for all of my passengers. I had to take a cab to the other side of the field. After filling out all the forms and buying a card to get the weather briefing I felt I had taken care of all the paper work. I stood in the airline passenger line for some time waiting for the official to stamp my flight plan papers, which he did. I took a cab to the private side of the field and I was told I needed another stamp. In looking back now I realize that they just wanted a bribe. I grabbed the papers, got a cab, and rushed over to the airline terminal on the other side of the field. I marched to the head of the line and thrust the papers in front of the official and said, "Stamp." He looked up startled and stamped without even looking. I then got a cab to the private side of the field. This whole process had taken at least an hour and a half. As we took off I said to Cecil "Please don't go back until they put the new private aircraft facility in." We came back the next year and had no trouble since the new terminal was in operation by then.

Upon landing back in the United States in Houston, there was a place that offered TV sets if you fueled up. An aircraft like ours held about 5,500 pounds of fuel, which is about 785 gallons of fuel. Of course it was not empty but it still took a lot of fuel. So, when you purchased fuel, it was a big purchase. Everyone was trying to entice you to there facility. The price of the fuel was the same so I opted for a TV set. They didn't have one since they were out and I figured that I would never see the set but a few months later I received it. Most aircraft would carry a small amount of fuel. Small aircraft capacity ranged from 30 gallons of fuel to 50 or 60 gallons of fuel. If you were to sell 700 gallons of fuel at one time it was quite a sale. All over the country there was advertising to "stop and fuel with us and we will give you a free steak" or "stop and fuel with us and we will give you terrific service as well as a gift." All the fuel operations were all trying to get the jet aircraft to stop in and fuel with them.

I can't remember the exact date this happened but the important executives always went to the New York Hardware Show in the Lear Jet. On one of these occasions I was there with Jack Nelson and we proceeded to see the town and have a great time. He told me that he thought he could get us in Jackie Gleason's penthouse apartment in the hotel we were staying at. Of course, he was always the kind of guy who would talk to someone and get things done. We took an elevator to an upper floor and then transferred to another elevator to go up to Jackie Gleason's penthouse apartment. During the course of this tour I was coming back down in the elevator and there was Johnny Carson, and Ed McMahon who had just taken over the show from Jack Paar.

Somehow I had gotten separated from Jack Nelson and I was alone in the elevator with them. They asked what I was doing there in New York and I told them that I was a pilot for Wheel Horse. They said that they were going to advertise for Wheel Horse so "Come on with us, we're going to go out and have a few drinks". Well boy, I was ready to go but I thought I better tell Jack that I was leaving. So, I told them to go ahead and I would catch them at the curb. I assumed (never assume) they would wait. Of course, I never found Jack and never found Johnny and Ed either. The brief conversation that I had with them was very cordial. Later on when they introduced the tractor on the show Ed said, "here's Johnny." He came out and stated that they had a new sponsor, Wheel Horse Products Corporation and went on and on about it. Ed said something about Cecil, Johnny said, "who the hell is Cecil" and he got a big laugh. He got on the tractor and had a mishap trying to drive it but it was great coverage for us.

The Skystream facility was on a piece of land that had been originally purchased to build a Holiday Inn. They had built the Holiday Inn and then used a portion of the land to build the airport; the city acquired that land and it became the Plymouth Municipal Airport. We based the Lear Jet in Plymouth and the people sleeping at the hotel at the side of the runway would be aroused early in the morning as we departed, because the Lear Jet is one of the noisiest aircraft in the world. When it left the runway everyone in town heard it and it was deafening to the motel guests.

Right across the street from the airport in the take-off path was a company that sold Chevrolet automobiles, Jim Labas Chevrolet. I was talking to Jim some time after we had opened the airport and I said, "What do you think about the aircraft flying over your business?"

"Well" he said, "it cost me a lot of money." I asked him what he meant by that and he said, "as soon as you fire that thing up, everyone stops working, the mechanics drop their tools and go to the door to watch the take-off." "One of his employees said to Jim that he wondered what it cost to get that aircraft off the ground?" I said "I don't know what it costs them, but it sure costs me a lot."

I decided to have an air show to publicize the airport. You don't want the people to think that you are a bunch of daredevils or they won't come around. But, you have to have something to get their attention. We hired a pilot to come in and do some aerobatics and another pilot to make some passes in a North American P51 Mustang. I elected to use the Lear Jet to make one pass across the field. We had a raffle and a couple of people were selected to go with us. I took off from the Plymouth Airport and circled around to the east and after I was about 15 miles to the east I radioed the airport and told them that I would make this pass across the field. I accelerated to the red line, which meant that was as fast as the aircraft could legally go. I think I was going about 350 knots, which is a little over 400 miles per hour as we went over the airport. As I reached the center of the runway I pulled back on the wheel and aimed the airplane straight up. With all of the acceleration you could just count one, two, three, four, five, six, seven, eight, nine and ten. At ten I was at 10,000 feet and not visible. Some said that it was the most spectacular thing that they had ever seen because it seemed to make the aircraft disappear right in front of them. I know the people who were flying with me were not too thrilled when they looked out of the window and saw that they were going straight up. The original airshow was a hit. We also did the penny a pound ride, which helped attract a lot of people that had never before thought about flying.

About that time I began a tradition that continued as long as I ran Skystream. Once a year in the fall we had all of the employees to our home for a dinner. My wife, Betty, purchased some real nice steaks and in later years we served lobster and steak because Phil Calvert, my vice-president, had an uncle who had a store nearby and Phil would have live lobster from New England shipped in. Most of those guys didn't eat much the day before the dinner so they could really pig-out. This was a very congenial dinner to show my appreciation for their help in getting Skystream going. At that time our personal income had not yet reached $12,000 a year.

Bill Lear's son was going to school at the Culver Military Academy, which is about 14 miles from Plymouth. He was a nice young gentleman and seemed to be real straight-laced, so we rented a Cessna 172, a four-passenger aircraft to him. Later on when he returned the aircraft there was hay on the landing gear indicating that he obviously landed at places that were not airports. Needless to say, we didn't rent him an aircraft again. These were the things that could and did happen.

We had the same problem with rental cars. I recall renting cars at our rental car business, Skystream Rent-a-Car, and one time the car never came back. Today that wouldn't happen because you would have it on a credit card. But in those days if the guy landed at the airport, and rented a car we figured he had to come back to get his airplane. Then we started renting to people who came out from town and needed a car, and one day a guy departed with the car and never came back. It took quite a while to run the car down and get it back. Those were minor things that happened in starting a business.

We begin to have a thriving charter business. Young Door Co. and Plasteel Co. chartered with us as well as many other companies. We would fly them to their various plants around the country and to Chicago for airline connections. Young Door had quite a bit of trouble getting from place to place without going on a train for a long distance and then renting a car. We flew them to their destination airport and one of their associates would pick them up and take them to their place of business. By charting a plane they would fly to the plant in the morning, take care of business matters and would fly back home in time for supper. We developed quite a large charter business. Later on we became the "largest charter operator" in the region. Since we were a Cessna dealer I always used brand new aircraft.

I would buy a new Cessna 310, six passenger twin engine charter aircraft. One of the most common aircraft used in our organization. If it was a $100,000 airplane, I could get it with radios in it for in the neighborhood of $80,000, and we immediately put it on the books for sale for $80,000 plus 15%. So, that would make it $92,000 when it was brand new. This was called our minimum no trade price. We used a one and a half declining depreciation, which basically meant that in approximately six months we could sell the airplane for $80,000 (which was cost), and have used it in the charter business for six months for nothing. We would put at least 50 hours a month on each aircraft, which created quite an income. The charter department had a wonderful deal since the aircraft was under warranty and their only cost was depreciation. The sales department had a better deal since they could sell the aircraft for cost (most times they sold it for much more than that) and make 15% profit or more after six months use. It wasn't long before we were selling many charter customers an airplane. They would see how beneficial it was to travel this way and perhaps become attached to one of our charter aircraft.

I would explain to the customer how they could benefit by owning the aircraft and it won't cost anything. They would say, "How could that possibly be?" I would tell them, "you're a company paying 50% tax and there is an investment tax credit of 10%. Let's suppose you bought a $100,000 dollar airplane you would save $10,000 investment tax credit on your taxes the first year. You could take double-declining depreciation, which was approximately 1/4 of the book value of the aircraft off your taxes also. In the case of the $100,000 airplane, that meant another $25,000 of which half was tax. So you save $10,000 in investment tax credit plus $12,500 that you saved in depreciation So, you had a total savings the first year of $22,500 on the purchase." The people I sold to were the ones who owned mobile home factories and small business, especially in the Elkhart area and they were interested in $250,000 to $1,000,000 aircraft (saving as much as $225,000). They would say, "Is that possible?" and I would reply "Yes, just get your accountant in here and, I will explain it to him." All bean counters are against purchases like that because they are very conservative. After backing them into a corner they would have to admit that what I said was true. We sold a tremendous amount of aircraft with this tax saving sales approach and became in relatively short order the largest multi-engine dealer in our zone. This took in Chicago, Milwaukee, South Bend, Indianapolis, Fort Wayne, and Minneapolis as well as all the smaller towns in between.

My oldest son Stephen graduated from high school and was working for Russ Repp our head of maintenance at the airport He was an excellent mechanic for his age but there are several requirements to obtain your aircraft and powerplant license (A and P). Stephen was ready for some challenges and chose to go to Lewis Lockport College to obtain his A and P. He graduated, took the test passed, and with his license at that time became the youngest A and P in the State of Indiana. Stephen received his Inspection Authorization certificate at twenty-one years of age, which was unheard of; he was the youngest in the state of Indiana to have an IA license. When the head of maintenance moved to Detroit with the airlines he recommended Stephen for the job. I thought he was just trying to gain favor with me, so I checked with all the pilots and they all recommended Stephen for the job. He was given the job and became our head of maintenance at Skystream and was in charge of all the Skystream locations.

My son Alan accomplished something that to this day I don't think any other person I know of has ever achieved. The first time I took him out for a lesson, he was fifteen years of age. It was a nice calm day and we had a lot of things going for us. Alan is very good at taking instruction. I talked to him about the aircraft and he had been attending ground school, so he had a good idea of how an airplane worked. It has always been my contention that no student would learn to fly if the instructor was on the controls all of the time. So, I thought I would see what he could do. I used this same procedure with all my students. I talked to him as we started our take off giving him verbal instructions and he made the first take off with no assistance. Later on, after about thirty minutes of instruction, turns, glides, etc. we came back to the airport and I talked him back down to the runway and he made a near perfect landing. I don't know of anybody who has ever done that, not in my experience, and I've taught a lot of people to fly. That was quite an achievement. His second accomplishment occurred on his 16th birthday September 14, 1967. He soloed a Cessna 150, a two passenger aircraft, came back down; soloed a Cessna 172, four passenger aircraft, landed; soloed a Cessna 182, a 230 horsepower with a controllable prop, that was considered a high performance aircraft. He went to school after his solos, because we did this early in the morning. Alan made his first solo cross-country after school the same day, going from Plymouth to Porter County Airport and back to Plymouth. He was an extremely good student. I've never seen anybody with the touch or feel with that little experience before or since.

Martin, my youngest son, went to Vincennes University to obtain his flying licenses. He told me that he felt that he would always be last in line to fly at our four flying schools. He graduated at nineteen with his commercial, flight instructor, instrument, instrument instructor, and his multi engine rating. The same licenses and ratings that had taken me until I was twenty-nine years of age to acquire. Martin was typed in the Lear Jet at twenty-one with a letter of competency and received his Air Transport Rating at twenty-three, the youngest that you can obtain such a rating. He flew charter for Skystream and was checked out in all the aircraft.

I have to be very careful in my bragging about my family because I am extremely proud of every one of them. They are all accomplished people, far ahead of where I was at the same time in my life. At the end of my term as President of the Rotary Club one of the guys said jokingly that it was nice that I was leaving because they wouldn't have to hear about my family every week. So I must get a little carried away. I'm not sorry for that because I am more proud of my children than anything in my life.

Rey Nelson my brother in-law flew for Skystream and was a hard working and competent pilot. Gloria, his wife (Betty's sister) lived in Morton Illinois, at their home while he stayed in Plymouth with Betty's parents, Jim and Lillian, and went home weekends. I have never known Rey to be drunk, but he was happy after one beer and hence the nick name "One beer Nelson." After a tough day of flying Rey stopped at the Holiday Inn to have a beer and when he left the police followed him since he had Illinois plates and had just left the bar. They pulled him over and questioned him. They asked if he knew anyone from around Plymouth and he said that I was his brother in-law. Immediately one of the policemen said, "Let him go Palbykin is my landlord."

For some reason or another people seem to connect me to the Mafia which is as far from the truth as you can get. I kind of blame my son in-law Michael Dickey. When he first started going with Ann Marie his father told him to beware of me since he thought I was a Don. Michael realized immediately that there was no connection but since he was full of the blarney he continues to this day to play the theme that I'm a Don. He is always saying, "That's not what The Don says." I had picked up a fake Rolex watch for him when I was down in the Islands. He told his friends that he could get one for them but if a guy by the name of Guido asked them to give it back to do so immediately. He had them believing him. When the Plymouth mayoral election was held I backed Greenlee, an old freshman football buddy of mine. Michael's friends were saying that Greenlee didn't have a chance but Michael said "The Don is backing him and HE WILL WIN." When Greenlee won they were fully convinced. That's how these rumors get started.

We had a problem with the telephone situation at the Plymouth Airport. We tried to help customers by installing a telephone at the counter. By putting in a phone with a separate line so they wouldn't tie up our line we helped them and helped us as well. That darn thing only worked occasionally. If there was any mist outside or the slightest amount of rain it didn't function. One day, in one of my tirades, I pulled the phone from it's roots, threw it out the door and told Velma to call the phone company and tell them to come and get their damn telephone since it didn't work anyway. That was one of the incidents that I became famous for. I wasn't always known for being the most patient of people (Betty says no kidding). I don't mind being thought of as just a little eccentric but some thought I was a little crazy.

When I was working at Wheel Horse in South Bend I would contact my distributors regularly. I would simply tell the Wheel Horse operator to get all of the distributors on the line and she would contact them one by one. Within a couple of hours I had talked to fifty distributors throughout the United States. That would have been impossible in Plymouth. I referred to the Plymouth Telephone Company as the "just a moment please Telephone Company" because every time you picked up the telephone to make a call they would say "just a moment please" or "could you hold a minute?" What choice did you have? You had to hold. The telephone system was antique and boy it showed. It would be difficult to call three or four people long distance in a morning. It was that bad. One time at home I was having a party and called the long distance operator and she said, "Is that you Mr. Palbykin?" And I said "yes". She said, "Oh, I didn't recognize you because you are in such a good mood." I told her that I wasn't always mad, but I was mad a good portion of time when I tried to use the telephone in Plymouth at that time. Fortunately they hired a man by the name of George Shipper and he was put in charge of fixing the phone system. In a couple of years he had it all straightened out and the service was much better.

When we brought our Lear Jet back to Indiana I believe it was the first based in the State. We were quite proud of having it based in Plymouth at this tiny airport after Skystream opened. There was no question about the fact that the aircraft caused considerable talk and caused people to speculate about our operation. It also caused the movie stars, politicians and rock starts to look us up for Jet charter. There just weren't many businesses that provided this service. We had calls from as far away as California. I recall flying to California many times to pick up customers. We had some really well known clients. Hubert Humphrey, Ted Kennedy, Governor Brown, Al Hirt, Olivia Newton-John, Perry Como, Helen Ready, Elton John, Jerry Lee Lewis, Governor Bowen, and many others would call us for charter service. Here we were just a little FBO in a town of 7,558 flying celebrities all over the country. It was great fun.

I was flying as much as I flew in South Bend and this job was also a seven day a week job. I had an extension on the airport telephone that came directly to my home less than a half a mile away. I covered the telephone, day and night, seven days a week. We were providing charter service to a lot of companies in the area, which gave us a great entree to sell corporate multi-engine aircraft. By the middle of 1967, we were buying and selling Cessna Skyhawks with a great deal of success as well as selling one of the most popular single engine aircraft the Cessna 182 Skylane, which was a 230 horsepower, 4-passenger relatively fast aircraft with a constant speed prop. It sold for about $17,000. Just recently I checked the pricing of the new Cessna Skylane the same kind of aircraft but with better radios, and the price given was $237,000. This increase was mainly caused by governmental intervention. I'll get into this later on in the book.

September 1967, the City of Plymouth started the Blueberry Festival, which now has become a phenomenal event in the State of Indiana. I was involved in the original planning of it and we flew a formation of three aircraft over the parade on opening day. We gave rides at the airport for a penny a pound. If you weighed fifty pounds you paid $.50, so if you weighed two hundred pounds you paid $2.00. We had people lined up clear out to the end of the road. We probably didn't make a lot of money on that promotion but we sure introduced aviation and Skystream to a huge number of people. We began making more and more extended trips with our new Cessna 310 charter aircraft for Plasteel Corporation out of Walkerton. We eventually sold them a Cessna 310. We also made many charter flights for Young Door Company, which had plants in different parts of the country. We would leave early in the morning, go to the plant, take care of their business, and return home the same day. In many cases it even saved money, even though it was a lot higher per mile cost.

Cessna had built a rather revolutionary new airplane called the Skymaster. It had an engine in the front and one in the back. The early models had a fixed landing gear, not a retractable landing gear. They were noisy and slow as sin. But, one of our charter customers was complaining about the cost of charter service yet insisted on multi engine charter. I was able to purchase one of these aircraft used at a very low price since it was not a very desirable airplane. Of the multi-engine aircraft that was about the only thing we could afford to use for the price he was willing to pay. The aircraft number was N 252 MD and I think it had been owned by a doctor. Velma aptly named it 252 Mountain Dew. I'm telling you it seemed like the name rang on for years to come. I can remember it after all of these years.

I became a champion sleeper because of my long hours, when I was out of town I would try to catch up on my sleep. I remember after a particularly long week I was on the road and checked into a hotel in the early afternoon and slept through until the next morning. I got up about nine AM and went down to breakfast and then back to my room and crawled into bed and slept the rest of the day and all night. I got up the next morning refreshed. When I had another pilot sharing a room with me I would always explain to them that I was a champion sleeper and if they got up to be sure and not wake me or they would be in trouble.

I was running myself pretty ragged so Betty and I decided that we needed to go on a vacation. On March 22, 1968, we departed Plymouth in a brand new Skymaster N2491S. This was a retractable gear airplane. My wife is so relaxed she falls asleep immediately after you put the wheels up in the airplane, so we put her in the rear seat with Barney Johnson. Martha Johnson, his wife, and Maxine Coursey were in the center seats, and Dr. Coursey was sitting up front with me. I looked back to the rear of the airplane and there was Betty with her head on Barney's shoulder sleeping away about as soon as we got airborne. I used to say, to Betty's consternation that Barney was the only guy that I ever let her sleep with. Two peaceful passengers, both sound asleep in the rear seat, even with all of the noise of the Skymaster. This aircraft was brand new and I was able to get a real good deal on it because somebody forgot to put a vacuum system in it. This meant that it did not have any gyros. No directional gyros, and no horizon. As such, it was not legal to fly instruments with this aircraft. The morning that we left it was a good time to fly instruments because the clouds were low and we worked our way down to Florida through some relatively low weather but eventually arrived in Stuart, Florida in good shape. We had three rooms at the Holiday Inn in Stuart. Coursey's had one, Johnson's had one and Betty and I had the middle room. We set up the bar in our room; all three rooms were bordering the swimming pool. Here we were, middle-aged people kicking up our heels and acting like a bunch of jackasses since we were out of town, footloose and fancy-free. No kids, no phones and we had a wonderful vacation.

We decided to return on the 24th, so it was just a long weekend. That was about all we could afford as far as time went. There were a lot of low clouds in the middle of our trip so I decided to go up on top and go across the top of Atlanta and by the time we would arrive in Indiana the weather will have dissipated and I would let back down. To make a long story short, about the time we got 50 or 60 miles south of Atlanta northbound, the clouds had risen so high that I was unable to go over them. I was forced to call Atlanta Center and file an instrument flight plan. This is a difficult thing to do if you don't have a directional gyro and you don't have a horizon. In fact, it was illegal. But in this case I didn't know what else to do. As we ground along in the rough air the compass would swing 20 to 30 degrees each way. Since I had just ball and needle to keep the airplane right side up, I would have to hold a heading as near as I could with the compass swinging side to side. When we got into the Atlanta area, which is a very busy area, they started to give us vectors, telling us to take up a heading and fly that, and then take up another heading of such and such. I did the best I could but I often thought they probably wondered what kind of guy is flying up there if he can't hold a heading. I'm sure that I wandered five or so degrees off of my heading from time to time. Anyway, we got through it, got back to Plymouth and all was well.

As the company began to make some money I received an increase in pay and eventually got up to $25,000 per year plus a bonus based on profit. In the later years this amounted to about $45,000 per year which was a very good income for that time.

Skystream started to sell several of the light twins, Cessna 310's primarily to small companies in the area. I realized that there was a great potential to sell multi-engine aircraft. I had hired a couple of pilots to help me with the charter service, however, they were not qualified to do instrument work and I was looking for someone who would be of the caliber that could be developed. Phil Calvert was working for Dalton Foundry at the time we sold them a Cessna 310 and they had a problem with one of the engines and brought it in for service. I had given them a full year warranty, and even though it was past the year on the Cessna warranty, we went ahead and replaced the engine. At that time I talked to Phil about coming to work for Skystream. He felt he had a pretty good job as pilot for Dalton Foundry and it would be a radical departure for him to leave an established company. I tried to explain to him that a pilot was a pilot but he could learn so much more working for Skystream and that the sky was literally the limit for him with his talent. This has proven to be true for he has had a phenomenally successful career. He did elect to come to work for us and from that time on we began to grow tremendously in the charter department. We had as many as fifteen or sixteen charter pilots including the managers and chief pilot at one time.

When I was working for Wheel Horse, John Ritzenthaler had approached me in an attempt to hire me to go to work for him to do basically the same thing that I was doing at Wheel Horse. In other words, sales work, supervising of a printing set-up for brochures, etc., and of course to fly an airplane. We had talked along the lines of buying a Twin Beech. I told Mr. Pond that I was going to take the job and he spent a day talking me out of it. I got to thinking about it and thought that I better stay with Mr. Pond because we were talking about going into business together if the opportunity arose.

My friend, Paul Meyers, who taught me to fly, was recommended for that job by me and he went to work for John. They bought a Twin Beech, N791A, and as soon as we opened Skystream it was based at the Plymouth Airport. John Ritzenthaler asked us to provide pilot service on their Twin Beech, since Paul was so busy in the company at that time. Paul came out on 5/31/68 and checked me out in their Twin Beech. It must have been okay since he gave me an extensive checkout and said that I was okay to take the Ritz-Craft people on trips. I checked Phil Calvert out in the Twin Beech so that I wouldn't be the only one able to provide pilot service to Ritz-Craft. We flew them on trips throughout the country as Paul became more and more involved with the day to day workings at the their plant.

I flew the first aircraft to depart Plymouth Municipal Airport direct to a foreign country, Bermuda, on 4/20/68. Upon landing in Bermuda I was asked to call the tower, which I did. They informed me that I had just landed at an Air Force base without permission. The airlines used this airport as well as all private aircraft so I assumed (never assume) it was OK. I asked them why they didn't tell me. They said that when they tell people they turn around and run out of fuel before they get back to the mainland and they were tired of fishing them out of the ocean. Since all the private aircraft and the airlines used the airport, unless you checked you wouldn't realize it was an Air Force base. The base commander came down and talked to me and it just so happened that he was a friend of one of the passengers I had on board on the airplane. He did fine me a hundred dollars but I think he spent more than that taking us out to dinner and entertaining us. Bermuda is a delightful place. It has pink beaches and a beautiful climate.

We departed Bermuda 4/24/68 and proceeded back into the United States. I was planning on landing in Columbus, Ohio, because the East Coast was socked in with real bad weather but Columbus was above landing minimums. As I proceeded on with the flight and kept watching the weather I could see that Columbus weather had deteriorated and they had gone below minimums, which meant that you were not allowed to make an approach. Ceilings too low even for an instrument approach. I called Center and asked them to advise Chicago that we going to be extremely light on fuel coming in from Bermuda and that we would request "preferential." I was not declaring an emergency but was asking in as nice a way as possible for them to give us every break they could on the approach. I called Chicago Center and ended with my number 969 Bravo as identification and Chicago Center came back with 969 Brave-O. I certainly didn't feel very brave at that moment. We were fortunate to get lined up early for our approach and landed in Chicago with no further problems. My logbook shows the total time of the flight as three hours and forty-five minutes. I have heard of Lear Jets being in the air for four hours and ten or so minutes but that is the maximum that I have ever heard of. That was too close for comfort.

I flew Mr. Pond on the morning of 4/28/68 from Plymouth to Stuart, Florida in 969B. I then proceeded direct to Wichita, Kansas. I left the aircraft there for the installation of a mini-mod electrical system and while we were there I decided to have the aircraft stripped, painted, and reupholstered. I wanted to get it up to snuff in every way that they could at that time including a new number 1968W. We went to Wichita 6/7/68, to pick up the refurbished Lear Jet and it was beautiful. It was a white aircraft painted with a red and maroon exterior stripe, and inside a real thick plush blood-red carpet with red and black seats that went extremely well with the walnut paneling in the aircraft and the Wheel Horse colors. The mini-mod for the electrical system had been recommended because I believe that they found out that the Rexall crash was caused by an electrical failure. So, I was beginning to believe that the skull and crossbones had been removed from the airplane. Lear Jet 1968 Whiskey, as we called it with its new number, was the premier airplane in our fleet. We were flying Jet charter service with it on a lease back arrangement from Wheel Horse. At that time there was very little Jet charter available. We had serial number 89 and most of the aircraft sold were sold to companies who were not going to put it out for charter service. Word got around that we had Jet charter available and we got calls from celebrities everywhere. I can recall times when we flew clear out to California to pick up people to take on trips, deadheading all the way, and them paying at least a dollar a mile for the pick up. It was really a fantastic time for that particular type of aircraft. They had not yet instigated most of the rules and regulations for private jet aircraft, so we could take off and get a clearance on the way up, and get up on top where there was no traffic, and go almost any where we wanted to go direct. We charged by the distance direct to the destination. We had a huge map on the wall with a string out of the center of Plymouth that we would stretch to the destination. We could tell in a moment what the charges for the trip would be.

People are always concerned about safety so we had to constantly be on the look out for ways to allay their fears. It's about eighteen times safer to fly than to drive your car. I had a sign made and installed on the inside of the gate so that when you left the aircraft for the parking lot you had to see it. The sign read "You are now leaving the safety of flying, please drive carefully."

There were some wonderful trips with Mr. and Mrs. Pond. I remember one time we flew from Plymouth down to Stuart, Florida, then down to Puerto Rico, then from Puerto Rico to the Virgin Islands, St. Croix, St. Thomas, San Juan, Puerto Rico, and back to Stuart, Florida and back to Plymouth. We had an excellent time and I became extremely enthused about St. Thomas in the Virgin Islands. It was such a heavenly place. No bugs and no windows, you just threw open the shutters and the house was wide open. The temperature was in the mid seventies through the day, with clean beaches, and crystal clear water. Orchids bloomed on the fences. Early settlers had trouble with snakes on the island and had brought in a large number of Mongooses to kill off the snakes. They are still there and will eat about anything that isn't metal. So, the island is litter free just like someone is policing it at all times. It's a very beautiful place.

A schoolteacher of Mr. Pond's had married a gentleman who decided to move to St. Thomas after experiencing Island life. He was a contractor who built homes. He sold everything and moved to St. Thomas and started building homes down there. He encountered a rather lackadaisical labor market and had trouble getting sufficient help to do what he wanted to do. He decided that he would start a perfume company. The Virgin Island Perfume Company. He came up with a scent he called Amalie since Charlotte Amalie is the capital of St. Thomas. He advertised it as Amalie, the scent of the islands. Everyone who went to St. Thomas wanted to take some home. Not only those who visited St. Thomas, but all of the other islands surrounding it. He took us out to his plant and it absolutely amazed me. It was a cement block building with a tin roof. That was his entire plant. It had a very small office with a linoleum floor and a metal desk. He had no full-time employees. He had two or three stainless steel mixing vats where he mixed the commercial perfume products that he bought from companies in the United States. He told me about the operation. He said the most expensive part of the perfume was the bottle, the second most expensive part was the cardboard carton it went in, and the perfume itself was extremely inexpensive. He hired some lady homemakers to fill the bottles, and place them in the cartons. They were only part-time help. He was able to sell over ten million dollars worth a year at a very high rate of profit. He told me that the small size bottle of perfume sold in the various shops for about $10.00. He was able to wholesale it to the shop owners for $5.00. His cost was much less than $1.00. He was making a tremendous profit. I remember thinking at that time that I was going to go back to Plymouth and bottle essence of Yellow River, give it a French name and make a fortune. He later became Governor of St. Thomas.

There was no airline service running in and out of St. Thomas at that time because there were no runways suitable for large aircraft available then. There was a large mountain to climb over after take off, and most aircraft just could not climb that quickly, especially airliners. Since the Lear had such a terrific acceleration and had the ability to climb it was no trouble getting in and out of any place down there. Betty and I went back after the airlines had established service, and it became a tourist Island and never had the wonderful ambiance that it had in the early days.

Traveling like I did there were many mornings that I woke up in strange surroundings and wasn't sure where I was. I do remember taking Cecil and Betty down to Arizona on 11/10/68 and dropping them off for a vacation with the understanding that I would pick them up on the 15th. The morning of the 15th I got up early and hopped in the Lear jet and flew to Harrisburg, Pennsylvania for a pickup. I departed Harrisburg, flew back to Plymouth, landed, jumped out of the airplane, ran over and jumped in the Twin Beech. I then flew some people from Plymouth to Pittsburgh, Pennsylvania. I dropped them off, returned to Plymouth, landed and ran from the airplane to the Lear Jet. I hopped into the Lear Jet with my brother in-law, Rey Nelson, sealed the door, and took off for Tucson, Arizona. After landing we fueled the aircraft and put Mr. and Mrs. Pond into the Lear Jet, and flew back to Plymouth. That was a day in Palbykin's life. I can remember getting up in the morning and flying to Stuart, Florida, back to Plymouth, back to Stuart, Florida and back to Plymouth in a single day. (It was exhausting!) The Lear Jet was truly a time machine, and at that date far ahead of its competitors.

Associates Investment called me one day; they had repossessed a Lear Jet and wanted me to ferry it from South Bend to Columbus, Ohio to have some maintenance done on the airplane. I agreed to do so, and I went to South Bend with Merlin Jones as a copilot and checked the airplane out and took off. We departed South Bend and after cruising along for a while the nose of the airplane dipped down almost like someone grabbed a hold of it and pulled it down. I didn't realize what it was because I wasn't indicating excessive speed and didn't get an over-speed siren indicating that my air speed was too fast. I pulled the power back a bit and the airplane became controllable. I had exceeded the design limit and the airplane did what was called a tuck. Just like a stall. I found out later that the airplane had a malfunction in the air speed indicator as well as the warning system. I flew the airplane back to South Bend and then to Philadelphia and back to South Bend. They finally sold it and were glad to be rid of it.

Cecil was an avid golfer and as such really took great joy going to the various places to golf. We went to Greensboro, Pine Hurst, Augusta, Hershey, Homestead, The Cloister, and The Doral, White Sulfur, all of the top-notch golfing areas in the United States. He told me that it would be a good idea if I learned how to play golf. I'm sorry to report that I never got very good at it. But, I did make an attempt, and at that time I probably shot in the high 90's, which was embarrassing to the people that I was playing with. Whenever we went anywhere I was the one who had to refrain from drinking in any way, shape or form. Since I was the pilot, we never knew when we were going to have to fly somewhere.

One time we flew up to a Tecumseh meeting in Michigan where they were having a golf outing for

President's Day. Cecil and the other Wheel Horse people were there and they were choosing up teams to play golf. Of course, I was the worst player in the group and was chosen last, and Cecil got stuck with me. They had a bar on every other tee and since I didn't have to fly for a day or two I decided to avail myself to some of their beverages. I had a high handicap and I had strokes on most of the holes that I played. I kind of got carried away as time went on and got very relaxed and started shooting way over my head. I was getting arrogant and would say "watch this" and sure enough the ball would drop in the hole. It got to the point where several of the opposing teams were throwing their clubs and cursing loudly. I think my score was 82 or 83, which was enough to beat everybody with the amount of handicap that I had. That was the good part. The bad part is it has never happened again. I wasn't as popular that day as I could have been.

We took a trip to Mexico; departing January 16, 1969, we flew to Houston to fuel up, and flew on to Acapulco. Two days later we flew to a town called San Luis Potosi, a very nice city, but certainly not very industrialized. I remember people coming out to the airport in wagons drawn by oxen. The fellow who met us there was a friend of Cecil's whose daughter had gone to school with his daughter at St. Mary's in South Bend. He made gum (similar to Chiclets) that was sold in Mexico and a lot of people, especially the beggars, would give you a few pieces of gum in return for a gift. As Mr. Pond went to his host's home, I told him not to worry about me. There was a real nice Mexican pilot (educated in the States) who came over to the door of the Lear Jet as I was shutting down, and he was in his glory to see such a modern aircraft. I turned all the lights on and let him see all of the bells and whistles. I think he had a Piper Cherokee or some such airplane. He recommended that I stay at a downtown hotel and provided transportation to the hotel. We had dinner together that night and it was an excellent evening. He did say that he didn't usually like Americans but that "I was okay." The next morning, sure enough, he showed up in the breakfast shop and we had breakfast together, and he spent the rest of the day with me. He showed me the town and all of the places of interest and some of the industry that was there such as it was. Many were very interesting places and it was great to have a personal tour guide.

A little girl was standing there when I came out of the hotel and she asked me for some money for ice cream. I saw a man watching her from around the corner and I had heard that they used children for begging. I thought what could I do to see that she gets her ice cream. I took her across the street to buy her an ice cream cone and then I gave her some money so that she wouldn't get beat up by going back without money. It was a real heartbreaking thing to see the poverty. I remember reading the statistics for that time; the average peon made something like $35 a year so you can imagine the poverty. We flew on the next day to Mexico City and spent some time there; we visited the Pyramids and some of the wonders of Mexico City and then flew back to Plymouth, Indiana.

Construction begins on Skystream completion in the fall of 1966.

The new years eve party t day before we opened for b

The Skystream Logo that would become famous in the future.

People waiting in line to ta penny a pound airplane ri

Skystream flies formation over first Blueberry Parade.

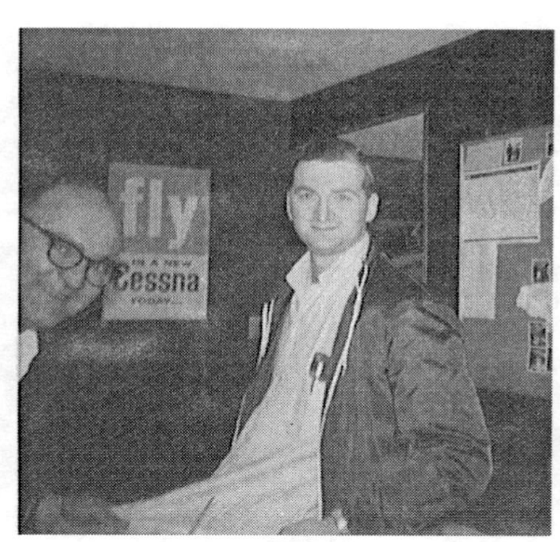

Bob Snyder cuts shirttail after Dr. Holm's first solo.

Bob Snyder cuts shirttail after Everett Colvin's first solo.

Velma on Ritzcraft Twin Beech (Paul Meyers pilot)

N1968 Wiskey ready to charter.
(We started getting calls early)

Joe Harmon with Fred Morro
President of the aviation boar

As you can see we were beginning to attract some business.

Hank Beard chief test pilot for Lear arrives at Plymouth.

One of our Cessna 310's on the line ready for charter.

Ernie Brovold at the helm in Canada on a fishing trip.
Ernie's log cabin with all the amenities including outhouse.

Skystream The Leader

The third month of 1969, we entered into negotiations to purchase the FBO and its assets at the Goshen Municipal Airport in Goshen, Indiana from Russ Miller, the fellow who had given me my private license when I first learned to fly. I thought it was time to branch out a bit and see if we could capitalize on some of the companies in the Goshen and Elkhart area. Therefore, I thought an operation in Goshen would give us an entrée to several of these companies, which proved to be true. On April 1, 1969, we took over the Goshen Municipal Airport. We purchased the building, tools, jacks, hangars, and all of the other assets that Russ Miller had at Goshen. In the next month or so we spent so much money on telephone calls back and forth that I decided to put in a radio connection. We installed a Motorola Radio System with a tower at Plymouth and a tower at Goshen and a receiver at each end. So Velma, with the touch of a button, could be in communication with the office at Goshen. This gave us the ability to be in close communication with them to schedule charters, swap airplanes, and to bring airplanes over to demonstrate to prospective buyers.

I talked Paul Meyers, my original instructor and a close personal friend of mine, into coming to work for Skystream and managing the Goshen Airport. I think he was intrigued by it. I think that since he had spent considerable time behind the desk at Ritz-Craft and since the company had been sold, he was ready to get away from it a bit and go back to the joy of flying and the job of operating an FBO. Paul moved to Goshen and from that time on I didn't have to worry about Goshen. He was right there at the airport, watching what was going on, protecting our interest, developing sales, and handling charter, and instruction. He was also responsible for the purchasing of fuel and oil, and the supervision of all help except maintenance.

My logbook shows that on May 27, 1969, I started getting Phil Calvert ready for his type rating in the Lear Jet. He had flown with me quite a little before that but he needed to concentrate on the Jet to get ready. We went on a pretty extensive flight where he was able to log quite a few hours and returned on June 2, 1969. July 14, 1969, both Phil and I went to South Bend to take flight tests. He acquired his type rating in the Lear Jet and I took my six-month ATC check ride. We now had someone who could back me up with regard to traveling for Wheel Horse in the Lear Jet.

Cecil had been talking for some time about how we would "some day" fly the Lear Jet to Europe. I took it with a grain of salt because it was a very marginal aircraft for that type of trip. At any rate, he called me one day giving me about five days notice and told me that he wanted to leave for Europe in the middle of the following week. I hardly knew what to do. I phoned around to see if anyone had made the trip and found that Faberge had made the trip in a Lear Jet. I called Faberge and talked to their chief pilot and he graciously sent me his charts. I wouldn't have been able to get charts in time to make the trip. He told me that we would have no trouble getting over there because we would be going with the prevailing winds. We might have quite a bit of trouble on the return trip since we would be running into the wind. He also told me to get permission to land in Greenland at Sunderstrom Air Force Base. I called and found it would take about six weeks to get permission. I tried to find a pilot who had experience in oversea flying in any type of aircraft, and heard of one in the Chicago area. I talked to him on the telephone and he said that he would be delighted to go with us if we paid his expenses.

On the afternoon of July 27, 1969, we departed Plymouth and landed at Goose Bay, Newfoundland. When we arrived at Goose Bay we were given quarters which were like barracks. Cecil, Betty Pond and I, along with a salesman for the European operation, departed Goose Bay the next morning for a direct flight to Reykjavik, Iceland. The trip was not a bad one, by today's standards. But in those days when you had an aircraft that was barely capable of staying in the air for four hours and you had to go further than the manual said the aircraft would go it was more of a challenge. The ocean under us was filled with crushed ice in which you could expect to have useful consciousness for only a few minutes if you were forced down. It did not make for an attractive adventure. I was required to take an inflatable rubber boat and I informed my passengers that if we were forced down they were to take the boat and go if they wanted to, but I intended to sail the airplane right into port. The compass in that area was off about 16 degrees because of the fact that we were flying closer to the North Pole. So you have to take this all into consideration when you flight plan it, because if you made a mistake and were off 16 degrees the wrong way, there was no way you could recover. I decided that the thing to do was to go out through the departure corridor coming out of Goose Bay and establish a heading and then turn the number of degrees that was indicated on the chart by my marks and take up that heading. Sure enough, in about an hour and fifteen minutes the ADF picked up the Prince Christian homer on the tip of Greenland approximately halfway there. After going by Greenland we proceeded to Reykjavik Iceland and upon arriving found instrument conditions. We went through the procedure for the approach and I noticed that I had to stay awfully high on final for a long time. I complied and when the time came to let down we looked back and I could see there was a cliff there. We landed and it was an excellent situation since it was early in the day and we were continuing on that day. We fueled the airplane and were ready to go in a relatively short time.

From there we went to London, England. In the United States we used what is called a transition level, in those days I believe 18,000 feet, was where you switched your altimeter over to a standard barometric pressure. When you went below 18,000 feet you took the barometric pressure from the field you were landing at and set it on your altimeter so it would be correct when you landed. The Europeans assigned a different transition level whenever they felt like it I guess. When we started down I received a message that said "transition level 8.0, altimeter such and such a millibar setting instead of standard barometric pressure setting." It was so difficult to understand we just looked at each other and blinked. Arriving over London we were put into a holding pattern. We were holding over Gatwick

Airport and I could see it below me very nicely and by that time we had used considerable fuel. Finally I got up my courage and asked the tower if we could possibly land "before we ran out of fuel" and they graciously complied.

The official language for aviation is English. All towers speak English and all of those involved in aviation, including the centers, as well as the pilots, speak English. The only place I found that I had trouble understanding the language was in England. It seemed that they spoke so quick and so differently that it was hard to understand what they said.

We stayed in London for a few days and then departed on the 30th for Antwerp, Belgium. We stayed there for a day and then flew to Oslo, Norway to meet with the representative of Wheel Horse Products in the European area by the name of Mr. Knut Eng. The copilot that I had so eagerly wanted to go with me was of little or no use. Evidently he had flown over in a small airplane, got into a lot of trouble and had to call for emergency help and didn't even know just where to go to file flight plans or anything, more trouble than he was worth. Cecil would have been more help. When you go from country to country you are continually going in and out of customs and the customs officer would come down and ask, "Are you the Captain?" and of course I was. They seemed to treat you with great respect. I really didn't have too much trouble but it is time consuming to file an international flight plan where you go in and out of several countries. You have to have a penetration time and they required a detailed plan of where you were going to be and when. Therefore, there was considerable time expended to prepare a flight plan and to determine when you were going to enter the next country and how long it took to get into the air and how long the decent would be etc.

We had arrived in Oslo, Norway on July 31, 1969, and didn't leave until August 4, 1969, returning to Reykjavik, Iceland. I knew this would be the critical flight because it was the farthest distance and it was into the wind. The only place to land on the tip of Greenland was Nanortalik and it was down a fjord and had an iffy approach since there was a mountain at the end of the runway which meant you couldn't take off the same way you landed. I had determined that the radio beacon on the tip of Greenland, the Prince Christian homer, was the halfway point. I wanted to be by that homer in an hour and thirty minutes so I would have a little bit of lee way on the other end, for weather reasons. When we went by the Prince Christian homer the time was exactly one hour and thirty minutes. We continued on to Goose Bay, landing without even having the red lights on. I was very pleased with the return flight. After landing at Goose Bay, we had lunch and got back into the airplane and flew to Detroit International where we went through Customs and flew back to Plymouth that afternoon. Of course we were running ahead of the sun instead of behind it.

On 9/7/69 we made another trip to Europe, departing Plymouth to Goose Bay, from Goose Bay, direct to Reykjavik, Iceland on the same day. Iceland was a beautiful little country with brightly colored rooftops, and very nice people. We had an excellent meal that evening of miniature lobster and we enjoyed ourselves immensely. We departed 9/8/69 for Oslo, Norway to pick up our distributor, Knut Eng's wife and the Crown Prince and Princess of Norway and flew them into Brussels, Belgium where we were met by the Belgium King. I must say one thing about having royalty on board; it really greases the airways. When we departed from Oslo, the tower called to confirm that we had VIP's on board and I said "That's affirmative," and that's the only time we had any waiting in the entire flight. We were given clearance to land in Brussels while other aircraft were in a holding pattern and when we landed they rolled out a red carpet and the Belgium King came out to meet the Royal Flight.

After staying in Brussels for a couple of days we departed for Paris, France and then on to Dusseldorf, Germany. We were staying in Dusseldorf, but we were actually attending a hardware convention in Cologne. We traveled back and forth by train, which is an excellent means of transportation in Germany. I talked to a man who spoke the language and I asked how I would know when to get off? He said when this train stops at the posted time, the door will open and you'll get off. We never missed any destination by more than thirty seconds. It was the same in Belgium after we landed, I knew we were a minute late to catch the train so I said to Cecil, "Let's run for the train." Cecil said, "You can run if you want but you'll only see the back end of it leaving." He was sure right because they really run on schedule. You either get there on time or you don't go.

Cologne is a wonderful ancient city and is famous for it's beautiful cathedral. The history of the cathedral was fascinating. Many generations worked on it while it was being built. There had been a cathedral there in that area for many hundreds of years. On 9/14/69 we departed Dusseldorf, Germany and went to Oslo for the evening and then back to Brussels, Belgium for a couple of days. On 9/17/69 we departed for Reykjavik, Iceland. We arrived on the 17th fueled and departed for Goose Bay, then to Detroit and through customs and then back to Plymouth that evening.

A real nice gentleman by the name of Bob Love and his wife Helen operated the FBO in Valparaiso, Indiana. We had become friends with them and tried to work with them as much as we could. On 10/26/69 I took him to Rochester, Minnesota to Mayo Brothers for hip surgery and he came out of it pretty well. Later I talked to him about selling the Valparaiso operation. Skystream bought it and Bob & Helen stayed on to help.

We departed 1/3/70 to go to Akron, Ohio, and to Wheeling, West Virginia, to Nassau in the Bahamas, staying there until the 5th. We went to San Juan for a couple of days then on to St. Thomas, in the Virgin Islands. We had with us on this trip the winners of the yearly Wheel Horse sales event. They had sold more tractors than anyone else had and this trip was their prize. We wined them and dined them and they loved it. We flew back to Miami, Florida, played golf, took them to some of the nightclubs, and brought them back to Wheeling and Akron. We then flew back to Plymouth.

At that time my hours had grown to 6,600 and we were really doing a lot of flying. The only incidents that I am relating to you here were some of the interesting flights, because I flew almost every day.

In the second month of 1970, Sollitt Construction Company, which was the large construction firm that Conrad Lesh "Tiz" worked for decided to get rid of their airplane. Of course I wanted Tiz to go to work for us in the worst way but I was reluctant to ask him because he had made a lot of money with Sollit. I knew we were still poorly paid by almost any standard. Mr. Sollitt came to Plymouth and talked to me about Tiz working with us because the Twin Beech was going to be sold. He wondered if we would be interested in it along with Tiz. I see by my logbook that we were flying the Twin Beech by the second month of 1970, so I assume that was when

Tiz came to work for Skystream. I needed someone to prepare the pilots for their instrument check rides and to make sure all were complying with the FAA requirements, which were becoming more and more intrusive in our business. Since Tiz was an examiner he was able to give most of the check rides himself and could also give private licenses. It was big advantage to have him on the staff. I really have to thank this man for so much in my life. He was the one that got me ready, he's the one who kicked me out of the nest, and the one who rode guardian angle on me in the early days of my flying career with Wheel Horse. He was so well respected by the other pilots that he had no trouble taking command of his position. He was really the glue that joined Skystream together and got our pilots off on the right foot.

In the early days of Skystream I had planned to maintain my half of the company no matter what. I wanted to share in the growth of Skystream and it was certainly obvious that it was growing. It was also painfully evident that I was not going to be able to finance the growth of the operation and do the things that I wanted to do with Skystream. Therefore in order for it to grow I would have to give up my ownership to Mr. Pond so that he could infuse money into it and make it grow the way it should.

In 1968 Cecil Pond and I had built an apartment building on some land close to where my home was. It was the first real apartment building constructed in Plymouth, Indiana. Prior to that the only apartments were remodeled houses and converted upstairs units. It was a beautiful brick building with three levels of apartments. The terrace level was down a few steps, you went up a few steps to the first floor and then up to a third floor. Palbykin Enterprises LLC still owns that building today. We were equal partners in that venture, Cecil having put some cash that was in a company he owned called Ecco, Betty and I put up a equal amount of equity in the form of some valuable land I had, we owned this property together. Eventually he bought out my share of Skystream and we bought out his share of Ecco, the company that owned the apartment building.

On May 5, 1970, Mr. Pond asked me to pick him up at JFK Airport since he was coming back from Europe. Betty Pond called and said that she wanted to ride along to pick him up. I gave her the time we had to depart in order to be there on time. That time came and went and after almost an hour past the time that I had to depart I decided that we would have to leave without her. When we got to New York we were late but not by much. As soon as I saw Mr. Pond he said "Boy are you in trouble." Evidently his wife had called him and told him that I left without her. He said, "well it's better that you made her mad than make me mad, by being late." So we flew back home, but I don't believe Betty ever forgave me for leaving without her. It's hard to please everybody.

With my printing background I realized that it would be expensive to prepare forms and advertising pamphlets and the other paperwork we needed at Skystream. To do this and to handle the mailings I hired a Plymouth man Lane Lafoon, and purchased an upscale duplicating machine. We printed mailers, addressed them and mailed them to all the businesses in the area. About that time we at Skystream developed a day stretcher charter form which had a vignette of each of the charter aircraft at the top of the page, and the price per mile. We used this form to show how we could take someone from here to there and what it would cost in the various aircraft. We asked the customer where he normally went on trips and gave him this form which showed what the trip cost and the time it would take in each of the aircraft, Lear Jet, Twin Beech, Cessna 421, Cessna 414, Cessna 310, and single engine. We had a lot of good vibes from our charter customers. We also developed a relationship with some of the aircraft owners based at Plymouth. We leased the aircraft from them when we needed them and gave them so much per hour for the use of their aircraft. We also instigated CAMS (Corporate Aircraft Management Service) so that they didn't have to employ a pilot and all of the extra expenses required to do so. They simply bought the aircraft; we provided the pilot and leased back the aircraft. This proved to be a very good situation for both Skystream and the customer.

I had been trying to sell a Cessna 421 cabin class pressurized aircraft to a gentleman by the name of Hal Gehring who owned Holly Park mobile home manufacturing company. His company produced an upscale unit with a lot of quality built into it. I had gone all over the tax advantages and he was definitely interested in the Cessna 421. He called me one day to come over to see him at his plant. I arrived and after coffee and a full tour of the plant we sat down in his office. I was determined not to bring up the airplane since I had told him all about it before and we had flown him many times in our charter Cessna 421. We talked about his new models we talked about fishing we talked about everything but the airplane. Finally he said what about the airplane? I said well the nice thing about having your own airplane is if you want a bomb or a hijacker you take them along and if you don't want them you don't take them along. I left without the order. The next morning I got a call from Hal and he said, "you silver tongued SOB I'll take it."

I had a young man by the name of Bill Smith employed as an accountant who took care of the paperwork from the various airports and compiled monthly reports so that I could see what the operation had done and what the accounts receivable were, etc. I would ride pretty hard on Bill, always calling him after the first day of the month for my report. I recall going in there one time and he was having trouble with his stomach. I said, "what do you think it is?" He said it might be an ulcer. I told him that I never get ulcers and he responded, "of course not, you're a carrier." I recall another incident when the IRS notified me that they were going to audit my personal tax returns and we were to be at Elkhart at a given time. I kept asking Bill if he was ready and it was getting late and he was busy doing something. He finally got into the car and I don't think we were ever much below 100 M.P.H. especially on the side roads where we weren't likely to get caught. Bill smoked a pipe and he had it between his teeth when we went over a raised railroad track out in the Amish country. The Oldsmobile that I was driving flew about thirty feet and when it came down Bill bit the end of the stem off his pipe. We got there on time, but after that Bill informed me that he would never, ever, be late to one of those meetings again.

We had a good charter customer by the name of Mr. Roy Beck a very nice gentleman who owned a steel company in the Elkhart area that made frames for mobile homes and made steel junior I beam's. We later found out that we had worked together at Studebaker way back in the fifties. In fact they called Roy "Missouri" and they called me "Nature Boy." (We both worked on the fifth floor putting in headliners) Roy and his wife Naydean were to become our close friends and still are. He bought a new Cessna 310 and later a Lear Jet through me. I knew about Roy as a customer but I had not had a chance to spend much time with him. He was at an LPGA outing at the Plymouth Country Club and I was a part of the committee to get the ladies professional golf tour started in Plymouth. A friend of his was with him by the name of Mr. Jeffries. I had sold a Lear Jet model 25 to Mr. Jeffries the largest sale I had ever made. As I came into the Country Club both of them greeted me cordially and Jeff looked at me and saw the question in my eyes and said, "you don't know who I am?" He was right. It was out of context, not at the airport, and I didn't recognize him. I had been doing some contracting and I assumed (never assume) he was a builder so I said, "I know you are a contractor." Then he said, "my God man, what do I have to do to impress you? Here I buy this Lear Jet from you for three-quarters of a million dollars and you don't remember me." Of course at that point I recognized him but it was too late. Roy looked at me and said, "well, I suppose you don't recognize me either?" I said, "I'm not taking any more chances today." Well, needless to say, I spent the rest of the afternoon trying to make amends for not recognizing them.

After I had become reacquainted with Roy he asked me to fly some of his Lear Jet charter trips. We often flew to Florida, Vegas, and on many golf outings to Pinehurst and to Red Lake, Canada for fishing trips. He had a good friend Abe Gibron who used to be the head coach of the Chicago Bears and later assistant coach of the Tampa Bay Buccaneers. Roy liked to go to Las Vegas and take Abe with him. Roy had requested Marty, my youngest son for his pilot. One time when they had gone to Vegas, Roy who is generous to a fault gave Marty a hundred dollars to spend for gambling. Marty needed a haircut and decided to go to the shop in the hotel. (He later said to me what could it cost?) A little trim a little styling and the cost was over a Hundred dollars. Marty was forced to charge it to his room and had to go to Roy and tell him he would pay him back. A year or so later when we were having dinner with Roy and Naydean Roy asked if Marty had told me about his famous hair cut. I said no he hadn't and Roy started laughing and told me the whole story.

The Lear Jet was an extremely good performing aircraft. It would fly higher and faster than most of the aircraft that the Air Force had. There was nobody in the skies that flew much higher than the Lear Jets. One day I was in our Lear 1968W westbound. You need to understand that the atmosphere extends up to what they call the tropopause, and above that is the stratosphere. Now if you are in the atmosphere down where the air is moving across the earth you normally run into head winds if you are westbound. When you run into head winds you won't be able to go as far as you can if you get up into the stratosphere because the air isn't moving much. In those days before the altitude encoder most Lear operators ignored the aircraft limit of 41,000 feet and would climb, keeping an eye on the DME, watching for the prevailing westerly winds to taper off, so we could go farther on less fuel. This particular day I was going westbound and below me was an eastbound airliner. The Lear Jet makes a contrail and the captain of an airliner looked up and saw the contrail. He called the center and asked what the traffic was at 12 o'clock high. The center came back to him and said that it was a Lear Jet at 410, and of course from his altitude, probably in the mid 30,000's, to where we were in the high 40,000's, was at least 12,000 ft higher. The Lear Jet is just a speck 12,000 feet higher than the airliner. There was pause and he came back and said "Mighty high 410."

Skystream was a multi-engine sales outlet for Cessna aircraft. We had done a novel job of selling aircraft in our area because of our association with the charter customers. Our distributor Aviation Activities was based in Valparaiso, Indiana. They had been trying to sell a gentleman over there for a long time and never seemed to be able to get it done. Chris Valo, was a kind of mysterious guy, and his advertising would just say Chris Valo Enterprises. No telephone number, just a promotion for Chris Valo Enterprises. He was a very mysterious person. He had an unpressurized cabin class multi-engine aircraft. One night he arrived in Plymouth and he wanted to see the Cessna 421 we had which was a pressurized eight passenger multi-engine aircraft. It had a lot of goodies, air conditioning, nice radios, etc. He was interested in it and I talked to him for some time and finally got him to agree to purchase the aircraft. He sent his pilot to his airplane and he came back with a cloth bag filled with money. He gave me a deposit of $50,000 in cash. The banks were closed and here is this mysterious individual and his pilot. I was concerned to say the least. After he left I went to the bank and dropped the money in the deposit chute, which is an awful way to do things. I called and talked to the banker to let him know that I was going to do this since it was cash. Aviation Activities had told me that if I could sell a plane to Chris they would buy Betty and me a special dinner in Chicago. They picked us up in a new airplane, flew us to Chicago and bought us a deluxe dinner at a Cantonese restaurant. On a later date, when we were out in Wichita, Kansas, to pick up the aircraft after some maintenance had been accomplished, Chris said to me, "you know Don, I would like to talk to Cessna about loaning them some money." I thought, boy why would you get a loan on an aircraft if you could loan Cessna.

He convinced me that he would like to. A few years later the Cessna factory called and said that they wanted me to pick up the aircraft at the Gary airport. I thought I might get shot or something but I went over there and had them pull the aircraft out of the hangar, started it up and left. As I took off I was thinking maybe the airplane was rigged with a bomb, or some other type of anti theft device.

In 1972 we began construction on 32,160 square foot maintenance building at the Plymouth Airport, which included more offices, and a new avionics installation and repair facility. In fact, I moved my office back there, upstairs in the Northwest corner of the new building. This was a beautiful facility and I was intent on developing an image that was uncommon in the aviation business. Most aircraft were sold in the hangar or a little office with a linoleum floor and a small cluttered desk. I wanted to have the image of Skystream as the great facility that it was. We built this hangar that was state of the art and beautiful. The floor was painted in a light gray. Mechanics were forbidden to wash the aircraft in the hanger. I was hell on pop cans, and windowsills. It seemed like everybody would get a can of pop and set it on the windowsills when done. I eliminated the windowsills but that still didn't get the job done. I talked to the employees several times and told them that this would stop or I would make changes. I found a few after that so we took out the caned pop machine, and put in a paper cup dispensing pop machine. The pop was dispensed into a paper cup and that solved the problem. I was intent on having a beautiful spotless hangar. If you take your aircraft in to be worked on you are not overly thrilled with seeing it pulled into a hanger with grease on the floor and trash setting around. I wanted it immaculate. I really didn't need that much space, but my office was 20'X 30' and had a private rest room and storage room as well as a separate entrance to the conference room. It had walnut paneling; drop ceiling with walnut moldings, ruby-red plush carpet, black leather sofa, walnut furniture, and it was very impressive in a garish way. Nobody ever forgot it and they all talked about it. No other dealer in our zone had the advantage of such an office and it was built at a very low price.

I rarely invited a customer into my office that I didn't get a signed contract for an aircraft or a new charter customer. As Skystream grew I now realize that I should have spent more time with the sales end of the business and less time worrying about the pop cans, etc. Another pet peeve of mine was scotch tape. Everyone knows that scotch tape is to be used on paper, not be used to stick signs on the wall. We had beautiful paneled walls and people would stick a piece of paper on there with scotch tape. After the sun hit it for a week or so the tape yellowed and melted into the paneling. I told everyone in the place "No scotch tape on the walls. If you want to do it on glass, that's okay. On top of your desk or on Formica tops, that's okay. Never let me catch you putting it on the walls." I once had a pilot land with the gear up because of a problem. He got out rather sheepishly, and I asked him if he was OK, and he said he was, he later told the other pilots that I didn't say anything about the gear up landing but I gave him hell for putting scotch tape on the hanger wall a week before.

I was bound and determined to develop this image and Bill Smith was telling me the other day about an incident he recalled but that I do not. We were getting ready for a promotion at the hangar and they had brought in some throw rugs for the lobby. Two or three feet wide by four feet long to cut down on the wear and tear of the carpet. I had come in and had a fit about them since I wanted the clean uncluttered look in the lobby. Bill says I threw them in the trunk of my car mumbling "they won't be able to get at them in here."

Mr. and Mrs. Pond occasionally flew to Acapulco for a visit and recreation. I recall one time I was there and they were staying at the Pierre Marquette, an exclusive place there, and I told them not to worry about me that I would go downtown to stay. It just so happened that there was a film festival and there was not a room to be had. After driving around for an hour or more the cabby said, "I think I know of a place." It was an exclusive place called the Hotel Maralisa. It was known as the Pearl of Acapulco and was situated in the center of the Bay of Acapulco. It had many celebrities staying there, including Kissinger. It had an outdoor walk-up reception desk. I approached the desk and said, "is there a chance I can get a room?" The lady manager behind the desk said "I can let you have a room tonight but you'll have to move out tomorrow." I thought anything just to have a room tonight. As I was signing the papers to register I remembered Carl Rinstrom had told me he had a hotel in Acapulco and I said, "do you know Carl Rinstrom. She said, "Don't try to pressure me!" That ended that conversation.

The next day I was sitting out by the pool and Carl Rinstrom came by. Carl had something to do with Duncan Aviation where we had bought the Lear Jet. He had made a fortune in the hair curler business. He had sold out to Clairol and made millions. I think he lent money to Duncan to start the Jet business. I met him on a demo flight to California while we were trying out the Lear Jet. He was going to California at the time. I talked a little bit with him and told him about the Wheel Horse garden tractor that we made. After we talked for awhile he wanted us to ship him one and since we didn't have a distributor in his area I did. His gardener started it up without putting oil in it and burned the engine up and he called me about the problem. I shipped him a new engine and that was the only contact I had with him.

On this particular day he came by the pool, noticed me and stopped and talked to me for quite a long time. He invited me up to his home that evening. In Acapulco as in most places the higher you live the more exclusive the neighborhood, and he was about as high as you could get. He purchased the land from Lana Turner after the Stephanato incident. It was a wonderful location. He dismantled parts of a castle in Europe and had them brought in to make this beautiful and stylish home which was open – open – open. It's hard to understand, but there is very little rain so you don't have to worry much about the roof. I met the Maralisa lady manager at his house that night and she didn't throw me out the next day after all.

He had a pilot who flew his Lear Jet that was a reformed alcoholic and looked and acted like Dom DeLuise. He was busy making Margaritas in the kitchen. In Acapulco limes are a staple, limes are on the table just like salt and pepper. They are used on papaya, pineapple, and other fruit to enhance the flavor. He had the girl's busy helping him squeezing limes and preparing drinks He came in with a tray full of Margaritas, in real tall frosty glasses. I tried one and it tasted like lemonade so I had another. During the coarse of the evening, I had three or four of these drinks. After while I thought I should get back to the hotel, but I found I couldn't get up. I stayed in that chair for quite a while before I could get my body functioning again. That was my introduction to margaritas and I love them to this day.

He also had a sauna right by the swimming pool. He had a home in Omaha and several other homes, and he had a sauna in each home. He had given instructions to his servants that they were to be hot at any time he might be there. He wanted them ready for him, whenever he arrived. He told me to go down and have his masseur give me a massage. I declined. In later years I flew Mr. and Mrs. John Ritzenthaler, Dr. and Mrs. Robertson, and Betty and I down there. We stayed at the Maralisa and Carl's masseur was working there since Carl was gone at the time. I decided that I would have a massage and it was quite an experience. They asked if I wanted a sauna first, and they said that's what most people did. I knew nothing about a sauna but I went into this wooden room which was suffocatingly hot. The wooden seat was so hot I had to put a towel down in order to sit down. There is a big hot rock with water dripping on it and there was a window that looked out to where the masseurs were. I figured they would tell me when to get out but finally after about a half an hour of sitting in there I came out, exhausted. I said, "I don't think I can stay in there any longer." The one guy said, "we were kind of wondering about you because most people only stay in about five minutes or so." They told me to go in and take a cold shower and wrap myself in a towel. After showering I came out and climbed up on the table and boy I was worn down pretty good. He pounded on me, cracked my toes and fingers and vigorously massaged my back. All the sudden I noticed another masseur, a great big Mama working on me at the same time on the other side. After about thirty minutes of this I went back to my room and, slept like a baby. I told Betty she should try a massage, but she declined.

Skystream had been in negotiations with the Warsaw Aviation Board for some time and on 8/1/72 we acquired the operation at Warsaw Municipal Airport. Phil Calvert, our vice-president, expressed a desire to be the manager at Warsaw. I thought that was a fine idea. Paul Meyers was taking care of Goshen and I had tried several young men at Valparaiso with mixed results. Valparaiso was a very difficult operation. Since the City sold the fuel on the field we had to make it in maintenance, aircraft sales, charter, and instruction. Another one of the problems associated with Valparaiso was that we were not the only FBO. There was an FBO on the West End of the field that was a Piper dealer and during the coarse of the time that we operated at Valparaiso there were probably two or three of them in and out of business. They started up and went broke, another one came in and started up and went broke. It is very difficult to compete with business like that because they come in and try to cut their prices below what they should to make it and we just went on as best as we could using the same pricing as Plymouth, Warsaw and Goshen.

By the middle of 1972 I had negotiated with Duncan Aviation to purchase a second Lear Jet N788DR. This was another Lear 23 that was kind of a sister-ship to 1986W. We had enough Lear Jet charter that we needed it. In the later part of 1972 I also negotiated for and purchased a Lear Jet 24, N907CS from a dealer who had purchased it from Computer Sciences. It was a beautiful airplane with lots of goodies in it. I couldn't afford to keep it and therefore I was actively pursuing a sale from the day I bought it. I was approached by Flying Tigers out of Detroit who had tried to buy the airplane and would have if we had not bought it when we did. They made me an offer on the aircraft for $25,000 more than we paid for it.

Mr. Hal Gehring of Elkhart had expressed a desire to purchase a Lear Jet. I had previously sold him a Cessna 421 aircraft, and he loved it, but he was looking for a Lear Jet since he had chartered our Lear Jet several times. This Computer Science aircraft was just a beauty. I remember calling Hal in Elkhart saying that I had this aircraft and that if he wanted it he had to do it today, or I was going to sell it to Flying Tigers tomorrow. He said that he was in a meeting and said for me to bring it up to Elkhart to him. I sent the pilots to Elkhart and he wasn't there but his accountant was. They flew up to their other plant at Blue Earth and the accountant called Hal and told him it was a great airplane. Hal phoned me and said, "Can't you wait any longer?" I told him I couldn't afford to keep it and had the opportunity to make some money on it and that I would sell it to him for the same price and give him a lease back on it. "He said well okay." Without anything other than his word I turned down the deal with Flying Tigers. Within a day or so I received a check from Hal written in pencil for the full amount of the aircraft. In the aviation business most of the people you work with are top drawer, good people. You can trust what they say and they will do what they say. You don't have very many trying to take advantage of a situation.

In the early part of 1973 we sold N788DR to John Ritzenthaler of Ritz-Craft, which gave us another lease-back aircraft without the expense of owning it.

Mr. and Mrs. Pond, my wife and I, departed Plymouth 10/7/73 for a flight to Milwaukee to pick up Mr. And Mrs. Knut Eng our distributor for Europe. After picking them up we left Milwaukee for Kenora, Canada for a fishing trip. We stayed at a beautiful lodge in a rather remote area. I noted that the waiters carried towels on their arms and served champagne with a great flourish. We went fishing and caught a bunch of fish, ate shore lunches and had a great time. Since Mr. Pond was spending time with Mr. Knut Eng, our European distributor, he decided to go further on this trip. We left for International Falls, and went through customs. We then went to Colorado Springs and stayed at the Broadmoor Hotel, a very famous and elegant place at that time. That was the night that Spiro Agnew resigned the vice-presidency. A couple of days later we departed Colorado Springs for Las Vegas, Nevada. On the way to Las Vegas as I was letting down, I dropped down into the Grand Canyon beneath the ridge. The Lear Jet had such an abundance of power that even if I lost one engine I could still climb 3,500 a minute on a single engine. My wife says to this day, "you haven't seen the Grand Canyon until you've flown through it." It is a beautiful sight with the Colorado River looking like a turquoise ribbon winding through this magnificent canyon. I am sure that today it would not be permitted since the government is restricting everything. After spending a couple of days in Las Vegas and seeing a lot of the sights and many shows, we departed 10/13/73 for New Orleans, Louisiana. Upon arrival, we went to dinner at Antoine's for a wonderful meal. We spent the night, had breakfast at Brennan's, a fabulous place to eat, and left New Orleans for Chicago. We landed at the Chicago International Airport where Knut and his wife were to catch their flight back to Europe. We then flew back to Plymouth, Indiana.

We took several memorable trips with our friends and I remember one of the most enjoyable was with Barney Johnson his wife Martha and Dr. Coursey and his wife Maxine. We had flown to Knoxville Tenn. in the Twin Beech and rented a car for a trip to Gatlinburg for the fall festival. Both couples had asked about reservations but I told them I never saw the time I couldn't get rooms. As we got close we started stopping and inspecting motels and they were all full. We finally found a gas station man by the name of "Virgil" who in retrospect must have owned most of the town. He said he had a large room that had three beds in it and since the people that had reserved it had not shown up we could have it. By that time we were willing to take anything. What a night. Barney and Martha were given the alcove and every time they moved that old bed made quite a racket and we accused them of making love. Maxine had always complained about Jim's snoring and sure enough we were treated to quite a serenade. Betty likes to sleep quite close to me and in the morning the other two couples swore there was only one body in our bed. We changed motels the next day and each couple got a separate room. We had a great time at the festival but the thing we all remembered was "Virgil's room."

On one trip Dr. Lloyd France and his wife Mary Ann visited our Oceana condo on Hutchinson Island which was right on the beach. Mary Ann drove down to see some of her relatives and after the visit picked up Betty who had flown to Orlando. They went to the condo a couple of days before Lloyd and I flew down in our Cessna 210. Lloyd remembers us missing a pelican as we flew low over the beach. We visited the Flagler Museum, which is quite an experience. We also went to Frances Langford's outrigger restaurant as well as Bert Renyolds dinner theater. At that time they were considering purchasing a condo in Islandia. We had a great trip with the girls shopping at Lohmans and lunch at Two Jays and a later dinner at Benihana's.

We also took several trips with Pat and Kay Flynn. We first met them through the church since both Betty and Kay were in the PTA. We found out later that Betty and Pat attended the same grade school in Chicago and knew the same families. They were godparents for our daughter Susan. We took trips to Florida, Callaway

Gardens, Tulsa, and several other adventures. We always had a lot of fun because Pat and Kay are always cracking jokes and are such good sports.

In 1973 Skystream had not only become the largest charter service in our area but the largest multi-engine dealer in our zone. Having beaten out the competition in many of the large cities such as Indianapolis, South Bend, Chicago, Milwaukee, Minneapolis, and Fort Wayne. We were number "ONE." I was called out to Wichita to receive an award. Del Roskam President of Cessna presented it. Mr. Pond was there and Angelo Marasco, who was the manager of our zone for Aviation Activities also attended. We had achieved something by building our charter business that most dealers had not. Everyone was talking about Plymouth, Indiana, since we were given the award and it was such a small town. In those days Cessna was making about 800 aircraft a month; Almost 10,000 aircraft per year. Aircraft sales were booming and gas prices were very low, with jet fuel selling for about eighteen cents per gallon and 100-octane fuel for about twenty-six cents per gallon. It was inexpensive to fly and a great time for a booming industry later cut short by government intervention and regulations.

I went out to Wichita often to pick up new aircraft and to take prospective customers out to show off the plant and meet the President or Vice President. One time when I was out there picking up a new aircraft I went to see a show in a nightclub. The featured act was Hines & Ford. Mimi Hines was best known for taking the part of Funny Girl after Barbara Streisand left the Broadway show. During her act she came by and sat on my lap and took the cigar I was smoking and used it in her entire act. After she was done with her act she brought the cigar back and gave me a big kiss on the lips. I can truthfully say that is the only time I was ever kissed by a star.

Mr. Pond had taken some studies at Cornell and had asked me to pick him up in the Lear Jet to bring him back to Plymouth. Phil Calvert was with me and as usual we fueled the aircraft before Mr. Pond arrived at the airport. We had assumed (never assume) he would be alone since he hadn't said anything about any other passengers. He brought some other people with him and a large load of luggage. Phil looked at me and I at him and we said, "I don't know if we want to go through the defueling procedure to get the weight back down." The aircraft had an abundance of power and we had a good runway. We loaded them all in and taxied out. I remember pulling out onto the runway and holding the brakes while pushing the thrust levers all the way forward so that we could get the use of every bit of runway that we could. As the aircraft started to roll it was sluggish. We had hot, damp weather conditions, which affects the jet engine. It develops considerably less power than normal. As we rolled down the runway we observed a pick-up truck on the road that ran crossways at the end of the runway on the other side of the airport fence. The pick-up truck stopped right in the center of the runway on the road and a couple of people got out and jumped onto the bed of the truck. As we were rolling along I was thinking that I wonder if they realized that this is one of the noisiest aircraft in the world and we're going to barely miss them. I waited until the last minute when I got the flying speed I needed before lifting the nose-wheel off and the airplane left the ground. I doubt if we missed that truck by twenty feet. It had to be a terrible experience for those people. As we climbed out and proceeded on our way, I looked over at

Phil and said, "I bet they won't do that again." Phil responded, "I know they won't."

The Michiana Regional Airport located in South Bend, Indiana, is a large facility and it is the airport that I had worked at when I worked for Stockert's, the largest airport in our area. It was 1973 or 1974 when I was advised that we had made more takeoffs and landings from Plymouth, Indiana than they had in South Bend. This was a major accomplishment. We had charter operations running out of Plymouth all of the time, we had a sales force operating out of there, and student instruction, and customers coming in for aircraft and radio maintenance. Plymouth became what was later referred to as the "Biggest little airport in the country."

Lear Jet had developed the Lear Model 25, a stretch version of the aircraft that we had, but built to more rigid specifications. We ordered a Lear Jet 25 for Wheel Horse and received it in 1973. We also ordered a Lear Jet for a lady out of Chicago. In each case we were able to buy these aircraft at a given price and by the time they were delivered the price had escalated considerably because of the rising costs. We ended up selling both aircraft and made a good profit on them. The Wheel Horse aircraft was bought for speculation and when the high fuel prices hit in 1973 and fuel became more expensive it became a very desirable aircraft because it used less fuel than most Jets. We sold the second 25 to Winnebago, a manufacturer of motor homes and we came out on that deal rather well also.

At one time we had two Lear 23's one Lear 24 and two Lear 25's in our charter fleet. We did really well with them. People in aviation began to look at Plymouth and wondered what in the world was going on there. I can remember people at the Holiday Inn, which was adjacent to the airport, waking up in the morning wondering if they were at O'Hare, as they heard so many aircraft take off.

We did a lot of work for Ford Motor Company. They talked to us about emergency parts flights where they had a plant that was going to have to shut down because of lack of parts. They wanted to know how fast we could respond in such an emergency. We wound up in some cases with the aircraft sitting on the ramp ready to go, and since I was only about a half a mile from the airport, I would meet a co-pilot at the airport and we would be airborne in about fifteen minutes. They requested that we call them as soon as we were airborne. As soon as we got the wheels up I would call on our aircraft phone and they were astounded that we could launch that quickly. We picked up parts and delivered them to various parts of the country. In many cases the plants would cease production if we didn't arrive. We were busy beavers for Ford Motor Company and they became a big part of our charter business.

With the completion of our new maintenance facility we were able to prevail upon Kerns Avionics out of South Bend to put in a facility at Plymouth. We now were able to provide aircraft maintenance and radio maintenance, an important part of aircraft service. With this expanded facility, we drew even more new customers. They knew they could take their aircraft to Plymouth and get Kern's Avionics (the best-known radio facility in the area) to take care of their radios. Skystream had the best and most up to date maintenance and our mechanics were sent to Cessna to keep them up to date, and we were highly regarded by the Cessna organization.

In May of 1974, we were featured in the Cessna Marketing News with headlines

"Service Means Sales at Skystream, 400 Attend Open House."

"The success of our business will be predicated directly on how well we can take care of customers. That's the feeling of Don Palbykin, president of Skystream, Inc., Cessna full-line dealer at Plymouth, Indiana. Who recently backed his belief with construction of a new, ultra-modern 32,160 sq. ft. facility devoted strictly to aircraft maintenance, service and dispatching.

"IT'S NOT often you build a new maintenance shop and avionics lab all in one year," said Palbykin. "We've made a deep commitment to maintenance because we think it's going to be the real key to the future of our business."

Apparently Palbykin's gamble is paying off. At its recent grand opening and open house to unveil the new facility, the dealership sold two new 421 Golden Eagles and two new Skyhawks to area businesses...due directly to the new shop complex.

"IN TODAY'S MARKET" Palbykin said, "customers want to know their airplane will be in good hands after the sale. And they want to know this before they buy. That's what our new facility provides. It means a great deal to our business growth now, and will mean even more as the years go by."

At its open house, Skystream invited all major business leaders in the community over 400 turned out – plus the Governor of Indiana and the mayors of Goshen, Warsaw and Plymouth. The complete Cessna multi-engine line was on display during the event, and TV and newspaper coverage was excellent.

"FROM THE open house," Palbykin said, "word of the facility and our expanded capabilities spread by word of mouth from businessmen who attended to other area business leaders...and we closed the two 421's and Hawks as a direct result."

"More important," Palbykin said, "we sold the new service facility. This was the real reason for the open house, since it will be the impetus from which our future growth will come."

Skystream's new facility features a large 120 x 125 ft. clear-span service/maintenance hangar staffed by eight well-qualified A&P's, a well-equipped 7,800 sq. ft. avionics shop staffed by two top-notch technicians, an on-purpose parts department, and 6,000 sq. ft. of additional executive, accounting and office space.

"ADDED TO the new airplane sales we've already picked up," noted Palbykin, "the open house also gained a huge amount of new service business for us and we obtained a lot of additional sales leads, too. Some are just hatching out now. Others are very near the closing stage."

In addition to its outstanding new maintenance facility and expanding sales volume, Skystream also operates one of the largest charter businesses in its part of the country, with a fleet of five jets and 22 piston-engine Cessna models available to suit every customer need."

The Cessna Marketing Newspaper went to all Cessna dealers and of course Cessna dealers usually leave these newspapers in the lobbies of their facilities. It was a tremendous advertising coup for Skystream.

With all this going on you began to wonder how we had time to do anything else, but sure enough we were about to become involved in an airline operation. Hub Commuter Airlines based in Fort Wayne, Indiana was in the process of going into bankruptcy. George Bailey came over to talk to Mr. Pond about purchasing the airline. I spent quit a bit of time trying to talk Cecil out of it. We went to Florida for a trip, sat around the table, and discussed the matter. I explained to him that very few commuter airlines ever make a profit. So, we decided to pass on the purchase of the airlines. Within a very short time the airlines went into bankruptcy. We were approached by the lawyers in the bankruptcy proceedings wanting us to purchase the assets of the airline. It was too much to resist and we purchased Hub Airlines. The airplanes were being leased from Pepisco and we purchased them at a good price. We bought the other airline assets at an extremely low price; way less than wholesale. Hub Airlines was a mixture of the large Commuter Airlines that had operated out of Chicago and had gone into bankruptcy a couple of years before. We now had Hub and Commuter Airlines as a combined airline. More about the airlines in the next chapter.

All of the advertising we had now and all of the people we taught to fly, thirty or forty a year, as well as the contacts and charters and a phenomenal sales history had made Skystream a well-known name in the industry. We could sell in Valparaiso, Goshen, Warsaw, and Plymouth, and shuffle airplanes between them since it was less than a thirty minute flight to each one. We sold an airplane to Petercraft Aviation Services that was used to transport Jimmy Carter in 1976 in his run for the presidency.

We were constantly flying trips to the various fishing villages in Canada. On 6/4/75 we flew up to South Bend to pick up a bunch of Mr. Pond's friends to fly to God's Lake in Canada and we had a wonderful fishing trip staying at a very nice lodge. This was so far up North that it didn't get dark at night. When we got there we chartered small seaplanes to fly us to the most remote fishing lakes. We also used Indians as guides. We flew back to South Bend on 6/7/75. That was a common type of outing for many of our customers.

I remember a trip with a close friend of mine, Ernie Brovold, in his aircraft. (He bought a Cessna 182 and later a Cessna 210 retractable gear aircraft). We flew to

Thunder Bay, then to Armstrong. We bought our food and supplies at a local store. Then took a train to the middle of the wilderness and were dropped off at Schultz's Point where Ernie had boats ready for us. We fished, had shore lunches, and some great meals in his log cabin which has about everything. It was just like living in God's Country. It was a wonderful thing to be able to spend time with friends in Canada on such fishing expeditions.

We also went on golf outings. I remember leaving Plymouth with a group of four, Ernie Brovold, Barney Johnson, Herschel Towns, and me and flying to Brownsville, Texas to spend a week playing golf. We played thirty-six holes each day and I even had some good holes before returning home. These were all wonderful experiences with great people.

I can see by my logbook that on 11/09/76 I gave some instruction to Betty Pond, who was a white knuckle flyer, and I think the instruction she took helped her to relax more during trips. She was pretty good. Women have inherently a good feeling for aircraft. They seem to sense that is meant to be controlled by pressures not movements. She did very well and I gave her quite a bit of instruction. Betty wanted to be in a position so that if she was in an aircraft and there was problem, she could get the aircraft down in one piece.

The new offices and maintenance hanger under construction.

The completed facility from the air. (We only had one runway.)

The charter room from which all flights were dispatched. Phil Calvert on the left, me, and Jennifer Campiti.

One of our new stretched Lear Jet's ready for charter.

At work in my new office, walnut, cork, and ruby red carpet, with black leather sofa and chairs. Visitors never forgot it.

Velma, my secretary standing guard outside my office.

Conrad (Tiz) Lesh in his chief pilot's office. (The professional)

Some of our piston engine aircraft that were used for charter.

Donald Palbykin, Cecil Pond, Crown Princess Sonja, and her lady in waiting; Baudoin, King of the Belgians, The aide of the crown Prince Harald, and Mrs. Knut Eng, after we landed at the Brussels Airport upon completion of the "Royal Flight."

Phil Calvert, Chris Schenkel (The bowling sportscaster), and John Sanders his pilot, upon delivery of his new Cessna 421.

Governer Bowen (Later to become head of HUD for the federal government) and his wife at Skystream for one of our sales parties.

Our sales parties were well attended with many in ball gowns and attended by the Mayors from all the cities we operated in.

One of Skystream's displays at the start of a new model year.

Aircraft being serviced in the maintenance hanger. (Note the immaculate floor and the lack of clutter)

From the left Del Roskam President of Cessna, Cecil Pond, Angelo Marasco, and Palbykin receiving the award, for the most multi engine sales in our zone for the year.

The author taking delivery of a new Cessna Super Skymaster from Del Roskam President of Cessna. (At the factory.)

Skystream Airlines

With the acquisition of Hub Airlines and the formation of Skystream Airlines Inc, we entered a whole new chapter in Skystream history. The Skystream FBO people were top quality people, unquestionably the best in the area. The airline people were an entirely different breed of cat. They mostly consisted of pilots who were trying to build time so that they could some day go to work for a major airline. They were a different type of person altogether from the corporation pilot.

When we first acquired Hub we started out with complete crews in place. The pilots were concerned about wages, and in many cases they had been passed over for increases for some time during the dark days of Hub Airlines. They were looking for some way to get an increase in their salary, which was pretty skimpy. The first thing we did was to try to blend them together. The cards and stationery had Hub in one corner and Skystream Airlines in the other. It was a difficult time but we had to keep it that way because, had we not kept flying as we were we would have had to go through a complete startup with the FAA. They required so many hours of line flight and so many hours of training for each of the crews, and it would have been very costly and non productive to change names at that time. After a while we were able to change the name from Hub Airlines to Skystream Airlines, Inc., which turned out well as far as start up costs were concerned.

The airline operations headquarters was near Midway Airport in Chicago, Illinois. Maintenance was being performed at several places, mainly Fort Wayne and Flint, Michigan. It became quite a logistic problem to manage, with each place buying there own parts and supplies. We needed order, teamwork, and organization when working with the different branches of the FAA. One of the first things I tried to do (and I don't think I ever succeeded) was to get all of the Skystream Airline personnel working together for the common good so that we could make Skystream Airline a viable and thriving company. I invited them all to a meeting in my office and I remember many of them sitting on the floor and all around the office as I talked to them about the plans to reinvigorate the airline. We had to organize everything and try to get it pulled together. I shared my thoughts about moving reservations to Plymouth and doing the maintenance in Plymouth where we had good, competent people, and where we had the ability to do the servicing of the airliners in the evening with the whole maintenance hanger to ourselves.

We had five airliners that we had bought from PepsiCo, a leasing corporation, and they were pretty sick looking when we took over. The first thing I did was to try to think of a way that I could somehow get them talking and thinking about Skystream Airlines and renovate the airplanes to make them look pleasing to the customers. At that time Braniff was using airliners that were painted all different colors, yellow, green, red, and

I thought that's not too bad an idea. But, I wanted a single color that would do something entirely different. At one time I considered painting all of the airplanes black but that had a very negative connotation. So after a lot of consideration I went with the color pink. I mean a bright pink, Pepto Bismol pink. We had a lot of things going with that. "We're in the pink" or "get in the pink." The other thing we could say is that we were "in the pink of condition." The exterior of the airplanes was pink with black lettering. The interiors were a blend of red and black and other fabrics that didn't show the discoloration if someone spilled coffee or something.

We also published for PR purposes in the early part of 1974 a little brochure called "Skystream Plane Talk" (Pink and black on white paper) edited by Betty. The first edition was the spring of 1974, just after the pink program was started and after we had the airplanes overhauled and painted. When we started to fly the pink airplanes, we received a tremendous amount of free publicity because it was rather shocking to see a pink airplane as we got each of the airplanes back after fresh engines and paint and upholstery they looked really good. We felt we were off to a good start.

We moved reservations from the location near Midway Airport to Plymouth into the new offices built the year before. We contracted with Braniff to go on their computer system the "Cowboy System." Skystream was literally riding the Braniff system. We installed monitors and the reservation girls were right by the Airline operation office. We had relocated the operations to the new offices and very shortly moved all of the maintenance to Plymouth. This made Plymouth one of the stations. We might as well take someone with us if we were going somewhere. In this way we often had a direct connection to Chicago, South Bend, Fort Wayne, or wherever we were going.

We had many excellent people in the airlines but some were problem children. There were times when pilots had to overnight because of bad weather. Early on they just went to the station manager and asked for money out of the cash drawer for hotel, etc. The girl at the counter gave them money out of the drawer. That was okay but we certainly didn't want to do it that way on a regular basis. I called the pilots all in and told them I would give each one a one hundred-dollar bill and I want you to put it in your wallet. I said, "if I tap you on the back, I want you to be able to show me the hundred dollar bill. It's our money; you just have it for your emergency situations. After the overnight you will file an expense report and the necessary receipts and be reimbursed. I don't ever want you to ask for help from our station managers again." I informed all of the managers of this policy. I'm pretty sure they spent their one hundred-dollar bill but none of them went to the station managers again.

We had a young lady by the name of Bonnie Kalina who worked in the Airlines with a background in the military. She was a firm no nonsense person. The more I talked to her the more I felt she should be put her in charge of all station managers. After installing her I knew she was the right person for the job. She came on the corporate management team and from that time on I had very little trouble with any of the station managers.

We had some transporting to do between two of our stations, Chicago O'Hare and Chicago Megs Field. We bought an old limousine and painted it pink with Skystream Airlines lettered on the side in black. We also used it in emergencies for transporting passengers or freight to Plymouth. It was sometimes used for events in Plymouth, when we had parades, etc.

In the spring of 1974 as we kicked off our pink campaign I wrote a letter on pink paper with the Skystream emblem and name on top. Skystream Airlines, Inc. was a separate corporation from Skystream, Inc. Underneath the Skystream logo on the letter was printed in small script, "The Sign of the Leader" and we were definitely the leader at that time here in our area.

"THINK PINK"

We're finally ready to begin an advertising campaign, the theme of which is "PINK". If we all take a very positive view of pink it will turn out to be a tremendous asset for Skystream Airlines. It would be wonderful if everyone thought that the pink planes were beautiful, but they won't. The important thing is that they talk about our airplanes. For example, many of Braniff paint jobs are atrocious but everyone knows Braniff by the colors of their aircraft. Even if you don't personally like pink, we want you to take a very positive approach with our passengers. You have been provided with pins that will help attract attention. Tell our customers you will give them one if they'll let you pin it on them. Even if the customer wears the badge for a few moments, it will stress the fact that Skystream Airlines and Pink are synonymous.

Very shortly now all of our Airliners will be pink, most of our paper supplies will be pink, our signs will be pink, our in-house newspaper will be pink and the ticket agents uniforms will be pink. One of the greatest points made by the advertising media is that when we get sick and tired of a theme, color or promotion, we're probably just beginning to penetrate the market and many themes are used for years before they catch on enough to be effective, so "THINK PINK".

D. J. P.

We were constantly developing more gimmicks to promote Skystream Airlines. We came up with a little pink heart that stuck on much like a name tag does which said, "Love at First Flight, Skystream Airlines." A small matchbook that said "Skystream Airlines" and had the 800 numbers for our reservations on it. We had 800 numbers for Indiana, Illinois, Ohio and Kentucky. "In the Pink" seemed to be working. On some of the flights we served pink champagne. The pilots' wings had an emblem with the Skystream insignia of black on a pink background and so the whole theme was coming together pretty well.

In the first edition of Plane Talk we discussed the various consolidations and what we had to do to bring Skystream people together. Some of the articles read:

THINK PINK

Skystream Airlines has chosen pink as the official color for our "Pink People Carriers" (Beech 99's to you).

If you're shocked by our choice of pink consider this: We wanted a really different color because we plan a really different kind of commuter service. (Truly dependable, with well-serviced airplanes that are in the pink of condition).

The color pink lends itself nicely to our advertising campaign and various promotional ideas.

But mainly we want people to notice us "cause we're on our way to the kind of service that will tickle people pink.

PASSENGER VOLUME UP

Skystream Airlines reports that air passenger volume at Kellogg Regional Airfield continues the trend of monthly increases and Commuter Airlines totaled a 72 per cent increase in traffic over this time last year.

Richardson Murphy, Chairman of the Battle Creek area Chamber of Commerce Committee, indicated recently that Skystream maintained the frequency of the local flights at a time when a number of other airliners curtailed their flights because of the fuel crises.

"Our local airlines have been able to obtain fuel and appear to have sufficient fuel allotments for the foreseeable future", Murphy said.

WELCOME ABOARD

This is our newsletter's first flight and we hope you find your journey through its pages enjoyable and informative.

Skystream can most certainly look forward to an excellent growth pattern in years to come. When Skystream acquired the assets of Hub Airlines I'm sure that there was a question in many peoples minds about the future of the company. At that time Hub management was located in Fort Wayne, Indiana, the director of Flight Operations in the Detroit area, maintenance was accomplished at Flint, Michigan, and accounting and reservations was close to Midway Airport in Chicago.
We have during the past few months consolidated all these activities here in Plymouth, Indiana. The economies that

we have realized are excellent. The spirit of cooperation between department heads is growing daily. The incidents of cancelled flights due to mechanical problems is down. Our accounting people are well entrenched and for the first time important data is available monthly.

Our new computerized reservation center was operational March 1st and with no hesitation, began to increase bookings.

The pink airplanes are already doing what we had hoped. They're causing all kinds of excitement wherever they're seen. Pink buttons are much in demand. The aircraft's new interiors are serviceable and good-looking.

The Skystream charter and sales operation, which is the backbone of our company, is better organized today than ever before. Our new avionics shop here at Plymouth completes our operation and makes it without question the finest maintenance facility in this area. Our charter aircraft jets, light twins, and even single engine aircraft are heavily scheduled and almost daily new customers are flying Skystream charter. I want to extend my congratulations to all the employees at Skystream whose cooperation and willing dedication have enabled us to accomplish all of these things in such a short period of time.

D. J. Palbykin, Pres.

THE COMPUTER COMMUTER

SKYSTREAM Airline customers now enjoy the advantage of a fully computerized reservation system.

On March 1, SKYSTREAM went online with the Braniff "cowboy" system, enabling our reservationists to handle your requests in a fraction of the time formerly required.

In addition to the tremendous time saving advantages, this system should minimize reservation-connected errors.

Each reservationist has a remote station tied directly to Braniff's computer bank, and all information stored therein is immediately available to each reservationist. Information is updated instantly, and replies appear on a "television" screen in front of the reservationist in a matter of seconds.This new reservation system is the most modern and efficient available, and is just one of the many things SKYSTREAM Airlines is doing to make your travel with us more pleasant.

The following article appeared in the Plymouth-Pilot Newspaper:

I have been noticing the advertising in the Pilot concerning the new service offered by our local airport and our new Plymouth based Skystream Airlines. It appears that our community is not taking advantage of this service, as they should.

A few weeks ago my wife and I needed to make connections with a United Airline flight to Los Angeles and used the noon Skystream flight to Chicago'' O'Hare. Our baggage was checked in at Plymouth to the L.A. Airport. The flight to Chicago was very pleasant and interesting. We were transferred by bus to the United terminal quickly, in plenty of time for our flight. Our baggage arrived with us in Los Angeles without our worrying about it.

Skystream Airlines is just another fine organization that should make all of us proud to say - I live in Plymouth, Indiana.

Mearl Strombeck
1728 Hope Blvd.
Plymouth

In the summer of 1974 Skystream Airlines acquired G.L.C. routes, Great Lake Commuter. We were now operating out of Plymouth, O'Hare, Chicago Meigs, Fort Wayne, Detroit Metro, Detroit City, Lansing, Traverse City, Marquette and Houghton Michigan. In the second issue of Plane Talk not only did we acquire the G.L.C. routes, but the headlines say, "Future Looks Rosy!"

FUTURE LOOKS ROSY!

In our first issue our President, Don Palbykin, stated that "Skystream can most certainly look forward to an excellent growth pattern in the years to come."

Little did we realize that these words would come true only two weeks after publication of our Spring Newsletter, and that we would almost double the size of the route covered by Skystream Airlines.

In May, Skystream Airlines, Inc. acquired some of the assets of Great Lakes Commuter (G.L.C.) and without a break in service accomplished the transition smoothly. As a result of this acquisition, Skystream routes now include stops at Lansing, Traverse City, Marquette, and Houghton, Michigan.

This extends Skystream Airline's routes to eleven cities in Illinois, Indiana, and Michigan.

In September, 1973, Skystream Inc. entered commuter competition when it purchased the assets of Hub Airlines which had stations at Battle Creek, Detroit Metro, and Detroit City, Fort Wayne, Chicago O'Hare and Chicago Meigs, and added Plymouth as the repair and fuel stops.

Today, with the addition of the old G.L.C. routes to four Michigan cities and five PINK Beech 99's, the future of Skystream Airlines and Skystream Inc. looks very "rosy" indeed!

October of 1974 Skystream added South Bend to our growing list of cities that we served. The fall issue of Plane Talk had articles as follow:

SKYSTREAM ADD'S SOUTH BEND

On October 1, Skystream Airlines instituted service to the city of South Bend, Indiana and the Michiana area with its fleet of PINK Beechcraft 99's.

Sixteen daily flights now connect Michiana Regional Airport with Chicago's O'Hare and Meigs Field, Detroit metro, Battle Creek, Lansing, Fort Wayne and Plymouth.

Northbound flights also connect with scheduled flights to Traverse City and with the Upper Peninsula stops at Marquette and Houghton.

The airline offers a computerized reservation service tied in with the Braniff "Cowboy" system for instant connections to all major air carriers. New joint fares are now offered with major airlines to reduce the costs of connecting air travel.

In addition to the commuter service Skystream Airlines offers a complete air freight service for area businesses.

The opening was inaugurated with a T.V. interview with WNDU on Channel 16 on September 30, a V.I.P. flight on the PINK plane to inspect the home base in Plymouth and followed by a press party.

During the T.V. interview President Don Palbykin was asked why after the failure of three commuter airlines in the Michiana area in recent years he thought Skystream could be successful.

"There are several factors in our favor," he stated. "First we are an established company in our field and have sound financial backing with a meaningful growth pattern. Secondly, our existing organization is unique in this business. I know of no other commuter that has our internal capacity. Others are forced to lease airplanes, farm out maintenance and electronics repair, buy fuel from others, etc. In every case we are self-contained, we even have a centralized accounting system."

Skystream has its own fixed base operation at four locations. This leads to profitable consolidation of management and maintenance for the entire group.

The third factor noted is that the timing is right because growth has caused the major airlines to graduate to larger planes. These larger planes physically and economically cannot use the smaller airport best served by commuter planes. This provides more opportunity for the commuters.

Even the fuel crisis of last fall and winter was a boon to commuter operators because major airlines were forced to cancel many of their less profitable flights into smaller regional airports. In closing Palbykin stated, "We intend to offer consistent flight schedules that the traveler can depend on. We have grown because of quality service and we do not intend to lose that reputation."

Skystream now serves twelve airports in Indiana, Michigan and Illinois, more than any other commuter in the Midwest and as a result the sight of those colorful PINK airliners is becoming more and more common.

We started operating out of South Bend Airport and got a lot of good coverage for nothing. TV interviews and some of the publicity photographs had a large impact on our start up. We also had good articles in the newspaper. The following article appeared in the South Bend Tribune 8/28/74.

AIRPORT OFFICIALS THINK PINK

Think pink.

That is the word circulating around Michiana Regional airport as Skystream airlines and its brightly painted pink Beechcraft 99's prepare for inaugural commuter flights here Tuesday.

Skystream, a Plymouth-based airline, will begin serving the Michiana area with a schedule of 16 flights daily to and from neighboring metropolitan areas. Eight inbound and eight outbound flights will connect the Michiana Regional Airport with Chicago's O'Hare and Meigs Field, Detroit Metro, Plymouth, Fort Wayne, Battle Creek and Lansing. In addition, northbound commuters may connect on the firm's scheduled flights to Traverse City and the Upper Peninsula stops at Marquette and Houghton.

The airline offers a computerized reservations service tied in with the Braniff "cowboy" system for instant service connecting to all major air carriers. New joint fares will also be offered with major airlines to reduce the costs of connecting air travel. In addition to commuter service,

Skystream will offer an air freight service for area businesses.

In the fall of 1974 I wrote a letter to all Skystream employees.

TO ALL SKYSTREAM EMPLOYEES

I want to take the opportunity at this time of the season to thank everyone for their tremendous effort during the past year. We have made considerable strides and we look forward to an even better future.

I particularly want to thank the department heads for their above-and-beyond the call of duty efforts during the acquisition of the Airline.

This is a traumatic time for all of us here at Skystream, but the promise of a more secure and bright future looms brightly. Many of you have been with Skystream for a number of years and have observed the growth we have enjoyed. To those of you who have recently joined us, we extend a hearty welcome.

I was particularly moved by the Airline pilots letters of expression of support. I want to assure you we will do everything in our power to make you glad you work for Skystream. I realize that all is not roses and that there are inequities. I can assure you that I intend to do everything within my power to make both Skystream, Inc. and Skystream Airlines, inc. a good place to work.

Things look good for the future! Charter's growing by leaps and bounds, Airline schedules are filling up, and our supply of fuel at the present time appears to be adequate. After three months operation of the Airlines we're pleased at the progress and looking forward to our fresh airplanes, new computer system and improved financial position.

Merry Christmas and Happy New Year.

SKYSTREAM

Don Palbykin

As things grew I appointed Phil Calvert executive vice-president of Skystream, Inc. in charge of the fixed-base operations.

Phil Calvert joined Skystream in 1968 and was one of the senior employees. He was one of those involved in the organization of the Skystream Charter Operation, which is the backbone of our company. Originally employed as a charter pilot, he rapidly rose to the position of Chief Pilot. He was later named manager and put in charge of the Warsaw operation, which became one of the most successful of Skystream's acquisitions. He has been involved in aviation since 1958 and as such has spent the major portion of his life flying. Before coming with Skystream, he worked for a fixed-base operation, and later as a company pilot for a large corporation. Phil is an avid hunter, and shoots skeet with the best of them. His latest hobby is gliding in his own sailplane. Phil and his wife Rose have a one-year-old daughter and live in Warsaw, Indiana.

I appointed Dale Johnson executive vice-president of Skystream Airlines, Inc. Phil was an extremely capable man and continued to do a wonderful job handling the fixed-base operation and selling airplanes. Dale had his hands full and had a rebellious group. I'm not sure if he ever got on board trying to pull for the Skystream image as much as he did for the airline's image. A negative reaction developed between Skystream employees that were in the fixed-base operation and the Skystream Airline employees. I recall one time when my oldest daughter was there and a Skystream Airlines pilot walked in with his uniform and she said "Gee, a real airplane pilot." Well, I can't think of anything that was less true. The Skystream Charter pilots were far superior to any of the Skystream Airline pilots with more experience, in more sophisticated aircraft and with the ability to make flight plans and go anywhere in the country with no difficulties at all. The airlines were more of a streetcar type of operation. Going from point A to point B time and time again. There is nothing wrong with either but the real problem was trying to get them to work in conjunction with each other. It worked pretty well simply because I wouldn't allow it to work any other way, but I think there was an undercurrent of distrust on both sides.

About the time that I was starting the Airlines I ordered a pink, and I mean pink, polyester suit to open up the various stations. When we opened a new station we made a big thing about it and I would wear the pink suit. Of course, it was quite a gaudy looking thing but it really attracted attention. I wore it one time to an Airline convention in California and out of the whole group of airline executives I was the one they talked about the most. The same thing was true in the various cities where we opened up. I recall a time when I was in South Bend for a meeting where I wore the pink suit. The meeting was at a hotel where Elvis Presley was staying. I stepped out into the hall and was mobbed by people who thought I was part of his entourage. It was just the kind of thing that drew all kinds of stares.

We later acquired Trans Michigan Airways. We had quite a group of airlines. Hub, Commuter Airlines,

Great Lakes Commuter, Trans Michigan Airways. There was a lot of various talent that we acquired and things seemed to be going very well.

In the spring of 1975 Pacific Airmotive, who were the people we had chosen to overhaul all of the engines on all aircraft, featured us in their publication called "Station 88" with an article about Skystream Airlines.

SKYSTREAM AIRLINES

AIRLINE IN THE PINK

On January 2, 1967, a small airport was opened in the Hoosier community of Plymouth, Indiana, a city of 7,600 population. The year before, the ambitious people of Plymouth, filled with determination to gain their fair share of business and industrial growth, recruited Mr. Donald J. Palbykin, who was then Assistant to the President of Wheel Horse Corporation of South Bend, Indiana, to fill the need of acting as the FBO, or Fixed Base Operator, and manage the new air field. Mr. Palbykin responded quickly to the idea, foreseeing a great future for a Fixed Base Operator as well as the possibilities of starting a new commuter airline to serve this area.

In partnership with Mr. Cecil Pond, SKYSTREAM, INC., was formed and entered into a Fixed Base Operator lease Agreement with the Plymouth Board of Aviation Commissioners, agreeing to manage the airport, construct buildings and provide the necessary services.

SKYSTREAM's operations began in 1967 with the Plymouth FBO, one single engine Cessna, one Lear jet, a Cessna aircraft dealership, and two employees. Work started almost immediately on the first of many buildings to come, an 80 x 80 building and one set of (T) hangars. Its first year of operations saw the realization of an excess of $600,000 in sales against what had originally been considered an optimistic projection of $125,000. An additional 72 x 80 building was erected the same year. With this phenomenal sales figure, 1968 and 1969 saw additional hangars being constructed as well as the acquisition in May 1969, of an air support FBO program in Goshen, Indiana.

In 1970 SKYSTREAM acquired the Valparaiso FBO and initiated a program called CAMS (Corporate Aircraft Management Services). This program provided many services previously unavailable to corporate aircraft owners. In 1971 increased sales were seen once more and the firm began to be recognized as a major name in charter air service.

June of the following year saw the acquisition of SKYSTREAM's third FBO at the Warsaw, Indiana, airport. By year-end the Cessna Aircraft Corporation recognized SKYSTREAM with the top Cessna regional sales award in an area covering Minnesota, Illinois, Indiana and part of Michigan.

A 32,160 square foot clear-span service and maintenance hangar was opened in 1973 and the runway was increased to 4,400 feet to accommodate increasingly heavy traffic and more Lear jet flights. A new avionics shop was also opened. This year, too, saw SKYSTREAM entering the commuter airline field. By acquiring the assets of a mid-Western commuter airline and stops at Battle Creek, Detroit's metro and downtown fields, Fort Wayne, Chicago's Meigs and O'Hare fields, and adding Plymouth as a fuel and service landing, SKYSTREAM entered the air commuter business. Along with this new commuter service, SKYSTREAM began to consolidate their acquisition operations into the Plymouth facility and by year-end, firm sales were topping $4 ½ million.

1974 saw Palbykin and SKYSTREAM concluding centralization of their new acquisition operations. This was a monumental task with Management being in Fort Wayne, Indiana, Flight Operations centered in Detroit, Maintenance at Flint, Michigan, and Reservations in Chicago, but by mid-February the job had been done effectively and with no loss in service.

In early March 1974, SKYSTREAM tied with Braniff's "Cowboy System" for instant and connecting reservations. Besides this being a tremendous help to SKYSTREAM and its passengers, it brought SKYSTREAM's reservations and ticketing programs up to a par with the major airlines. In May yet another area commuter airline's assets were added to SKYSTEAM's fleet expanding its stops to Lansing, Traverse City, Marquette and Houghton, Michigan. In October SKYSTREAM again increased its routing with 16 daily flights plus two new direct flights to Chicago from Traverse City and a stop at South Bend, Indiana. Joint fares with many major airlines are in the offing.

By late October SKYSTREAM's personnel complement exceeded 150 employees with a full range of aircraft, including single engine Cessnas, small and large twin engine crafts, SKYSTREAM AIRLINES' Beech 99 airliners, and stretch Lear jets. Naturally, this phenomenal growth, although spearheaded by Mr. Palbykin and Mr. Pond, was too big a job to be handled by two people. Merlin Jones, Assistant to the President, has responsibilities encompassing almost every facet of SKYSTREAM AIRLINE'S operations and is ably assisted by Jim Murray, Director of Flight operations; Bob Howard, Chief Pilot; Bob David, Director of Interline Services; and Bonnie Kalina, Director of Stations and Reservations. Good personnel are a necessity at SKYSTREAM with operations ranging to a point which is only 20 miles from Canada all the way down to the mid West. SKYSTREAM AIRLINES currently operates five Beech 99's, that are powered by the PT6A-20 engine.

Before initiating SKYSTREAM AIRLINES' first flight, all engines were completely overhauled as well as the refurbishment of the craft themselves. Jones and Murray strongly contend that their maintenance personnel supervised by Bill Savitsky, Director of Maintenance are as good as the best in the industry, and SKYSTREAM AIRLINES' record, as well as its Fixed Base Operations' growth would indicate that this is true.

Although Merlin Jones and Jim Murray are the first to admit that the PT6 powered Beech 99's are among the finest commuter aircraft in current use, they are researching suitable larger equipment for expanded activities. When asked about expanded routing, Jones stated that any expansion would be routing by evolution and not revolution. Deliberate and careful planning and programming seem to be the byword at SKYSTREAM. With average flight duration lasting less than 45 minutes and some being as short as eight minutes, reliability is a necessity. Weather conditions can vary from extremely hot sometimes to below freezing winters, and SKYSTREAM's Plymouth facility is busy checking each engine on each aircraft on a daily basis. SKYSTREAM performs much of their own maintenance at the base in Plymouth, and in 1974 signed an agreement with PAC in Burbank for overhaul of the –20s.

The thing that stands out most about SKYSTREAM AIRLINES is their theme, their corporate colors, and the color of their aircraft. In Spring, 1974, seeking to provide SKYSTREAM, an admittedly young entrant into the commuter field, with an identity all its own, Don Palbykin came up with the idea of going pink. It isn't a subtle, barely noticeable pink, but a "hot" pink! This brilliant pink became the new corporate identity, and aircraft color. It's quite evident that it worked from the start because "on the second day our pink aircraft, N410SA, was in service, Chicago radar did a radar identification as follows: "I've got a pink blip' and a Chicago disc jockey promised to give up drinking when he saw it."

SKYSTREAM's plans for the future are difficult to ascertain at this point. Continued growth is obvious in both Fixed Base Operations and the airline itself, but this growth will be accomplished through judicious expenditures and cautious thinking. As Palbykin stated at a recent interview: "Apparently we are pushing the $6,000,000 sales mark, and there are now over 150 employees and a full complement of aircraft ranging from single engine Cessnas to small and large twin engine craft to our Beech 99 airliners and stretch Lear jets. We have experienced steady growth, profitable growth. It's a tough, aggressive organization with great people and facilities unique to the commuter air business. This is the time for real commuter air growth in the market place, too. Its time has only meaningfully come during the past year and SKYSTREAM is going to grow with it."

PAC's PT6 Marketing, Customer Service and Engineering team think that says it all!

On the back page of that publication was one of our advertisements, which shows a lady in a pink hat and pink top and a pink belt saying, "Arrive in the pink." Underneath was a picture of Skystream Airlines with black stripes and Skystream Airlines printed on the side of the airplane. It also says "The airline that's in the pink."

I was running around like a chicken with my head cut off. I see on one particular day I left Plymouth went to South Bend, then to Battle Creek, on to Detroit, to Traverse City, Michigan, Marquette, Michigan and then to Houghton and back to St. Joseph, South Bend, and back to Plymouth. That's a lot of moving around. At various times I would be in bad weather. One time when I was coming back into Plymouth after one of those safaris I was flying instruments solid for two or three hours and it was l: 00 a.m. I knew I was really pushing the envelope out there all alone in the middle of the night dodging thunderstorms and trying to get home.

I still made a lot of trips for Wheel Horse because if it was at all possible Mr. and Mrs. Pond wanted me to fly for them. I could not take them all but I still flew a good number of trips for them.

Many of the people I had taught to fly at South Bend came to Skystream to buy their new aircraft. I remember selling Gran Godley a multi-engine plane. Mr. Darnell bought a multi-engine aircraft. I sold a 210 to Dr. Schmidt from South Bend, and the list goes on, as well as the people we sold here in Plymouth. But by far the biggest sales came from Elkhart. We had a built-in stream of customers who came to Plymouth and admired our maintenance hangars and the great airplanes.

In May of 1975 I was asked to speak at the Indiana Aviation Conference held in Chicago and I spoke about the difficulties of meeting the governmental regulations being thrust upon us at that time and, the difficulty of operating a Commuter Airline.

I assumed (never assume) Mr. Pond was pleased at the progress we were making with both Skystream and Skystream Airlines.

Mr. Pond had thought for some time about instigating a conglomerate. On June 10, 1975, I received a letter from him.

June 10, 1975

D. J. Palbykin, President
Skystream, Inc.
Plymouth, Ind. 46563
Dear Don:

Enclosed is an Organization Chart for POND ENTERPRISES, INC. AND ITS ASSOCIATED COMPANIES. Please note that there is a direct line and staff relationship between the POND ENTERPRISES, INC. or its designated employees and subsidiary companies.

Accordingly POND ENTERPRISES, INC. will require the below listed reports from your organization on the dates specified.

Any liaison necessary to accomplish these reports will be handled directly between the Controller of POND ENTERPRISES, INC. and the SKYSTREAM department heads involved.

Reports are to be submitted directly to POND ENTERPRISES, INC. by the department concerned, with copies to the management of SKYSTREAM, INC.

Yours very truly,
POND ENTERPRISES, INC.
Cecil E. Pond, Pres.

CEP/vh:encl

Receipt of this letter acknowledged:
SKYSTREAM, INC.
D. J. Palbykin, Pres.

I signed the letter at the bottom and that designated acknowledgment of receipt of the letter. Mr. Pond had gone to Europe.

This was a totally unacceptable situation for me and I wrote him back on June 18, 1975,

June 18, 1975

C. E. Pond
Pond Enterprises Inc.
P. O. Box 127 Harbert, MI 49115

Dear Cecil:

Monday, June 16th, Roy Caperton delivered your letter of June 10th regarding your "NEW" organization chart for Pond Enterprises and Its Associated Companies and advised me you were in Europe.

I note that it shows Skystream Airlines as a separate company. It advises me that liaison will be handled between the Controller of Pond Enterprises and the Skystream Department Heads involved.

He also delivered a letter from him regarding a purchase order system you have directed be instituted. Since we could not even buy parts (many parts cost over $1,000.00) under this "NEW" directive without prior approval from Pond Enterprises and since all liaison is between Engle and the various Department Heads you have in effect emasculated the job of President.

As per our conversation before, I cannot work for you under these conditions.

Therefore, please consider this letter as my resignation. This resignation is final and irrevocable and I will not consider changing my mind. I have advised Roger Engle of this fact.

If you would like I will stay one month to help you make the transition, but I will not be available after July 18th.

I am sorry you chose to have Roy deliver your "NEW" directives since you knew I would be leaving upon receipt of this information.

I have told no one that I have resigned. I will make the announcement Monday morning, June 30th at the Managers' meeting at 8:00 A.M. I will also send Cessna and our related companies notice on that date. I would recommend that you attend the meeting so that you can advise the managers of your decisions with regard to who to report to, etc.

Since we have known each other for approximately seventeen years and I have worked for you for over fifteen and one half years, I am sure you know of my warm personal feeling for you. I do appreciate all that you have done for me and I wish we could have parted differently.

Best Personal Regards,
SKYSTREAM, INC.

Donald J. Palbykin, Pres.

P.S. Enclosed please find our check for Betty's expenses in Canada.

Mr. Pond had the feeling that somehow you could make more than one profit out of the company. He felt that he could set up Pond Enterprises, Skystream, Inc, Skystream Airlines, C. E. Pond Inc. and each entity would make a profit. He wanted to transfer all aircraft and cars into C. E. Pond Inc. and lease them back to the FBO's (I had depreciated many of them to very low book values). He wanted to have each of the various department heads report directly to his people and so I said, "what the heck, he doesn't need me any more and I'll just get out of his way." I wrote a letter to the employees dated September 8, 1975.

9/8/75

TO: *All Skystream Employees*

FROM: *Donald J. Palbykin*

As you no doubt have heard by now, I have resigned from Skystream. It has been my pleasure to start Skystream and watch it grow to its present position in the industry. I am proud of our organization and I am sure that the future is indeed bright.

I want to take this opportunity to thank each and every one of you for your excellent cooperation. I can assure you that a company is only as good as its employees and that is what makes Skystream great. I think we have the finest group of people that I have ever seen in any FBO organization.

I am sure that Mr. Pond will need your best efforts and all of the cooperation as you have given me. I worked for Mr. Pond for over 15 years and found him to be a fine individual as well as an excellent businessman.

I will miss you all.

Best personal regards,

Don

After my resignation as President of Skystream and Skystream Airlines, Inc., there was a gap and neither of the entities did very well. I was approached by Mr. Pond to come back and take over Skystream, Inc. the FBO operation. We entered into an agreement with him where Phil Calvert, my son Stephen Palbykin, and I would operate the airport. Within a relatively short time we had it turned around and going in the right direction. At that time Mr. Pond decided he wanted to run things himself again and on 2/8/77 he sent us a Notice of Termination. That was the last that I had anything to do with Skystream.

Several years later Mr. Ralph Kerns and I decided to enter into an arrangement with Mr. Pond in which he would lease the buildings, office equipment and tools to us. It had disintegrated down to a hangar with a bunch of birds flying in and out, a second or third-rate operation at best. We were willing to go back in there and make things go. We were all set when we received a copy of the contract that we had negotiated with Mr. Pond and it was entirely different than what we had agreed to. I decided that I didn't want to go through the trauma and I called it off.

I feel a great debt of gratitude to Mr. Pond because of the opportunities he gave me at Wheel Horse and the many years we were together at Skystream. Without the insight I received in the operation of Wheel Horse I don't think I would ever have been able to start and operate the companies I have. This knowledge was invaluable to me in the years to come as I put together several profitable ventures.

In the fall of 1975 after leaving Skystream I formed a company called Pal-Air, Inc. I began to buy and sell used aircraft, which turned out to be very effective. I would locate a company that wanted to get rid of their airplane and purchase it myself. I would have it cleaned up and promptly resell the airplane. Actually I made a lot more money after I left Skystream than when I worked there. I think I made twice as much the first year with very little trauma at all. I used to sit in my back yard in the hot tub with the portable telephone and run my business. I bought a new Cessna 310 for myself and we used it quite a bit, and leased it out and made a good profit. I bought a Cessna 340 and used it for a while and sold it to Mr. Lebolt who was a jeweler in Chicago.

Phil Calvert was working for Muncie Aviation selling Cheyenne Turbo Props and he got me the Piper line of aircraft covering the northern part of Indiana. During the time I was working for Muncie I had the opportunity to spend some time with one of the men I admire most in aviation, General Chuck Yeager the man who first broke the sound barrier. He was doing the promotion on the Cheyenne. While we were at the NBA meeting in Atlanta Stephen, Phil and I had the opportunity to have dinner with him and a few other Cheyenne pilots and got to know him. Since we were both in the same booth at the meeting and both selling the Cheyenne we had a lot of time together and he was just a fantastic man to talk to. I have a picture of Chuck standing in front of a Cheyenne and a card saying, To Don good luck, and signed Chuck Yeager.

By this time my flight time had grown to over 10,000 hours total time. My logbook shows 9,879 and there were times I didn't log any of my flight time for months on end.

Almost thirty years after starting Skystream I wrote a letter to the original Skystream employees as follows:

DONALD J. PALBYKIN
310 N. Michigan Street
Plymouth, Indiana 46563

April 15, 1995

Thirty years ago next spring I started SKYSTREAM INC. I recall with fond memories the early days when we were all starting the company. When I left SKYSTREAM I said that it had been my privilege to lead the organization and watch it grow to become the best FBO in our part of the country. The SKYSTREAM employees made it happen; the best group of aviation pros around at that time, maybe ever!

As you might remember we would frequently gather all of the employees together at our house for dinner each year. Everyone seemed to enjoy these gatherings and it became a tradition.

Mark your calendar for July 15, 1995. I have reserved a large room at the Plymouth Holiday Inn for a SKYSTREAM INC. reunion. I am going to treat you and your spouse/guest to a dinner. We have an entire room reserved beginning at 5:00 pm with dinner at 7:00 pm. Those of you that come early will have an opportunity to talk, tell flying stories, and renew acquaintances. Additionally we will have SKYSTREAM pictures and memorabilia. Please bring anything you might have to share with others.

Through the years I have talked to many of you who have expressed a desire to attend a SKYSTREAM

INC. reunion and I am anticipating a large turnout. Enclosed is a list of names, addresses, and phone numbers for as many of the former employees as we have been able to locate. If you know any of the old SKYSTREAM INC. employees we might have omitted please let them know of our plans and ask them to contact me.

Please complete the accompanying form to allow us to plan the number of meals and create name tags for all attendees. Your earliest response would be greatly appreciated.

I hope you will be able to attend the reunion, I am looking forward to seeing you again on July 15th.

Warm regards,

Donald J. Palbykin

I sent this letter to all of the original Skystream employees we could locate. I was amazed at the reaction I received to my letter. I received many calls from all over; California, Texas, Pennsylvania, and Phil Calvert came from Saudi Arabia where he was flying. Many local people that were Skystream pilots attended as well as chief pilot Conrad (Tiz) Lesh. Rick Huff a Plymouth attorney was one of our Lear Jet pilots as well as Tom Leininger now an airline pilot. Bob Brown, Mark Kurtz, Harry Sheetz, and my brother-in-law Rey Nelson from California all attended. My son Stephen Palbykin the chief of maintenance from Arizona, Addison Clingerman from Pennsylvania and Bill Coppernoll part of the maintenance team were there. We had a great turnout and a wonderful evening. They kind of roasted me telling all about my failings. People reminisced and I remember Bill Smith, the accountant, said it was the best place he ever worked because he couldn't wait to get to work to find out what was going to happen next. There were a lot of very fond memories as far as I am concerned and I think the employees felt that way too.

In the Plymouth Pilot newspaper there was an article. 7/20/95 about the get together.

SKYSTREAM celebrates 30th Anniversary "in the pink"

PLYMOUTH - In the md-1960's the chamber of commerce decided a new airport was a must for the growing city of Plymouth.

They hired a corporate pilot to operate the new facility, not realizing that this pilot would take the airport and the city of Plymouth into the limelight of aviation.

In the spring of 1966 Don Palbykin not only began operating the airport but also formed a new corporation, Skystream, Inc.

No one, including Palbykin, at the time had any idea that Skystream would "take off" like it did. In less than six years, Skystream became the number one Cessna airplane dealer in the Midwest.

In addition, Skystream supported the largest charter service operation in the area and was the only service to have three Lear Jets in operation.

At one point there were only 120 Lear Jets in the world; Skystream operated five of them.

Believe it or not, at that time it was possible to charter a jet to Europe from Plymouth, Indiana.

One of Skystream's overseas trips took them from Oslo to Belgium as they transported the Crown Prince and princess of Norway on business.

Back here in the U.S., Skystream was busy flying American celebrities as well.

The likes of Pat Boone, Senator Edward Kennedy, Olivia Newton John, Indiana Governor Otis Bowen, Perry Como, and even Elizabeth Taylor all flew with Skystream.

Palbykin downplays his brushes with the rich and famous saying; "We hauled them all."

Skystream began with only two planes and three employees; but its first year saw the realization of an excess of $600,000 in sales. What was thought to be an optimistic projection of $125,000 was the company's goal.

Before Palbykin left in 1976, Skystream had a staff of 168 and over 23 planes.

At one point Skystream was serving over 10,000 airports nationwide with non-stop service. It was a custom airline, flying whenever and wherever the customer wanted.

Skystream was indeed a colorful entrant into the aviation industry, but in 1974 Palbykin took Skystream's colorful image to new heights.

Palbykin ordered the company planes be painted - hot pink. The new image worked from the start as Chicago air control was picking up "pink blips" on its radar.

The often-flamboyant Palbykin took the new company colors to the extreme when he had a custom-tailored pink suit made to wear at a press conference.

Palbykin resigned from the company in 1975, which eventually folded in 1984; but has fond memories of his time as president of Skystream.

This past weekend Palbykin hosted a reunion at the Balloon Wurks Restaurant in Plymouth that was not unlike the many gala parties he hosted in the hangar of Plymouth Airport.

About 60 people returned to Plymouth to celebrate the 30th anniversary of Skystream's inception.

Pilots from all over the world, one from as far as Saudi Arabia came back to fellowship with old friends and look at the many pictures and memorabilia Palbykin had brought.

"Thirty years ago next spring I started Skystream, Inc. I recall with fond memories the early days which were filled with enthusiasm and team spirit," said Palbykin. "The Skystream employees made it happen; the best group of aviation pros around at that time, maybe ever."

For over a decade, Skystream helped the Plymouth Airport become what Palbykin called "The biggest little airport in the country."

PLANE TALK

1ST EDITION | SPRING 1974 | PLYMOUTH, INDIANA 46563

SKYSTREAM GOES PINK!

THINK PINK

Skystream Airlines has chosen pink as the official color for our "Pink People Carriers" (Beech 99's to you).

If you're shocked by our choice of pink consider this: We wanted a really different color because we plan a really different kind of commuter service. (truly dependable, with well serviced airplanes that are in the pink of condition).

The color pink lends itself nicely to our advertising campaign and various promotional ideas.

But mainly we want people to notice us 'cause we're on our way to the kind of service that will tickle people pink.

Passenger Volume Up

Skystream Airlines reports that air passenger volume at Kellogg Regional Airfield continues the trend of monthly increases and Commuter Airlines totaled a 72 per cent increase in traffic over this time last year.

Richardson Murphy, Chairman of the Battle Creek area Chamber of Commerce Committee, indicated recently that Skystream maintained the frequency of the local flights at a time when a number of other airliners curtailed their flights because of the fuel crisis.

"Our local airlines have been able to obtain fuel and appear to have sufficient fuel allotments for the forseeable future", Murphy said.

WELCOME ABOARD

This is our newsletter's first flight and we hope you find your journey through its pages enjoyable and informative.

Skystream can most certainly look forward to an excellent growth pattern in years to come. When Skystream acquired the assets of Hub Airlines I'm sure that there was a question in many peoples minds about the future of the company. At that time Hub management was located in Fort Wayne, Indiana, the director of Flight Operations in the Detroit area, maintenance was accomplished at Flint, Michigan, and accounting and reservations was close to Midway Airport in Chicago.

We have during the past few months consolidated all these activities here in Plymouth, Indiana. The economies that we have realized are excellent. The spirit of cooperation between department heads is growing daily. The incidents of cancelled flights due to mechanicals is down. Our accounting people are well entrenched and for the first time important data is available monthly.

Our new computerized reservation center was operational March 1st and with no hesitation, began to increase bookings.

The pink airplanes are already doing what we had hoped. They're causing all kinds of excitement wherever they're seen. Pink buttons are much in demand. The aircraft's new interiors are serviceable and good looking.

The Skystream charter and sales operation, which is the backbone of our company, is better organized today than ever before. Our new avionics shop here at Plymouth completes our operation and makes it without question the finest maintenance facility in this area. Our charter aircraft, jets, light twins, and even single engine aircraft are heavily scheduled and almost daily new customers are flying Skystream charter. I want to extend my congratulations to all the employees at Skystream whose cooperation and willing dedication have enabled us to accomplish all of these things in such a short period of time.

D. J. PALBYKIN, PRES.

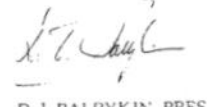

D. J. PALBYKIN, PRES.

First edition of Plane Talk our Skystream News Letter. (In Pink)

Four of our "Pink Airliner's" on the ramp at Plymouth Municipal.

"Tickets to anywhere" Operators at work at the keyboards of three ticket reservation computers at Skystream Airlines, Plymouth, IN.

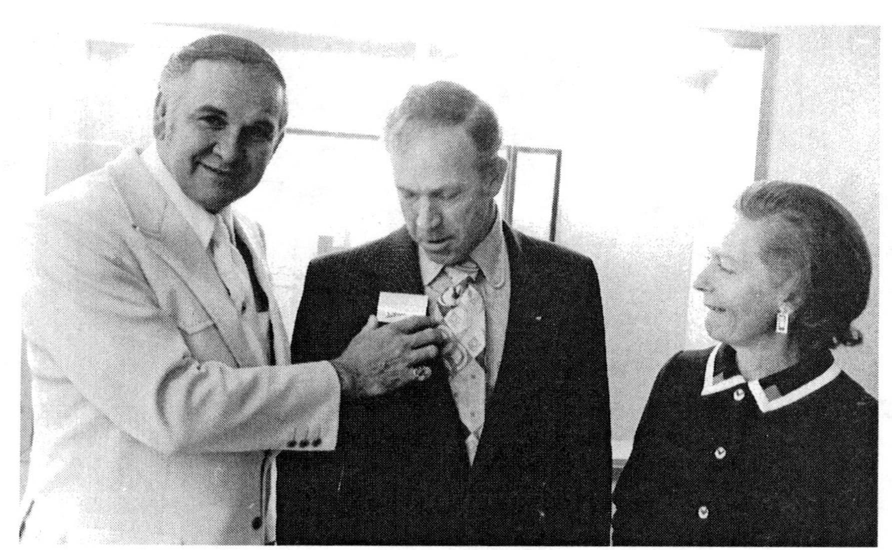

Pining a name tag on Cecil Pond chairman of the board of Skystream Airlines while his wife Betty looks on.

In front of the Holiday Inn in my "Pink Suit" with Cecil Pond.

The airport manager, unknown, South Bend's Mayor, Cecil Pond, and "Pink Suit" at the Michigana Regional Airport South Bend.

Cecil and me inside the airplane for a TV interview about the new South Bend station which included freight service.

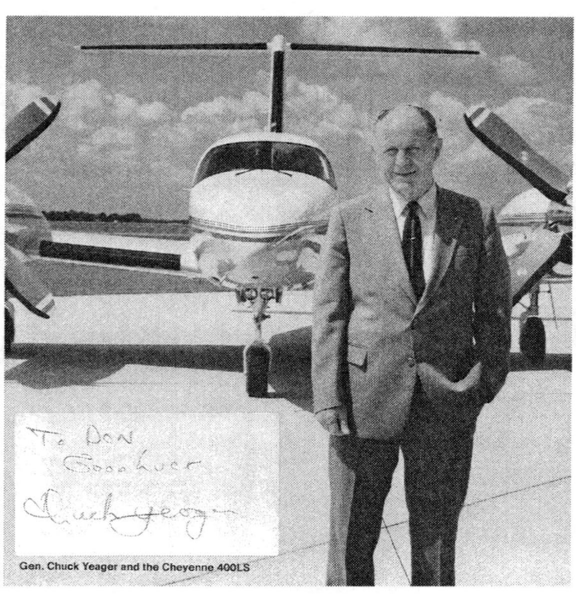

Gen Chuck Yeager in front of the Piper Cheyenne in which he set a world record. We were selling it as the fastest biz turboprop.

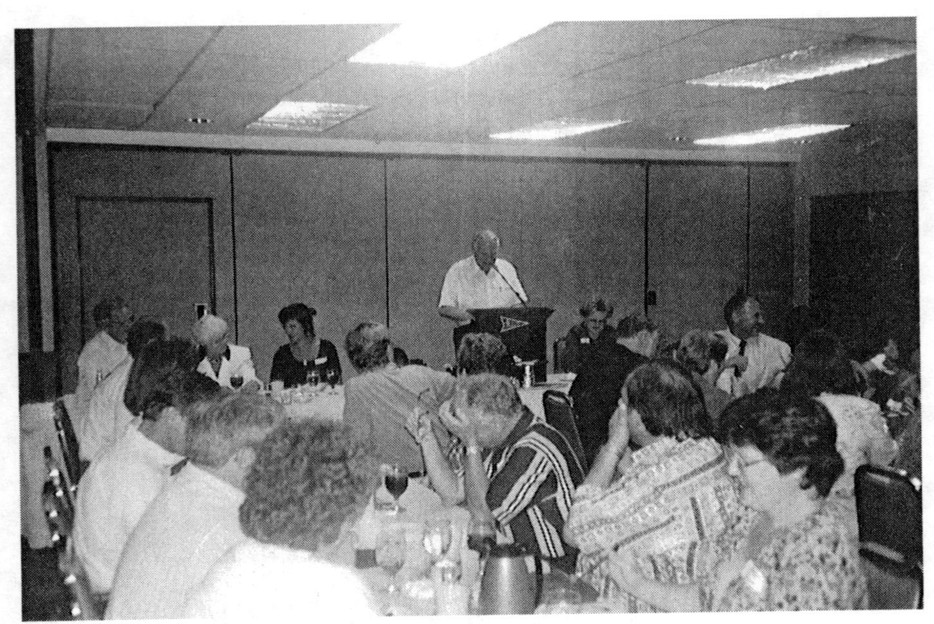

Skystream's 30 th reunion at the Holiday Inn in Plymouth, IN.

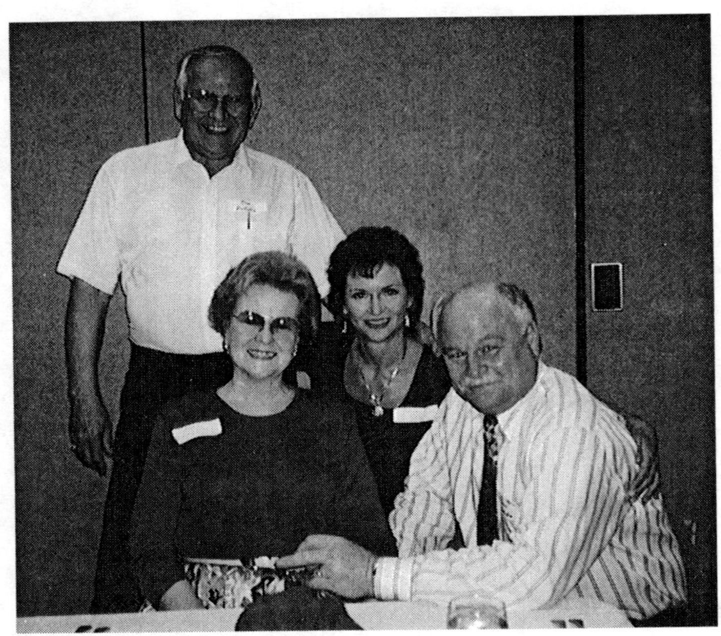

Seated Betty, my daughter Julie, my son Stephen, I'm in back.

On the left Tom Leininger and wife, Rick Huff's wife and Rick, On the right Bill Smith and wife, (Note pictures on table and wall)

Tom Taff, Carl Wilson, Conrad (Tiz) Lesh, and Phil Calvert.

Reynold (Rey) Nelson, his wife Gloria, (Betty's sister) Julie, (My daughter) me, Lane Lafoon at the microphone.

From the left Al Troyer, Steve Palbykin, Addison Clingerman.

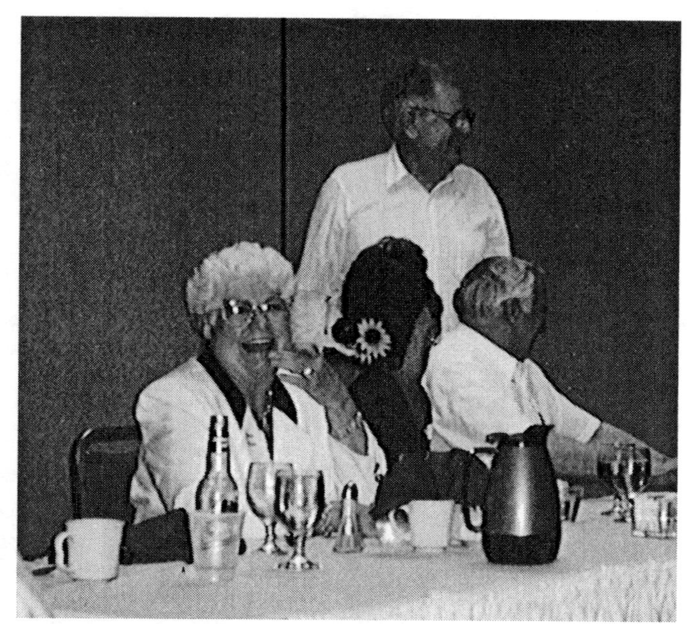

Gloria, Julie, me, and Rey delivering some cheap shots.

Rey Nelson, Tom Taff, Carl Wilson, Phil Calvert, Tiz Lesh.

Homes & Properties

When I think back to the many places that I have lived in my life and the many places that Betty and I have lived and the properties we have owned after we were married, it's a really amazing thought. Of course, I lived on Grandfather's farm from the age of one until he passed away. Then we moved to 817 N. Center Street with Grandma in Plymouth, Indiana. When my father came home from WWII, my Mother, Father and I moved to 844 West Windsor, in Chicago's uptown section. After graduating from Lane Tech High School and after Mom and Dad separated, I rented a sleeping room at 4325 McVicker's, right across the street from my cousin, Tom Bock's home. When I moved back to Plymouth I lived in a sleeping room at 310 N. Plum Street in Plymouth, Indiana. After Betty and I were married we rented the west apartment at 317 W. Monroe Street, the building that became the Historical Society Building and now is again apartments. That was our first home and we had a lot of fun making it really cozy.

Betty's parents had given us a sewing machine for a wedding present and she was very good at sewing.

Betty had worked as an assistant tailor at Sears for some time before coming to Plymouth. She made so many nice things. She also brought with her after our marriage her "hope" chest, which was filled with sheets, towels, doilies, accessories, drapery material and the various items to make a house a home.

We went shopping for a rug. A 9' x 12' rug was a standard size for living rooms at that time. I remember quite a pile of them, at least four or five feet high. Betty was on one end going through the pile like a woman who knew what she wanted and I was on the end with the price tags. She found it all right, the most expensive rug in the pile. So all of the money we had saved for our furniture went into "the" rug. It was an excellent quality Firth rug and we had it for years. When we put it in the living room that was the only thing in there.

We went to Montgomery Wards and purchased a very inexpensive bedroom set, along with the springs and mattress and put it on a time payment arrangement. My Mother gave us a chrome kitchen table and chair outfit as a wedding present. We purchased an old green gas stove. It was one of those old stoves that you had to light with a match and the oven was raised on one end of it. Today it would probably be an antique. We cleaned it up and got it as near perfect as we could. We also bought a used refrigerator that was quite modestly priced.

When we moved into the apartment Betty had put the drapes up and we had the bed, a dresser, one chest, and a nightstand and "the" rug in the living room. After we got married we bought a sofa bed for guests. It was one that you lifted up the seating portion until the back was flat and then put the seat back down. The padding of the sofa became the bed. It was gray mohair with a nubby pattern. We later purchased a radio phonograph combination that acted as an end table. This was not our most successful piece, because if you put a lamp on top, every time you wanted to use the record player you had to move the lamp. We were still learning but we were so pleased with our first home.

The apartment had a couple of peculiarities. It was a modified home. There was a closet just inside the kitchen that contained a metal shower and then at the other end of the kitchen was a tiny bathroom with a toilet and a corner sink. It was an odd set-up with no privacy at all if we had guests. In another corner of the kitchen there were a couple of doors, probably about three feet high, that opened up into a storage area under the stairs that went to the upstairs apartment. I took that as my workshop. It seems rather peculiar that you would crouch down to go into an area like that but I had all of my tools in there. There was a little short table and it was my pride and joy as my first workshop.

Betty loved cats. I do too now but in the days on the farm I used to sic Fanny on the cats whenever they came close to the house and I regarded them as sneaky creatures. But, they do make wonderful pets. After we were married Betty really wanted a cat so we got this tiny gray and white kitten and named him Tuffy. He was a doll baby and a lot of fun. We kept him in the apartment and he was of great joy to Betty when I was working nights at Studebaker.

Right across the back yard was my Aunt Mildred's home and my Grandmother and Mother lived in the upstairs apartment. Well, one day Betty was over there visiting with Tuffy and they had the window on to the roof open for ventilation and Tuffy got out on the roof. He managed to slide down the eave-trough that had been freshly painted. He had paint all over his belly. Betty got out the turpentine and cleaned him up. I was coming back from downtown and Betty came running towards me screaming about the cat going crazy. We both rushed into the apartment and the cat was making a racetrack out of the living room. He was going around in circles with his rear legs retracted dragging his rear on our new carpet. I said, "What in the world did you do?" She explained to me that she had just used turpentine to remove paint from his underside. When I realized what had happened and what she had done I asked her to fill the little corner sink in the bathroom with warm soapy water, and we put him in and soaped him all over. He was panting something fierce. He finally calmed down and Betty learned that you never use turpentine on a cat.

We were married May 29, 1948 and we had our first child August 25, 1949. When Stephen arrived he was a beautiful baby with red hair and the grandparents and his great-grandmother (my grandmother) were all huddled around admiring their first grandchild. We were only nineteen years old. The feeling at that time was that you couldn't have a cat around a baby. Because the cat would smell the milk on the baby's breath and suck the air right out of the baby and cause it to suffocate. That, of course, was an old wives tale but since my mother, "the doctor", who was an authority on such things had given us that information it must be true. So, we had to get rid of Tuffy. We took him out to a farm and later found out that he had been run over by a tractor. We sure felt bad that we had made him so trusting and dependent.

After living in this apartment for awhile we started thinking, "Why should we pay rent?" we should buy a home. We finally found one we felt we could afford; a garage house that was built far back on a lot by a Mr. Watkins. He was the shop teacher at the high school. It was a poorly built building, not meant to be a house since he was going to build the house on the front of the lot and it would just be a garage. So, there were a lot of problems inherent with the place. Pipes would freeze up and the bathroom was nothing more than a tin shower, a hot water heater and a toilet. It was not the greatest place in the world but it was in a good neighborhood so we purchased it. We paid $3,500 for the house and Watkins also wanted to sell us the next door lot for $500 and we said, "boy, we don't need the debt." It later sold for $1,500 and it dawned on me that we had made a big mistake. After Mr. Watkins moved out I showed the house to my buddy Joe Harmon. Someone had nailed a dishpan on the wall for a sink. The pipes were mounted on the wall and one of the faucets was higher than the other one. Joe said you don't want that, and ripped the dishpan off the wall. That forced me to buy some metal kitchen cabinets with a sink in them. We got them at Montgomery Wards since we had established credit buying our bedroom furniture there. That was the beginning of many years of bringing the house up to snuff. I put the new cabinets in the kitchen, put down some linoleum and we moved in. We were so pleased because we had our first little house. I remember the living room, which we later turned into a dining room, was about 9' by 10', an extremely small room. It had one bedroom and that was it, no closets, no laundry facilities, and no storage cabinets.

Betty was ready for another cat. She got a black and white male cat that we named Mr. Magoo. The way he got his name was because when Betty wasn't looking he climbed into the dryer to sit on the clothing and she threw some more in and turned it on. She kept hearing this muffled yowling, and it took her quite a while to figure what had happened. When she rescued him he came out dripping socks and was dizzy, and for some time we wondered whether he could see very well. We had a couple more cats Magoo II and another pair named

Skippy and Peanuts. They were all short-term residents. Our first cat was gray but every other pet since that has been black and white.

As time went on I built a breezeway and garage and then we had a place to put the laundry. Later I added on to the front of the house and built a nice big living room, entryway, and closet. I also got enough room for a closet for the down stairs bedroom. I dug the footings mixed the cement by hand and poured them. I had some help from buddies and Betty putting up the studding and roof. I was on the roof one day yelling for Betty to hand some lumber up to me. She came out with a baby in her arms and informed me that if I kept yelling she wouldn't help at all. I also did the wiring and when the inspector checked it he said to Betty "he obviously has done this before." She said, "no, he just went to the library and read up on it." We then built a bathroom with a sink and tub. Slowly but surely we made this into a nice house. We had acquired a large tractor tire and filled it with sand for the children to play in. The tire was given to me and we picked the sand up by the side of the road out where I used to live at no cost. Alan was about two at the time and was playing in it when a neighbor's son who was about four years old came over and tried to take away Alan's toys. Betty and I were watching out the kitchen window and were tempted to help Al but decided to see what would happen. The boy took the toys away a couple of times but Al just climbed up on him and took them back. This happened time and time again and finally he went home a rather dejected boy.

The children slept upstairs in the attic. As time went on I raised the roof and built an upstairs area with windows out the back and we were able to get two more bedrooms and two more closets. We did this in the winter since there was no roof on the house for a couple of days and I felt we could sweep up the snow but not rain. Then we converted part of the garage into a family room and put an Indiana limestone fireplace on the east wall. I then built a large laundry room on the back.

The evolution of the house was dramatic. But, no matter how much it grew, it didn't keep up with our family growth. My brother-in-law Rey would say he knew when Betty was pregnant because I started hammering on the house again. No matter how much it grew, it wasn't a big enough place to raise the bunch of kids we had. We needed space for them to play and more bedrooms and definitely more bathrooms.

When television came into prominence in Plymouth you needed a high antenna to get a good picture. I had fought a valiant effort to do without the high antenna but I was forced to put one up if we were to get good TV reception. I purchased a used twenty-foot section of tower and a turnmotor to mount on top. I planned to put the antenna on top of a twenty foot piece of pipe on top of the tower on top of the garage which would give me about sixty feet off the ground, barely enough for good reception. My buddies came over to help with the installation. Joe Harmon and I went up the tower and slowly lifted the pipe that was in the tower higher and higher, but then it slipped and came down on top of Joe's head almost knocking him out. Joe had to give up and go home. I had four other guys, one on each guy wire and we finally got it up. I thanked everybody and they left. After gathering up the tools and putting everything away I went in the house with a satisfied feeling to watch some good TV. Within twenty minutes a terrible storm came along and tore the whole antenna system down. I found out the next day it was covered by my insurance so it wasn't as bad as it could have been.

I have a bad habit of opening my mouth when I shouldn't. We had Paul Meyers and his girl friend Helen Depew over for dinner. Paul and I talked airplanes while the girls made the meal. After we had eaten we had coffee and I said "Betty this is the worst coffee I have ever had." Betty tried to hush me but I just went on and on about how bad it was. Finally after I had finished Helen said, "I made the coffee." Paul said my face dropped and I started to turn red and he will never forget the look on my face and laughs about it to this day.

I had just gone to work for Wheel Horse when we discovered a forty year old brick home for sale at 2111 north Michigan on the north edge of town. The sign out in front said "Trails End." (My son Alan still has that sign). It belonged to a Mr. Sharp and his wife. Their daughter owned the lot just north of it. We would not buy the home unless he could persuade his daughter to sell us the lot next door, which she didn't want to sell. She finally agreed and we purchased the home. We later sold part of that lot to a bank for more than fifty times what we paid for it and we built the first apartment building in Plymouth on the back part of it which by then was a very valuable property. We paid very little for the lot so that gives you a good idea of what we learned at 710 Ferndale. Always buy all the property that you can buy around the location that you are purchasing.

During the course of negotiating for the purchase of the 2111 North Michigan house Grandma told Betty she hoped we wouldn't get it. Betty said why? Grandma said, "Because that house is a woman killer." The house could best be described as the type of house that you would expect Frankenstein to answer the front door. It was a dark foreboding looking place. There where overgrown trees and bushes all around it. It had a grape arbor in the back yard that was just a jungle of vines and several fishponds busy breading mosquitoes. A big old coal furnace heated the place and of course there was no air-conditioning.

The house was actually three stories high. The first floor was raised quite a bit and had a bathroom, bedroom, dining room and living room, kitchen, recreation room, and a room for the laundry, and upstairs it had a bathroom and three bedrooms and the basement was even with the ground and had a garage. It was located on seven acres of land on the edge of town and the main north south highway ran right by our front door. I figured that much acreage near town would eventually be worth a lot more than I paid. It became an excellent place to sell anything because anyone going to South Bend went right by our house. There was a railroad going across the back of the land that was still being used. So, it wasn't the quietest place, because you had the car traffic in the front and the trains in the back. I remember when people came down to stay with us they thought there was a train going through the house at 1:00 a.m. but you get used to the sounds.

I had told everybody no pets in the house since we now had a small barn and pets bring in fleas that like me better than animals. Betty loves animals and the children do too, so it was no surprise to me that we got a puppy, who grew into a large black and white Border Collie by the name of Bingo. I found out later in a dog book that Border Collies are the smartest breed of all dogs. He was a pet to all of our children from Steve to Ann. Bingo was known by almost everyone in town. When the children were in school he hung out at Kroger's which was newly built and was adjacent to our property. He felt he was off duty. He would sit by the front door and look up with his big brown eyes and people would give him food.

Next Betty acquired a black and white female cat named Maggie Magoo that she dearly loved. Then came the Shetland ponies; Sugarfoot, being hilarious and the most stubborn of them all. Later we had to have horses when my oldest daughter felt she was too big for ponies. She bought Tarby a beautiful black quarter horse. I would go on a trip and come back and there was another animal. We originally had two rabbits and one time we came home and Steve had Harry the hare and Bonnie the bunny out of their cages. We said "You can't do that" and he said, "They were only out for a minute or so." After that we had more rabbits than we could handle and we finally had to have a man come and take them all away. We had four pigs we had everything but chickens because "I hate chickens." I got to where I was afraid to take a trip. I thought, "What's next elephants?"

We started a project right away after moving in to renovate 2111 and Betty set up the kitchen down in the basement using the washtubs as her sinks. She was pregnant at the time and said the lower wash sinks worked better for her. Water pipes dripped from condensation whenever there was humidity, and we had no air conditioning. Whenever those bricks on the outside of the house got heated up in the summer it felt like an oven inside. First I tore the kitchen apart with the boy's help and rebuilt some cabinets in there and purchased some appliances. I put ceramic tile on the kitchen walls about four feet high so that it would be protected against soiling. There wasn't that much of a problem keeping things clean in our family but you never could tell what a baby would throw. Doing everything myself it took a year to finish the kitchen.

When we first moved to 2111 we decided to install carpet in the living and dining rooms. I went down to see what we needed to do the job. One of the things needed was tack strips, the little one inch strips of plywood that have nails in them that are used to hold the carpet down around the edge of the room. I decided they wanted too much for them, so the boys and I made them. We picked up scrap ¼' plywood at the lumberyard and drove each of the nails ourselves. I also made my own stretching equipment. I bought the carpet wholesale. It sounds silly but in those days we had very little money.

Since I was working at Wheel Horse and was responsible for service I would buy a new garden tractor each year and use it to mow the lawn and take care of the garden as well as try to find it's weaknesses. The boys were great at this; if they couldn't break it we were in good shape for that model year. I remember a cintered metal steering gear that the boys broke right off the bat. I told engineering we had a problem and they checked and changed the way the gear was made. We had to change them all that year, but we found out so early that we were ready for the onslaught of problems.

Not only did the children have the tractor to play with but also they had go-carts, motor scooters, and motorcycles. One time they tore the engine off the go-cart (the base was still bolted to the cart.) Wheel Horse bought engines from a company that built go-cart engines and I was able to buy them wholesale. The kids always wanted the most powerful engines but I always bought the ones that had the least power. We allowed the children to have motorcycles but required them to ride them on our property. I often said we saved their lives with this policy.

There were always things to get into at 2111 since we had so much land. I remember the time the boys plowed the yard. We had a man with a Ford tractor come each year to plow the truck patch. He had left the tractor in the yard to pick up later. The boys were climbing on it when one of them said, “Let’s start it.” They started it and drove off and since it had a hydraulic lift on the plow one of the boys pushed the wrong lever and the plow came down and they plowed quite a furrow. I came home and said “They not only ruin the yard with their motorcycles but now they are plowing it.”

The girls were not all angels either and they got into as much trouble as the boys did. Julie and Debi went looking for tadpoles on the back of the land in a small woods they called the forest and got their boots full of water so they started a fire to dry out. The fire got away from them and Julie sent little Debi to get help but Debi went after water. Julie tried to stomp out the fire but it got so big the fire department had to come and put it out.

Julie, Debi, Al, and Marty were playing one day and Al climbed up a lilac tree and fell driving a broken limb through his side and leaving the muscles and the sinews showing. Betty was at school signing up for the next years classes when she got a call from Marty telling her that “Al’s guts were hanging out.” She was in the process of writing a check and just closed her check book and left to take Al to the doctor. She was an expert at how many stitches were required to close a wound.

My Dad was always looking for something he could do for the children. He got a rather elaborate playhouse with a stove, refrigerator, table and chairs and it had a beautiful outside with shutters and a nice front door. The girls spent a good deal of time playing in it and years later complained that Marty smoked in there and left his butts in the stove. (We now think its possible that Marty was smoking when he was in diapers)!

Julie loved horses and ponies and seemed to have a way with them. I can remember many times seeing Julie reading a book lying on the back of Sugar Foot. Julie got the chicken pox and was required to stay in the house.

Missing her beloved horses she persuaded the other girls to bring the horses into our newly built kitchen in the downstairs. Sugar Foot was no problem but Tarby got excited and pooped all over the wall and floor and then started sliding around in it. Susie said she saw it and just turned and fled afraid I would kill them all. We never found out about it until years later. Not only did they bring animals in the house but size was no factor.

When Susie was a small child she was impossible to keep in bed for her nap. Betty would be working in the house and someone would knock on the door and hand Susie to Betty saying she was in the middle of the road. I decided I could stop that easily so I wired a crib side on the top of her crib and thought that would do it. I was no sooner downstairs than Susie was out the door. I wired her in again and stayed by the door to watch and immediately her little arm came out and she unwired the top. I decided to use a piece of hardboard so she couldn't get her arm through the top but again she was out in seconds. We just had to live with the escape artist.

Some of the children liked to sneak out at night by climbing down the TV tower that was fastened to the side of the house. Steve was particularly good at this and was one of the "Rock of Gold" repositioning operators. The Rock of Gold was a large rock painted gold that was placed in front of a store in downtown Plymouth indicating that if you shopped in the store you had a chance to win a large amount of money. He and some of his friends would move the rock at night sometimes putting it in very peculiar places such as in front of the police station in Bremen. Later this required bolt cutters (Ten seconds) to remove since the storeowners chained it down. (I found out about this 25 years later).

Marty would be put in charge of the girls when Betty went somewhere and the girls just begged her not to leave him in charge. As soon as she left Marty took over the couch and required Debi and Susie to fight during TV commercials to entertain him. Al and Marty also talked the girls into touching the electric fence transformer telling them “it feels good.” It shocked them real hard since it was a weed chopper and would burn weeds off when weeds touched the fence.

Marty also had a habit of feeding lighted cigarettes to Sugar Foot who just loved them and would entertain Marty with his fancy lip work. Sugar Foot got even by going as fast as he could with Marty on him and then just stopping short and throwing Marty off headfirst. I don’t think Marty liked Sugar Foot since the first night we got him. Marty had volunteered to stay in the barn with Sugar Foot since we had not yet made a gate to keep him in. Marty was sleeping in a sleeping bag and during the night Sugar Foot stepped on Marty and stayed on him and Marty was unable to get away for quite a while because he was pinned in the sleeping bag. When he did get away he came in the house to get the shotgun but we got him calmed down. We had a large pond behind the barn in the winter. One of the funniest things you ever saw was when Sugar Foot tried to run on ice. He would realize that all was not well and just sit down on the ice and then he would spin around.

Ann and Eric (Gloria’s son) were playing in the loft of the barn when Ann fell through the trap door into the manger and was pretty well banged up. Eric came running into the house to tell us and of course everything was done to soothe her because everyone loved little Ann. Bingo our dog would bite anyone that came near her. This was a problem since she liked to play in a large magnolia tree in the front yard near the road. Anyone that went by on a bicycle or on foot had to flee for his or her life. Several times the police came and we had to fight to save Bingo.

We didn't have any picky eaters in our family or if we did we didn't know about them. We would have thought it absurd to ask the children what they wanted to eat. In fact if one of them said "I don't want any carrots or peas," I would say "What made you think you were getting any." We didn't have time to coddle them and in hindsight I think it was all for the best. Some of the children have said we rationed food. That's not true, but we did try to give an even distribution of goodies. For example Betty would buy ten pounds of bananas, bring them home and they would all be gone that evening. Some of the children had paper routes or school activities and didn't get home until late and they wouldn't get any. Betty decided to write the child's name on their share of the bananas to insure each child got the same amount as the others. The boys were particularly good eaters and I always said they would eat a pine board if you put butter on it. Alan would drink a gallon of milk at one setting if you would let him. When we had fresh sweet corn some of the children would eat eight or ten ears. I came into the kitchen one morning and Steve was frying some eggs. I asked him how many he was cooking for himself, and he said "only six." Betty would make ten pounds of French fries and they would be gone when she came to the table unless we saved some for her. Betty said she was afraid to leave the house to go shopping, because when she got home she would have lost ground, the kids would have eaten more than she bought home.

Boys will be boys and even though they got along pretty well they did at times have altercations. One evening as we sat down to eat I noticed that the table was really wobbly. After dinner I turned it over, found the screws torn out and spent quite a while fixing it. I didn't find out until the boys were grown that they had had a fight and tore the legs off the table. They didn't have much time so they just stood it up in place and hoped that I wouldn't notice, which is exactly what happened.

We were really pleased with the house and lived there for over seventeen years. It evolved into a better and better home and as time went by we were faced with the prospect of either spending more money on the house, which we felt we wouldn't get back, or live in it as it was. We elected to spend the money after Betty talked me into remodeling it so that it would become three apartments when we moved out. It was designed in such a way that by turning the stairs from the first floor to the upstairs around I could then make the upstairs into an apartment. One of the bedrooms became a kitchen (during the remodeling I had put in the pipes), and another became the living room and the third room was the bedroom. The center section was a good apartment as it was. In the previous years I had built a really nice downstairs in the area that was the basement and garage and replaced the old coal furnace with a new furnace and central air conditioning. We eventually built a brick fireplace in the large downstairs family room; we also built two bedrooms, and a bathroom, a nice kitchen with built-in stools and a big recreation room with a Brunswick pool table. The house eventually had sixteen rooms, seven bedrooms, an upstairs and downstairs kitchen, three baths, two family rooms, a large formal living room, a huge dining room, a big laundry room and two recreation rooms. Many years later when we left that place we were able to turn it into three large apartments within a week and it worked out well because then we didn't feel that we lost the money we spent renovating the house, and it became an income property.

Marty put on quite an act one evening, yawning and saying he was going to bed early. After a little while it dawned on me that this was not normal since we had to threaten the children to get them to go to bed. At that time Marty had one of the downstairs bedrooms. I went down to check and the door was locked. I got the passkey and sure enough the room was empty. It had a large sliding window so I knew how he got in and out. I just climbed into his bed and went to sleep. Late that night the window opened and he came in and I grabbed him by the neck. He says he lost several years of life that night and to this day he is reluctant to enter a dark room.

We had some great parties at 2111 and some memorable times. The children now tell us that they listened to all of our jokes and laughter through the large old heating ducts. I was quite famous for my margaritas after I learned to make them in Acapulco. At one of our parties for about twenty people Pat and Kay Flynn who were among our closest friends brought a large bottle of tequila with them and asked me to make some margaritas. A grand time was had by all and not only did we use their entire bottle but one of ours. Kay was in great spirits when she crawled out the back door and talks about that night to this day.

In 1977 Debi and some other girls were accused of laughing at the vice-principal of the High School along with the rest of the students at a pep rally. After the rally, the vice-principal screamed at the girls, "Get to my office"! In the office the girls tried in vain to explain that they had not laughed at "HIM" but at the joke that was made by one of the students. He screamed "You are all liars" He told each one to write a 10-page report and the girls decided to comply even though they were not guilty. Later that afternoon he called Debi into his office and with a sarcastic smile on his face tore up her permit to graduate early. She was one of the top students and more than met the requirements needed to graduate early. With all of our children I had never interfered with the school in any way. In fact I told the kids they better tow the mark in school or they would be in more trouble when they got home. I told Debi that there must be something else she had done. I called the principal and was told that graduating early was a privilege and even though he could remember only one student that had been turned down, he told me there was nothing I could do. I told her not to write the 10-page report. After being tipped off by another principal that we could appeal we took it to the Indiana State General Education Commission and "WON." The principal and the vice-principal were gone in a year and I had a numerous calls thanking me. When you are right never compromise.

A few years after we bought the 2111 property the City of Plymouth approached me about donating some land so that they could run a street through part of our property from U.S.31 to Western Avenue. I donated a small strip of land but most of the required land came from the Franklin school property just to the north of us and from Mr. Price. We helped name this street Skylane Drive. It opened up the back of our property and gave us a very valuable corner. We later sold the corner for a huge profit to a bank.

After we opened this land up the back of our property became very valuable and Mr. Pond and I built a 12-unit brick apartment building using a company he owned called Ecco Incorporated. He had some funds in it and Betty and I put in an equal amount of equity in the form of the land. It was a very modern unit and actually the first apartment building ever built as such in Plymouth. At that time I was thinking income property.

I felt that I would buy anything that was reasonably good that would pay for itself. I bought an old apartment building from Paul Meyers on Pennsylvania Avenue and was able to increase the number of apartments in it by a little judicious planning and it became a pretty good income producer for us. In Plymouth at that time that was what apartments consisted of, old homes turned into apartments.

We had taken Mr. and Mrs. Pond to Stuart, Florida, on the east coast about fifty miles north of Palm Beach several times a year for some time because that is where Cecil's father, Elmer, had established his winter residence. In looking around down there Betty and I came upon a property called Cabana Point Apartments. Mae Cabana, whose husband had just died, owned it, and it consisted of two four-plexes. There were eight apartments on the south fork of the St. Lucie River. The apartments were all completely furnished and many of the people who used them in the winter came back year after year. So, there was a built-in rental arrangement. Across the river was a wildlife preserve that had been dedicated by Mr. Kiplinger as a refuge for birds and wild animals. When you looked out of the windows on the St. Lucie River it was like being on the Amazon. There was no visible sign of any man made object around you. If you went into the back yard you could see other homes and man made things but you couldn't see them from inside. We had a couple of banana trees that had real bananas on them and orchids that bloomed on one of the fences. It was a gorgeous location.

I had learned my Ferndale lesson well and purchased the lot next to the apartments from Mae Cabana at the same time I purchased the apartments. So we actually had three huge lots on the St. Lucie River. One of which was still empty and each of the others had a four-plex on it. The children all loved the apartments because we would take them to the beach and let them sunbathe. We also had a dock for a boat.

I purchased a speedboat and made arrangements with Harold Strauss a friend of mine who operated the airport at Stuart to leave it in one of his hangars. I told him he could use it whenever he wanted. When we went down to Florida I hooked his jeep on to the boat trailer and pulled it to the slip. We would go up and down the river and out into the ocean. We called the boat the "Itsy", the pet nickname I had given Betty years before. The kids all loved to water ski behind the boat. Once when Debi and Susie were water skiing behind the boat they saw a dolphin fin in the water. They became terrified, jumped off and walked through the coral to get up on the shore and away from what they thought was a shark. They cut themselves quite badly on the coral.

Fishing at Cabana Point was extremely good. We caught blue point crabs, catfish, sheep's head, snook and we even caught a manta ray, and larger fish, some of which we were never able to land. It was brackish water, which is salt water from the ocean mixed with fresh water from Lake Okeechobee. Ann loved to play in the big tree that hung out over the river and we were worried that she would fall in and be mistaken for the loaves of bread that our neighbors fed to the alligators. We sometimes called Ann crabby when she was tired and feeling bad. We caught some blue point crabs and showed them to Ann in a bucket and they snapped at her. After that when we said Ann's crabby she would say very loudly "I am not crabby."

A short boat ride in the speedboat south from Cabana Point Apartments made you feel isolated out in the everglades. It was a wonderful place to be unless you had engine problems. I remember one time Joe and

Velma were with us and the engine quit. Joe tried to play Humphrey Bogart by getting out and wading along towing the boat. Finally a guy come by and towed us back. We later found out it was just a loose wire. During this whole adventure Velma kept right on fishing.

We gave an apartment to a couple in return for taking care of the apartments and managing them. They collected the rent, deposited it in our bank account in Florida, and sent the receipt to Plymouth. We did this for quite a few years. It later became quite a problem because every time we went down there people approached me wanting something done so my vacations down there became working periods with Betty scrubbing and cleaning and me fixing things. I remember thinking that this wasn't the way to enjoy what little leisure we had.

In 1973, while I was still operating Skystream, we purchased a building in downtown Plymouth called the "Plymouth Building". It was four stories high, had a brick front, and contained 25,600 square feet. It had originally been built as a hospital for alcoholics and drug addicts. It was built about 1910 and was the latest state of the building art at that time, with poured concrete and steel reinforcing. I still have the newspaper article about how wonderfully the building was constructed. When I was living at 710 Ferndale I had worked in my spare time for a Mr. Lee O'Connell who owned the building at that time. I had built several apartments in it and was fascinated by the quality of the building.

When Lee died, it was on the market for some time. I was approached by Al Collins, about buying it. There weren't too many takers because the income was very low for the building. I think it took in about $17,000 a year which was just terrible. After you paid the taxes, utilities, and other expenses there was nothing left to make the payments. The bank across the street wanted us to buy it. I had been doing business with them since I was a child and had a savings account. The reason they wanted us to buy it was because they didn't want to end up having a tenement across the street from their beautiful new bank. I remember Mr. Gidley the President of the bank calling me to his office and asking me, "what kind of a deal would it take to get you interested in that building? What kind of interest?" I asked for an extremely low interest rate and he said, "well, we can't go that low." At any rate we made an offer on the building, and Mrs. O'Connell accepted it. Her son John O'Connell worked for Skystream Airlines at the airport and he wanted to get the burden of operating the building off his mother's back. She said she really wanted us to have the building since I had worked on it earlier. I told the bank that I wasn't interested in buying the building as it was unless, I had the funds to renovate it to make it a real first class operation. They agreed to lend us the money for renovation as well as the money to buy the building. They already had a mortgage on everything we had so there was very little risk for them.

One of the first things we did was to put an elevator in the building to make the top floors accessible. There was already a rope elevator so it had the shaft and location. We put in a hydraulic elevator that cost some where around $20,000 a tremendous sum at that time but I think it ended up "making" the building. There was a first and second story with offices, and the third and fourth had a few apartments but most of the area was unfinished when we purchased the building.

The building sat back from the sidewalk forty some feet. In order to give it a new face we built a two story front addition to the building, which had a large 40'x 80' office upstairs and two large offices downstairs. From the street you hardly noticed the big brick building behind. When you first looked at it from the front it looked like a brand new building. There was a twelve-foot wide hallway inside and Ohio Sandstone on the front with brown soffit. Within a short time we were able to rent the offices and had all of the apartments full. Over the years we modified the third and fourth floors more than doubling the number of very nice apartments. One of the apartments was the one that Lee O'Connell had built for himself on the fourth floor and we rented it to our good friends Dr. James Coursey and his wife Maxine. It is a 3500 square foot, seven-room apartment and has a large twenty by forty-foot family room and an excellent view of Plymouth. They lived there from 1973 to 1982 and seemed to enjoy the huge apartment.

When I put the elevator in I let it stick up on the roof. Several people asked why I had an elevator door that opened up on the outside on the roof. I said that someday we would build a house up there. After all the lot didn't cost anything. I spent a year and a half designing the penthouse and getting it approved. We had an architect in the building by the name of Wilcox and after designing the apartment and making a scale drawing I took the plans to him. He said, "You don't want an architect you just want someone to get your plans approved." I said, "Now you got it." We completed it in 1976 the United States BI-Centennial year. Ann and Susie spent the first night in the penthouse the day before we moved. It has 3,500 square feet, four bedrooms, five bathrooms, a huge living room and a formal dining room, a brick fireplace, oak woodwork, and a large backyard, 80' x 40', with a hot tub, barbecue, trees, and flowers. It turned out to be a real haven because mosquitoes don't get up that high, "they spin out."

The first time we left Susie and Ann alone they threw some eggs down on Bud Treats parking lot and of course we found out about it from Bud. I couldn't help but think about Tom and me and our egg incident on the farm but we got rid of a whole basket full. History repeats itself, what goes around comes around!

One day Betty was in the hot tub au natural as usual assuming (never assume) she was safe five stories up, when she heard two guys talking real close to her. She dashed into the house just in time to see a bucket truck come up over the side of the building with two workers in it. They just wanted to see what was up there.

We also put a closed circuit TV in the downstairs hall to see who was ringing our doorbell. We then talk to them on the phone provided, and activate the elevator to bring guests up to our home. With the new addition and our penthouse the Plymouth Building now has 35,500 square feet. To the best of my knowledge it is the only penthouse around. I always said I wanted my tombstone to read "He finished the Plymouth Building" because the process took over twelve years.

Betty and my youngest daughter Ann wanted a pet. They tried hamsters but they kept getting away. I was listening to the radio and I heard about a family giving away kittens and told Betty about them. She went out and picked out a very small male kitten, which we named Tuffy. He was probably the most loved pet we ever had. He was (of course) black and white which all of our pets have been for the last fifty years. He roamed our penthouse and back yard in a lordly manner for over sixteen years. He wasn't too bright as cats go but he was a real clown.

After I resigned from Skystream we purchased a brand new Cessna 210 aircraft and flew to Cabana Point quite a bit. The first time Betty and I flew down to spend some time we awoke in the morning and opened the drapes and were in awe of the scene. We watched a couple of egrets walking through the back yard. We sat there enjoying our coffee and having breakfast and had nothing to do but enjoy the surroundings. The second day it was still wonderful but by the third day we were bored to tears. I don't think I was cut out for retirement. Betty tells me that I have flunked retirement five times, because just sitting there with nothing to do is not my idea of living. I began to fix up the buildings and I thought, "When I worked at Skystream I hired people to do these things, what am I doing out here fixing this place" so we decided to sell it.

One of the couples who came to see the apartments was an elderly couple who had a condo in the Wilshire Apartments on Lake Worth, just west of Singer Island in Palm Beach. They fell in love with the place and really wanted to purchase it. I went down to the Wilshire Condo and made an appraisal of what I thought it was worth. We were able to conclude a deal. We sold them the Cabana Point Apartments, but not the lot next door.

We took their condo in partial payment for the sale. It was a beautiful condo on the top floor of three floors, overlooking Lake Worth. The lake was full of sailboats and had a wonderful community of people who kept things spotless. We were quite taken with the unit. We also were able to sell the lot next to Cabana Point Apartments at a tremendous profit. Once again, I learned my lesson well at 710 Ferndale about always buying the additional land.

In 1981 my daughter Debi who was the manager of a Kentucky Fried Chicken restaurant in Warsaw and her husband Jim who worked at a Pizza Hut in Warsaw decided to start their own restaurant. I helped them design and build Bo's Restaurant on the first floor front of the Plymouth Building. We used lattice and mirrors to make it look twice as big as it was and large plants to help make the ambiance tropical. Bright apple green trim, Naugahyde chairs, and stools brightened the atmosphere as well as daffodil yellow walls. They also had many Coke signs and decorations. It became a very popular breakfast and lunch café. Many times people were lined up in the hall to get into Bo's. A few years later Debi and Jim had a job offer and an opportunity to move to Florida. We bought them out and leased the restaurant to two or three operators. In 1989 we decided to put an old-time soda fountain in featuring the best ice cream and all kinds of old fashion drinks. We had Phosphates, Black Cows, Green Rivers, real chocolate and cherry Cokes, Ice Cream sodas and sundaes as well as other specialties. Besides banana splits we had the specialty of the house "turtle sundaes" built around three scoops of ice cream, in a banana boat, it included caramel syrup, a crushed Heath candy bar with hot fudge on the center topped off with pecan halves and whipped cream and a cherry. We also put in a Wurlitzer jukebox with lighted tubes of colored liquid exactly like the ones made years ago. The lunches and sandwiches and salads were very good and we ran the restaurant for a couple of years before leasing it out again. "It's not the way to make money." You can make a good living but that's all.

When I sold Skystream to Mr. Pond he sold Skylane apartments to us. We proceeded to build three four-plexes in the next year and sold the old apartment building that we had on Pennsylvania Avenue for a pretty good price to finance building the new ones. We now had twenty-four new modern apartments at the complex called Skylane Apartments. As time went on I contracted with a very enterprising builder, Richard Day, to build some more apartments for us on the back of

Skylane Apartments and we built four more four-plexes giving us a total of forty apartments.

In 1980 I started a company that built QualaBilt Homes. It was a modular home manufacturing company. Dick Day the man who had built my last apartments and I went together to start Paladay Industries Inc. which built QualaBilt Homes. We built a modern new building and designed dollies to support the 14' by 32' modules so they could be moved anywhere in the plant. I developed plans for the units and got them approved by the State. We sold several units the first year and were able to pay all the bills and the workers as well as the payments. Not a bad record for the first year in any business. That was at the time that Jimmy Carter was in the White House and interest rates for homes were going past 20%. After the first year of operating the business it became obvious that it was going to be a pretty tough row to hoe to continue on because no one out there was buying anything. Dick Day wanted to get out so I bought his portion of the business. I kept it for a couple of years until I could sell it. We both came out of it well and I don't think either of us lost any money in the venture.

In 1983 my mother moved into Millers Merry Manor nursing home and we added the duplex at 700 Walnut Street to our rental properties. We had built that unit for her with the understanding that she would live there for as long as she wanted to using the rent from the other apartment to subsidize her income. She had decided she didn't want the hassle of keeping her own place any more and was anxious about her care.

In about 1984 Ralph Kerns and I had agreed to lease the Skystream operation at the Plymouth Airport and I realized I would be extremely busy starting that operation up again. I put the Skylane Apartments up for sale and they were immediately purchased by the company we had listed them with, Al Collins of Collins and Collins Company. I had assumed (never assume) the airport deal was firm. As you know by the previous chapters, the airport deal fell through. I tried to buy the apartments back but Al Collins said that he was going to make too much money and couldn't sell them back to me. He then proceeded to build thirty more apartments in the form of three buildings on the remaining land.

When we decided to abandon the purchase of Skystream, I was left without an income so I purchased the land across the street from Skylane Apartments. This was an L-shape piece of land at 310 Skylane and on it we built the Pal Apartments. They consisted of six four-plexes, twenty-four apartments. They were erected in 1985 and were leased as fast as we could get them built.

In 1987, the large tire store just to the north of the Plymouth Building was up for sale. I had very little interest in it until the realtor told me that one of the people looking at it was thinking about putting a used car lot there. That got my attention. We purchased the building and immediately started a complete renovation. The same type of thing we had done to the Plymouth Building. Since the building sat forty feet back, we built a brand new section on the front with four offices downstairs and four apartments upstairs and completely remodeled the back portion of the building into new office space and a laundry. This building became known as the Pal Building and we received the 1987 civic improvement award. Another modern building that fits nicely with the Plymouth Building,

The Wilshire Apartments in the Palm Beach area had gone up so much in value that we just couldn't resist an offer and sold the condo to the people we had leased it to a couple of times. We received more than twice as much as we had valued it at when we took it in trade.

We then went back to the Stuart area and north on Hutchinson Island to St. Lucie County on the ocean and purchased an Oceana condo in a high-rise building on the beach. It was on the eighth floor, well above the bug line, a nice new apartment with a living room, dining room, kitchen, two bedrooms and two baths. It was a very nice place to stay in Florida. You could sit out on the porch and look over the ocean to the eastern horizon.

During the time we had the Oceana Condo another Oceana unit became available next door to us and we purchased it on speculation. Within three weeks we retailed it for a nice profit. It just seemed to me that people would get the urge to sell something quick and if they wanted to sell it that cheap I would buy it and resell it and get the going price.

The strip of land along the ocean was Hutchinson Island and the water between the island and the mainland is called the Indian River. It is a lush tropical paradise and one of the most sought after areas on the East Coast. There had been several high rise condos built in St. Lucie County and they were all very beautiful places, Oceana, Islandia, etc. But the premier place was called the Admiral Building at Island Dunes. It was a very upscale, beautiful building in a great community. It had a set of elevators that only served two apartments on each floor. There were three or four elevators in the building so each apartment had only one neighbor across the hall. Downstairs was a garage underneath the building so that you simply drove into the parking garage and put your groceries into the elevator and went up to your apartment. We made a very low offer on a fully furnished beautiful condo that had less than one months use since new (three couples had bought it together and couldn't get along) so we bought it at an excellent price. In this complex there was also a golf course and swimming pools, hot tubs, right on the ocean with a beautiful beach. There were barbecue areas, billiard rooms, libraries and card rooms in the main building area. Looking out the other side of the building you looked over the golf course and slips for sailboats or yachts. You could play tennis, handball, croquet, horseshoe pitching, and golf as well as having a slip for your boat. We were very happy with it. After all, who wouldn't be happy? We had a Rolls Royce parked downstairs and a station wagon out at the airport and a nice new airplane to go back and forth from our penthouse in Plymouth to our second home in Florida. So we were delighted with the situation for a while. About that time we realized that we were just not cut out for life in the fast lane and were more accustomed to a less ostentatious life style and in a few years we became disenchanted with Florida. We got to the point where we only went down there one week out of the year. We were taking care of Betty's aged parents and our business interests. We were reluctant to leave for any length of time. So, just before we repurchased the Skylane Apartments from Al Collins, I decided to sell out in Florida and Betty concurred, and we agreed we probably would never own a second home again. The children were disappointed since they used it from time to time especially Debi since she spent more time down there than we did. All the children loved the beach and the ocean as well as the condo.

In 1990 Al Collins approached me about selling the Skylane Apartments back to us. We were agreeable but the bank that held the mortgage wouldn't let us assume the mortgage. We still held a second mortgage on the property and we put in a couple hundred thousand dollars as well as our second mortgage but we still had to borrow one million dollars. I was able to secure the loan and purchased the seventy units. At that time I was doing almost everything myself. Mick Overmyer my assistant was helping some but I could see that I would be pushing to take care of the 106 apartments as well as both office buildings. I turned the whole operation over to a Management Service, but after a year I could see that they weren't able to handle it.

Our mayor, Jack Greenlee had given me a resume about a man by the name of Charles Arnold who had applied for a job as a maintenance supervisor. He had an excellent background and had worked in the apartment business most of his life. He worked from 1978 to 1992 at Park Jefferson Apartments and Castle Point Apartments both owned by Ralph Williams Co. a large firm in South Bend. I checked with them and got a favorable response as far as maintenance. He didn't have any sales experience but it has been my observation that a clean well priced apartment sells itself. I did not want any employees at that time of my life. We talked at some length and he said he would set up Arnold's Management Service with Palbykin Enterprises as its first customer. He has been the manager of our properties ever since.

We re-purchased a piece of landlocked property that was our original truck patch back of the home at 2111 north Michigan after Collins sold the frontage to Dunkin Donuts. We built Homestead Apartments on this plot of land; four duplexes, eight new apartments. These were wonderful little two bedroom units with built in laundry equipment. Velma Harmon suggested the name Homestead Apartments, because it was the site of our family home.

The next year we added eight new duplexes to the Pal Apartments making a total of forty units in that complex. This was the same model duplex we had built at Homestead, and one that I had designed originally for the Skylane apartments.

The following year we purchased seventy-two apartments called the Webster Apartments on the south end of town. This complex has a variety of units, two bedroom townhouses, two bedroom apartments, and completely furnished efficiencies. They are built around a large pond that is home to a lot of Mallard ducks and the apartments have a very nice view.

In the following year we purchased the Nipsco building in downtown Plymouth, renaming it the Executive Building and leased it to Sprint Telephone Co. for their offices. This building is 10,360 square feet and is one of the best built business buildings in Plymouth. It was built in 1966 and has an all brick exterior with concrete and steel construction.

Betty's sister and her husband, Rey Nelson, had purchased a condo in Las Vegas, and they wanted us to visit them. Since we were visiting our son in Tempe, Arizona, and our daughter in Gilbert, Arizona we drove up to see them. I was quite taken with the area. While Betty and Gloria were shopping Rey and I went to look at some condos. I found one that I thought would be fine for us close to where her sister lived. When Betty and Gloria returned from their shopping, I took her up to see the condo but it had been sold in the hour that I had been gone, and there weren't any more available until they started a new project. It became quite obvious to me that things were selling very well in the Las Vegas area. I went up to take a look at the condos in Sun City. We were looking for a "little" place because we thought we wouldn't use it very much. After looking through them I told their saleslady, Susan Rosland, to save her time because all I wanted to look at was the Garden Villas. After about ten minutes I went back to her office and told her we wanted to buy the Charleston, which was their lowest priced model. She said, "You and everybody else, those are on lottery." I had never come across a place where you had to get in a lottery to buy a home. She said she didn't have anybody on her list and she would put our name on it and they would have the lottery in about a week or so. When we got back down to Tempe there was a call waiting for me. Susan Rosland said she was putting my name in the lottery the next day.

We went back to Plymouth, Indiana and we received a call from her that we didn't get it. She said not to give up because maybe one of those who were picked would back out because they wouldn't have the money to make the deal. (You have to pay or arrange payment for the home before they start building) Within a few days she called me and said we got one and to send a deposit. We now had to pick the extras, the lighting fixtures, the tile, the carpeting and all the other decisions that had to be made before the building got started, so we went back out to take care of these items. We picked out everything and it was built the next year. We bought all new furniture because we had sold Island Dunes Condo in Florida with everything in it. We had to buy everything again, not just furniture and beds but all the small things, salt shakers, napkin holder, dishes, etc.

We sure didn't go to Las Vegas for the gambling since we learned our lesson about gambling when we were first married. We were attending the Argos fair with Joe Harmon when I was called over to a booth that had bowling pins set up and rope hoops to throw and try to ring the pins. I told the operator I wasn't interested but he said just try a couple for nothing. You had to get ten rings to win a cash prize. I threw seven in the first ten I tried. The operator said I could keep the seven and only had to buy enough to get the remaining three. I thought how can I lose so I bought several until I ran out of money. Joe loaned me ten dollars with the comment that I would just lose the ten. He was right and we did without a lot the next week to make up for my stupidity. The good thing was that I was cured of gambling for life. Sure it was fixed but so are all games of chance.

The Villa was a split floor plan with a bedroom and bath on one side and a bedroom and bath on the other side of the apartment. It had a nice living room, dining room, a kitchen big enough to eat in, and a two-car garage. What more could you want? I had told Betty if she liked Sun City we would build a house. After a couple of months she said, "Let's build a house." I said, "What's wrong with the one we have?" Betty said, "It's just fine for me but where are you going to live?" We went looking for another home. I had wanted to get one further up on the side of the mountain with a view of Las Vegas and the strip. I was told that those units would go on lottery in a year or so. I was concerned about the lottery since my brother in law Rey Nelson had been in two and didn't get either one.

We bought a lot just across from the design center with a western view of the mountains and a lot of grass. We built an 1,800 square foot Marquis home, with a lot of amenities. The next year we went out to move into the new home. Steve and I put ceramic tile in the garage and on the front porch. We built a desk in the laundry room and built cabinets in the garage and moved the laundry to the garage. As we worked there we kept looking out the window and saw we were about where the golf balls roll to a stop from the drive on the first hole of that golf course. (There are three eighteen-hole golf courses in Sun City). We looked out the window and people were about fifty feet away looking back at us and talking in loud voices. After living on top of the

Plymouth Building in the penthouse we were pretty use to our quiet and our privacy. Unless people can fly or have a bucket truck they can't look into our home at the penthouse. We weren't used to the lack of privacy.

About that time Susan Rosland notified us that the lots we really wanted were being put up on lottery. She said, "Don, the one you wanted is gone." I asked her how that could be if they hadn't had the lottery yet and she said "I don't know but they must have a lot of juice because someone got it." I asked her why she thought I would get one now. She said, "you'll get it." I think she went to management and told them that I wanted that lot over a year ago, and that she put it in her computer to get it for me and now I come back and find out that the lot was sold and didn't go up for lottery. She asked which one I wanted and I chose the one next to it that was almost as good, and we got it.

Now we had three properties in Sun City including the lot up the mountain that we really wanted to build on. They would not allow us to build the 1,800 square foot house on that lot since it is a pretty exclusive community. Some of the houses are approaching a million dollars. We were required to build one of the top three models. We chose the Buckingham, a 2,500 square foot house. It has 12-foot ceilings, three bedrooms, three baths, a three-car garage, an oak kitchen, a couple of fireplaces, and a large breakfast nook with a bay window. It is high over the golf course with beautiful mountain views and overlooks the City of Las Vegas. No one is able to look into our home because the golf course is about fourteen feet lower than our back yard.

Now the problem was that I had the other houses to sell. I put a sign in the front yard "For Sale By Owner" (we had never occupied it) and sure enough a few weeks later a guy drove up in a Lexus, and I showed him the house and explained the extras. I told him the price and within a couple of days he sent me an offer within $5,000 of what I asked, I said, "no." I sent him a counter-offer for the full price and he accepted it.

The next year we went out there and had to start all over again. It was the third house in three years that we had decorated, and landscaped, which is an exhausting experience. After completing it we sold the condo and moved into our new home at 2320 Airlands. We spend at least seven months a year in Las Vegas. Neither of us enjoys gambling since you know you are going to lose in the long run. Betty loves the shopping which she says is the best she has ever seen. The children love to visit Vegas frequently and like the excitement of the city as well as the good airline prices and convenient schedules.

Sun City is a beautiful little community of about seven thousand eight hundred homes, probably over fourteen thousand people. It is one of the safest and most secure areas west of the Mississippi because of its security patrol. One of the owners must be at least fifty-five and so it is a group of very lively adults. There are over seventy clubs in Sun City with all kinds of activities for every interest. We have four recreation centers, each of, which has a swimming pool, hot tub, exercise room, billiard room, and every conceivable type of accommodation. There are three eighteen-hole golf courses and numerous tennis courts. We are in the quietest community I have ever seen, but we can be on the strip with the most phenomenal shows on earth in fifteen minutes and at the airport in about twenty. We don't have a State tax and no estate tax. It's a wonderful place to live and is our legal residence, but we still think of Plymouth as our home and come back every year for four or five months in the summer and fall.

Our first apartment 317 W. Monroe St. Plymouth, IN.

At home with the Palbykin's. Betty with our first kitten.

Our little garage house at 710 Ferndale when we first moved in.

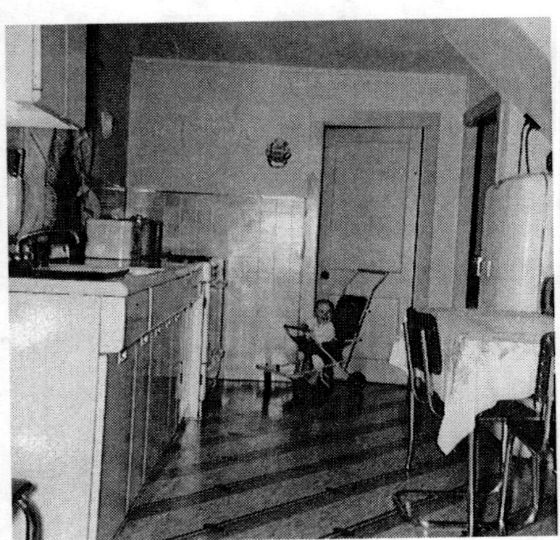

Our kitchen with the new cabinets, and new linoleum.

Starting the garage and the work required to complete.

Garage complete, starting the living room, and the finished home.

111 N. Michigan before, and after, (Cape Cod Colonial) remodeling.

laggie the cat, Ann, Bingo, by ie back steps after remodeling.

Julie, Debi, and Sue with some of our livestock.

The Plymouth building when we first purchased it in 1973.

After adding the front offices (Note elevator shaft on roof.)

Starting construction on the penthouse and the completed home.

Our backyard with trees, flowers, barbecue, spa, (No mosquitoes.)

ffy roaming the backyard.

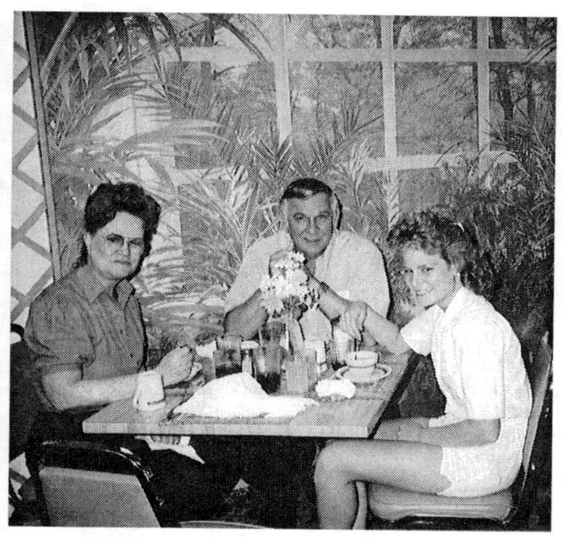

Bo's restaurant, tropical decor.

Cabana Point Apartments, our boat and dock, Stuart, Florida.

Wilshire Condo on Lake Worth, with a beautiful view.

Oceana Condo, living and dining room with an Ocean view.

Admiral Condo with parking under the building, on the ocean with all the amenities as well as luxury living accommodations.

Skylane Apartments our first building. (Now 70 units)

Pal Apartments we now have 40 units in this complex.

Starting the addition to the tire store north of the Plymouth Bld.

The finished 322 Michigan
Civic improvement award

'he little duplex Mom lived in
'ith Grandma. 700 N. Walnut.

Homestead Apartments built
on our old truck patch area.

Vebster Apartments on the
Mallard lake south of town.

QualaBilt factory we built to
manufacture modular homes.

The Executive Building that formally was the Nipsco Bld.

Family reunion in Las Vegas with a real good turn out.

Our home in Las Vegas with the back yard overlooking a golf course, and a beautiful view of downtown Vegas and the strip.

Father

My father, Albert Palbykin, was born in France in 1898. At that time his name was spelled "Palabykian." He was one of ten children, two of whom died very young. His father, Simon Palabykian and his oldest brother Francois, came to America through a relative to get established, so that they could bring the family over. The Palabykian family sailed for America in 1909 from France. A daughter Antoinette died at age sixteen. Her passing left three daughters, Lucy, Madelaine, and Annette, and four sons Francois, Robert, Albert, and Leon. The family settled in Chicago, where Simon worked in a garage on the lower floor of the building in which the family lived. It was a large rambling apartment at 2009 Prairie Avenue. He later secured a job with The Standard Club where he worked until his retirement at age sixty-five. He died in 1942 at the age of eighty-two.

Dad's mother, Grandma Palabykian was the backbone of the family. Madelaine said of her mother "She was the strongest woman we ever knew." Her maiden name was Elizabeth Kirikonan. She was born in

Tashkent, Russia. Her mother was Russian and her father was Armenian. Her parents were not suited or happy. Her father took her at age twelve and left her mother and a brother whom she never saw again or ever even heard of. They went to Greece where she worked in a Greek household under the guidance of a very fine Greek woman. No one knows how she met her husband Simon Palabykian, but she must have been less than eighteen when they were married. For awhile their lives were spent in Turkey and Armenia. They later found their way to France. All the children were given French names as grandmother fell passionately in love with everything French.

By diligent saving and with Grandmother working nights in a restaurant they were finally able to buy an old house in Oak Park, Ill, where they lived until about 1926. They then bought a home at 5111 Hamlin in Chicago and it is this home that I remember. Madelaine, Annette, and Leon were still living at home and I feel sure they contributed to the household expenses.

I remember staying with Grandma during WWII and she had a three star flag in her window to show she had three sons in the service. I remember shopping for groceries with her. Each day she went to the store to get fresh meat (She never served anything that had been frozen) and vegetables and fruit. She made wonderful meals and I am sure that is where Francious learned part of his trade. Antoinette Pope Francois wife started a cooking school in downtown Chicago called Antoinette Pope School of Fancy Cooking. Francois started a cooking show on TV and it was the longest running local show on Chicago TV. Many of the best restaurants in Chicago had a "recommended by Francois Pope" decal on their front door.

Dad went to school in the Chicago Public School System and was quite talented at painting. I still have some China plates he painted with roses on them and they are excellent. I know very little else about his early life.

On June 1, 1918, he wrote a letter to his mother:

Dear Mother:

I have enlisted in the U.S. Army. I am leaving today at 11 o'clock. I have passed the examination so far. Do not worry about me at all. I have good friends of mine who are going too. I have sold my Liberty Bond to our firm so I have everything I need. I did not want to be drafted. This way you are treated nice. I have a recommendation from the University of Chicago and perhaps I will have a Corporal position. Please do not worry. I have nothing else to write but later I will give you my address.

Lots of Love
To everybody

Albert Palabykian

P.S. I have laid two 5-dollar bills in back of the big clock; it's underneath the big glass vase. I don't need it but you do.

He was in the Calvary in World War I and used to talk at some length about how they would wear the hide off their bottoms riding so much. The Captain on one occasion dropped his pants turned around and said; "I'm bloody too. Let's go out and ride those sores off the back side of us."

There was very little else that I knew of about his early life. At the end of World War I he became very interested in aviation. Aviation was a fledgling business at that time. I have a business card of his that's older than I am. It shows Chicago Aero Sales Corporation Stinson Airport Flying School, LaGrange, Illinois, and it features Stinson, Waco, and Argo airplanes. He had changed his name to Palbykin by then because I see his card has the new spelling. After the war he was appointed field manager of Chicago Aero Sales Corporation. Stinson Airport at that time was located in LaGrange, Ill. He became a friend of many of the pioneer aviation people. Lindbergh used to fly mail in and out of the Stinson Airport and Dad knew him well. Dad said he was real quiet and stayed to himself, sometimes sleeping in the hanger.

The people who flew in those days were wealthy and were doing it for kicks. Dad told me about a young lady who insisted on making a parachute jump. She had no experience and when she jumped from the airplane, she immediately pulled the ripcord and the chute caught on the tailskid of the airplane. There she was, dangling below the airplane on the tailskid. A German pilot on the field went up to assist and he climbed down on a rope barefoot trying to take hold of the chute to pull it loose but eventually he fell to his death trying to release her. Finally the pilot was able to do some gyrations and shook her loose. She landed with no trouble.

Father use to regale me with various incidents about pilots at the airport. He would say, "He was really good. He could fly upside down and pick up a handkerchief off of the ground." I would always say, "How was he killed?" Father would give a reason like "The engine quit" or something of that sort but all the "Real good ones" were killed in those days. Dad was a pilot too but that was not his calling. He became one of the earliest aircraft mechanics licensed in the country. I forget what his number was but it was one of the first in the Chicago area. When mechanics got ready for their license, those with experience just went to the federal building and signed up and were licensed. There was no way to check them in those days because no one in the government knew anything about aviation. (As usual the non-participating experts were in charge, just as it is today).

They started to construct Midway Airport in Chicago, Illinois, which in those days was the largest airport around. Dad was offered the manager's job at Midway but he turned it down. I feel like that was a big mistake. Midway became the largest airport for several decades and until O'Hare came into being was the major airport in the Chicago area. When the stock market crashed in 1929 it was a real blow to aviation. Dad was having a lot of trouble making enough money to keep his head above water. That was when Mom and I moved to Plymouth to stay with my grandparents on the farm. Dad had a room in Chicago and sent money to us. He did everything he could to help as well as giving Mom and me gifts as he had the money to do so. I remember when I was living on the farm; he bought me a very special scooter and brought it to the farm. This was the one that I stole the wheels off to make my first car. He also bought me my first bicycle. He dressed very well, had a small mustache and a twinkle in his eye.

After his position of airport manager dwindled down to where he couldn't make a living at it, he flew with a very popular pilot named Harold Johnson, barnstorming the country. Harold Johnson had a Ford tri-motor; an old corrugated aluminum three-engine aircraft and a Laird aerobatics airplane. He would fly over a city and do a lot of aerobatics and make a lot of noise. People would gather at the airport and they would load the people in the Ford tri-motor and take them for rides to make a living. Dad did maintenance on the airplane and I have a picture of him with dark glasses standing by the Ford. I also have a picture of him as manager of the airport at Hinsdale Stinson. Dad was a true pioneer in the aviation business. He later became a top-notch automobile mechanic.

Dad was very much of a patriot and very proud that he was an American citizen. You certainly didn't want to say anything against the country in front of him or he was apt to hit you right in the face. After the start of World War II, even though he was over 44, he again enlisted in the Army. I recall having had a quarrel with him and I was really mad at him. He was leaving for the service from Plymouth and Mom and I took him to the Indiana Motor Bus. He had gotten on the Bus to leave and my Mother had bid him farewell. She said, "You know, you may never see your Father again." I stepped up in the front of the bus and apologized to Dad in front of everyone in there. I was never sorry that I did but it was a very embarrassing thing to do in front of every one, a thing that should have been done in private.

Dad went through basic training and was based at Hamilton Field in California. Imagine a man almost forty five years old going through basic training. That's how much he thought of our country. He appreciated his freedom very much and he felt that was what the United States gave to everyone. He was an excellent marksman and while in the service received several metals for marksmanship. I remember Dad sending us large burlap bags of English walnuts during the war that he had picked in the groves in California.

Prior to Dad's going into the service he had fooled around with model airplanes. He built the first gas model airplanes that I ever saw. He would bring them down to the farm and we would go out into the fields and fly them. They had pretty primitive engines in those days. You held them up and when you got the engine started (which took a long time) you released it and away it would go. It circled and when it ran out of gas it returned to the ground. (Hopefully not in a tree).

In the period of time that I was living with Grandpa, Dad would come down, possibly every other weekend, on the train, and he would spend weekends with us. His trips to the farm were the times we had to spend together with the scooter, bicycle, and model airplanes, etc.

Dad was a very loving person and very good to me but he was very insistent that you do what you were told to do as soon as you were told to do it. I recall one Sunday after we had returned from church, I was lying on the floor looking at the comic strips and Dad was looking at the paper. He asked me to hand him another section of the paper and I said "Just a moment." That's all I remember because he whacked me on the side of the head and set me spinning across the room. When he said to do something, he meant NOW. The other side of that coin was that whenever he came down to see me he almost always brought me something. One of those trips he bought me a brand new model airplane gasoline engine, of which I was extremely proud. Those engines were quite expensive at that time and very few of them had been made. A rather primitive but excellent piece of equipment. They had a tiny Champion spark plug on the top of the cylinder, and a set of points in the front that had to be properly set, and a needle valve to adjust the carburetor. There were wires going to the coil and condenser and a battery pack in the airplane. It was a good way to learn about gasoline engines and their wiring. I was as proud as punch with it as you can see by some of the pictures. I was ready to learn as much as I could about aviation. Dad helped me tremendously by explaining to me that I had to put a little bit of balsa wood in front of the wing to give it more lift or a little tab on one wing in order to keep it from turning too much. He was just invaluable in his explanations of how an aircraft flew.

Dad brought down to the farm a beautiful wooden tool chest that he had made. He had it sitting upstairs in Mother's room at the top of the stairs. In there were all of his airplane engines, spark plugs, coils and condensers, battery packs, etc. Of course, I got into it regularly when he was away in the service and when he got back I had used up a lot of things. I wouldn't have blamed him if he would have been upset with me, but he felt that I enjoyed it too, and was learning about aviation and engines.

Dad made a Curtis Hawk P6E model for Bocks that I would have given my right arm for. He had even painted the hawk talons on the wheel pants. They kept it in a china cabinet with glass doors in the dining room.

I also recall before WW II Dad taking my cousins and me to River View Amusement Park. Even though he didn't have much money he was very generous paying for everyone to go on rides. I discussed this with my cousins and they remembered those times. You could easily spend a lot of money with three or four kids.

I never knew Dad to be cheap in any way. When he purchased a pair of trousers he bought the best he could buy, he just didn't buy a lot of them. When he bought a shirt, he bought a good silk shirt. When he bought a belt or shoes, he tried to buy good ones and took very good care of them. He was a very dapper dresser. I recall after he returned from World War II, he had an Army belt. He took the buckle off the belt and polished it to a shine and it looked better than any buckle I have ever seen. The belt itself was made of webbing and was washable and he kept it spotless. He always wore that belt and buckle. He looked exceptionally good when he was dressed up. He was handsome, very strong, and had dark black hair and a thin mustache. I remember one time we went to the train station to pick him up and I actually ran away from him. I didn't recognize him because he had shaved off his mustache. After that time, he always wore a mustache.

He would come down to the farm and would always try to do something to help out. I remember one time he cleaned Grandma's windows, but she still checked them. She was always pleased that he offered to do the extra things. When he came to the farm and the sweet corn was ready he would eat eight or ten ears at one sitting. He just loved sweet corn. He also loved wild strawberries and would search the woods and gather bouquets of them when they were in season.

In the later years, just before World War II, Dad had built a U-control model airplane called the AJ Fireball. He kept it in the attic on the farm so that when he came down it was ready to fly. A U-control had a tiny thread-like wire from the hand control out to the airplane. When you turned your hand up the airplane would go up and when you turned your hand down the airplane would go down. The wires operated the elevator on the airplane. It went around in circles, and it was quite an exciting airplane to maneuver.

During the war Dad was transferred to Attu in the Aleutian Islands and spent a lot of time making various things. I still have a P-38 on my desk that he made out of Japanese shells. It has shells for the fuselage on both sides and shells for the nose. It stands on a large upright shell with an aluminum wing and tail surfaces. It is quite a startling piece. It's an example of the craftsmanship that Dad exhibited in almost everything that he did. He also made several rings out of aluminum and used whalebones or ivory to mount in the ring. They were quite exceptional too. I did lose one to a girl in Culver one night, but I still have a couple in my possession.

There were times when I would spend time in Chicago with Dad. He would pick me up after my Mother had put me on the train to Chicago. I would spend the weekend with him and then he would send me back home. Quite often Dad would take me to the Tom McCann store and buy me a nice new pair of shoes. Dad loved Chinese food and we would go to the Golden Pheasant, a very exclusive and fine Chinese restaurant in downtown Chicago. Then we would walk back to the room where he stayed. Of course, if I was wearing my new shoes it wasn't such a good time, because Dad could walk miles without a problem. He had a small desk in his very small room where he worked on his model airplanes. We had to sleep together in a single bed. The accommodations were pretty sparse because the whole room was the size of a closet, and the bathroom was down the hall but I loved visiting Dad.

When he returned from World War II he and Mom decided it was time to set up housekeeping again. At the time Mom and I lived in Plymouth at 817 N. Center Street with Grandmother after she sold the farm. Dad, Mom and I moved to Chicago and I entered my third year of high school, when I was about 16 years old. Dad got a job at Herman Magnus & Co. It was one of the largest automobile repair shops in the Chicago area. He was affectionately refered to by his fellow workers as

“Frenchy.” Mother also went to work for Kemper insurance company. We had a two-room apartment with a fold-down bed in the living room for Mom and Dad and a little cot in the kitchen for me. The bathroom was down the hall and was shared with the owner. The address was 844 West Windsor, Chicago, Illinois, about three or four blocks from the Aragon Ballroom in uptown Chicago.

I attended Lane Technical High School, at that time the largest technical high school in the world, right next to River View Amusement Park. There were over 5,000 boys in that school and it was a “Boys only” school. It was a wonderful school that taught every conceivable type of trade including mechanics. It also taught linotype operating which was the way newspapers and most printing was done at that time. They taught plastics, foundry, forge, welding, wood, and machine shop with huge lathes, automobile repair, and airplane and airframe repair. They even had a florist shop on the top floor.

I remember the driver’s education class. I had already learned to drive like most farm kids even though I wasn’t allowed to do so without a driver’s license. In taking this class it was pretty obvious to the instructor that I knew enough to be of assistance to him. He arranged for me to help him because he was on crutches. I asked him what happened and he said, “A student ran over me, and if that wasn’t enough, he then backed over me again.” You had to be careful because some of these city people had no idea how to drive. We had 1941 Ford Coupe’s and 1941 Studebaker Champion Coupe’s for driver’s education. There was a regular road course with driving lanes, and parking areas. We had a classroom with steering wheels and the other appropriate pedals and switches to help you to learn how to drive.

Lane Tech was famous for it's swimming team. I don't think they lost a meet in Chicago for many years. Johnny Weismuller, who played Tarzan in the movies, came from Lane Tech and swam in the Olympic pool. It was the type of place where you had to be very careful about fights. I recall one guy physically running into me every day on our way to class. Finally, one day, I busted him in the nose and then went on to my class. One of my friends asked me if I knew who that guy was. I didn't of course, and he said "Before you start a fight with someone I suggest you find out who they are first." If he was a gang member, "you are in serious trouble." Fortunately, he wasn't a gang member but I went out of my way to stay out of fights after that.

I believe my parents loved each other very much, however, it was very difficult for them to live together. Mother constantly told Dad "That's not the way my father would have done it." And he would say, "Well, you forgot the catsup again" or "You forgot to bring the salt." I know there wasn't anyone else involved but after high school I got my own place and my parents separated and later divorced which in those days was a big "no no." Mother went back to Plymouth to live with her mother and Dad took an apartment for himself in the Chicago area. It was extremely hard on me emotionally, because I always thought that some day I would get them back together. That was never to be.

When I came back to Plymouth I had to work really hard to keep in touch with Dad, since he didn't have a phone, I would have to drive to Chicago, go to his address and wait till he came home from work. By then I was married and living in Plymouth. Once in a while he would just show up on our front porch and we would have a very nice visit. After the divorce took place Dad spent a lot of time taking care of his mother. He had several brothers who were perfectly capable of doing so but didn't have the time, or weren't close enough, and I think they were against their mother going into a nursing home. It became obvious that she was going to have to do so, after trying to live with Madeline, in a one-room studio. Eventually she had to go into the Woodbine Nursing Home. Dad helped pay her bills until her death. This pretty well cleaned him out financially and then the company he worked for went out of business. He was only 62 but it was difficult for him to find employment, so he took early retirement even though he received a lesser amount from his social security.

He moved to Plymouth and stayed with us for a couple of weeks and that was okay, but it did cause some problems. He would order the kids around and they weren't used to anyone but Betty or me telling them what to do. I could see a problem coming, so I talked to a friend of mine John Ritzenthaler, who manufactured mobile homes in Argos. I was able to secure a new mobile home for Dad at dealer cost. As a result of this he moved into a trailer park on the East Side of Plymouth and was just as tickled as he could be with owning his own first home. In order to finance this we had to sell his new Ford Fairlane. I sold it from my front yard at 2111 N. Michigan at retail price and together with his savings he was able to pay cash for his new mobile home.

Mr. Bradley owned the mobile home park and was an ex WWI GI and he and Dad became good friends right away. Dad use to take Mr. Bradley to Indianapolis to the Veteran's Hospital for his health problems. I believe he may have been gassed in World War I.

After Dad sold his Ford he came home with a Hudson Jet and it was one of the first Uni-Bodys that was made without a frame. That car was coming apart in the middle but I believe he only paid about $50.00 for it. It moved down the road pretty well but if you hit a bump the doors would pop right open. At a later date he bought a Studebaker which was pretty good. It would not go into reverse and he wasn't about to tear it apart at his age to fix the transmission so he parked it so that he didn't ever have to back up. After some time he was able to acquire a brand new Volkswagen. It was his pride and joy and he would take the kids with him as he drove around the country. He changed the oil every thousand miles and took real good care of it. At that point, in his mind he felt the Volkswagen was the best car there was. Dad had a way of enjoying what he had in life and feeling that his mobile home was the best, or his Volkswagen, was the best or his shoes were the best. This is a wonderful trait. Most of us are always envying someone else's things. Dad just didn't feel that way, he was not just satisfied, but happy with what he had.

Coming to Plymouth I think proved to be the start of the best years of Dad's life. He would come over to our house in the afternoon or evening, almost every day. Betty would invite him to have supper with us and he spent a lot of time with the kids. He was so good to them, but I had to watch him a bit because he had his favorites. Susan idolized him and he would give her just anything she wanted. I had to have a talk with him and I said, "I don't care if you want to give Susan candy but you have to treat all of the rest of the children the same too." He took this to heart and became very fair about it. He definitely thought Susie was really something special. Dad taught the children to drive out in the orchard and he was known to let them steer when they were so small they had to sit on his lap. He used to take a car full of kids out in our old Cadillac limo and go trick-or-treating on Halloween. He was also very good to everyone at Christmas time. He used to wrap his gifts in white tissue paper with red string. He bought Betty her first paintbrushes when she started to paint oil colors to encourage her in her studies.

Dad came out to the airport when we opened it in 1967 and did anything he could to help. He washed airplanes and cleaned the insides and helped move them. He took several trips with me and he seemed to relish the fact that I flew such nice aircraft. I remember one trip in the Twin Beech when he was up front with me and seemed to be amazed at all the controls and adjustments that had to be made. When we went in the Lear Jet he just couldn't believe the speed and power.

I recall him bringing one of his radio controlled model airplanes to the airport and telling me to fly it. I had my hands full. That little devil zipped around so fast I was hard pressed to control it and I sure didn't want to bust it up. I was finally able to get it down on the runway and only broke the propeller. I was a nervous wreck at the time. They require a lot of skill to handle.

At the trailer park he helped people fix their dripping faucets. He also built a lot of aluminum skirts around the bottom of trailers for the residents at the park charging them only his cost for material. This helped people a lot and kept the wind from freezing pipes under the trailers as well as helping with the heating of the units. He was a very well liked man.

Dad always came over to help around our place and one day Dad was helping Julie clean out the barn and one of the ponies got out and ran away. It was the middle of winter and Dad chased the pony down to Centennial Park at a full run at the age of 72. As he came back after he corralled the pony, one of the neighbors later told me that he saw him lean on the mailbox as if he almost couldn't stand. He got into his car and went back to his home. Much later I got a call from one of the people at the park and they said "You better come out and get Al, I think he needs to go to the hospital." My first thought was Al my son and that he somehow had gotten hurt. When I realized it was my Dad I looked at Betty and said, "Dad is dying," because he would never go to a hospital unless there was something really wrong. I picked him up and took him to the hospital. After they were done with his check up and he was in his room I went in to talk to him and he said, "Don't tell anyone, I learned my lesson; I'll never do that again." The next day he had another major heart attack and died, that was in 1970. I couldn't believe it. He was so strong that he would Indian wrestle with the kids and win, Indian wrestle with men and win. He was so vibrant that I thought he would live through the heart attack.

It still brings tears to my eyes to this day thinking about him because I thought he would live forever. I didn't have much money in those days but I always thought later that if he could have lived longer I could have helped him more with a little money to partly pay for all Dad had done for me. Just before he died he had bought an aluminum boat and a new outboard motor with the understanding that I would take time off to go fishing with him. I wonder if I would have been smart enough to do so.

Dad was laid out at the Johnson Funeral Home. Barney Johnson was a friend of mine. The funeral home was packed and you could hardly get into the room. All of the friends that he had made in the short time Dad had lived in Plymouth, about eight years were crammed into the funeral home. He had many friends from the Model Airplane Club, friends of mine came and friends from the aviation business. Dad as very much loved by all that he came in contact with. There were a lot of tears in the eyes of those at the funeral home, not the least of which was mine. The kids always talked about the times they stayed with Grandpa at the mobile home and how he would make crepe suzettes for them in the morning and how they looked forward to seeing his new radio controlled model airplanes.

After the funeral we had a large buffet dinner at our house. Bob Pope and his wife had brought Madelaine and Annette down and we were so glad they could attend and share memories with us and we had an excellent get together. Our friends brought in food and the house was full of Dad's friends and people who knew him. There was a lot of talk about what a wonderful person he was. My Mother kept saying how she never thought he would die before her since he was so strong.

My Father may not have made a lot of money in his life but he had something that most people don't have. Almost everyone who knew him liked him. He was the kind of person who always helped everyone. I think the children all remember him fondly. I loved him very much and miss him to this day. He was a Father to be proud of.

The only picture I have of my Father during World War 1.

DEPARTMENT OF COMMERCE
AERONAUTICS BRANCH

MECHANIC'S LICENSE

This Certifies, That Albert A. Palbykin
whose signature and photograph accompany this license
is licensed as Airplane MECHANIC
of aircraft of the United States of America.
Unless sooner suspended or revoked this license expires
March 31, 1932

Stinson *Waco* *Argo*

CHICAGO AERO SALES CORPORATION
CHICAGO

ALBERT A. PALBYKIN
FIELD MANAGER

STINSON AIRPORT
FLYING SCHOOL
LA GRANGE 5490
LA GRANGE, ILL.

Dad's Mechanics License and his card from Chicago Aero.

Dad during the early days of aviation. (Note radiator)

Dad in front of his office at Stinson Airport La Grange,Il

Dad and the Ford Tri-motor, he and Harold Johnson barnstormed in.

A look at the tin goose from afar. (It was considered big)

Dad and Leo beside a beautiful Waco Bi-Plane ready to take off.

Dad on the farm when I was a boy the way I remember him.

Grandma, me, and Mother at 5111 Hamlin (Note three star flag)

Uncle Leo (A favorite) and me when he was in the service.

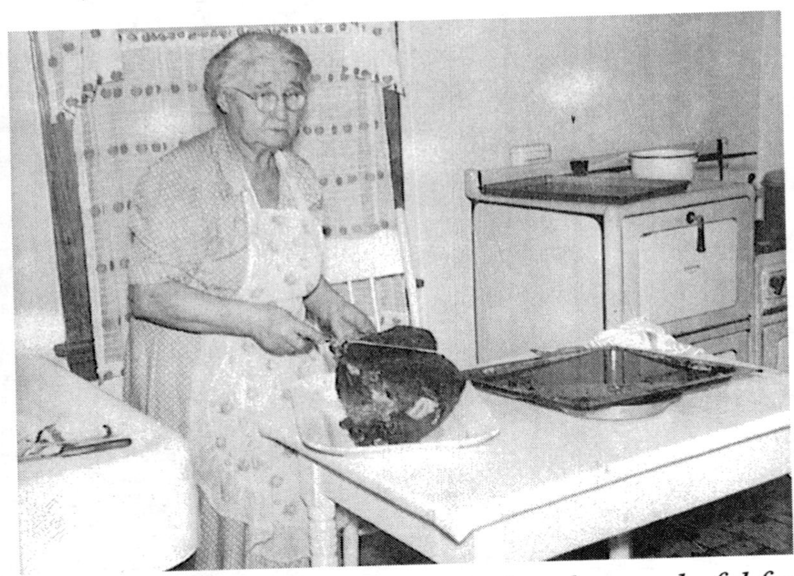

Grandmother in her kitchen, I remember the wonderful food.

Francois Pope, and his wife Antoinette, in front of portrait.

Bob Pope, Antoinette, and Frank Jr. (Note food display)

Annette, Leo, Grandma, Grandpa, and Madelaine. They lived at 5111 Hamlin Chicago, Ill. when I was a boy.

Dad on Attu in the Aleutian Islands (Note P38 on hood)

The P38 that Dad made out of Japanese shells on Attu.

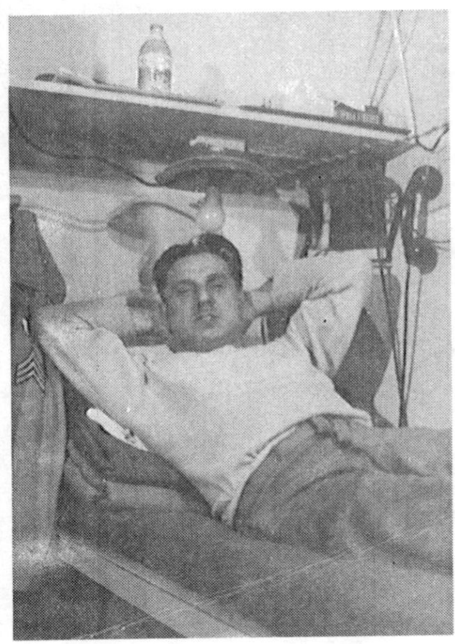

Dad in his bunk on Attu. Not bad shape for 46.

Dad in foxhole on Attu with radio ready for trouble.

The Globe Swift with Dad in June of 1956

Dad with one of his radio controled model airplanes shortly before his death in 1970 (See what I mean about healthy)

Mother

Cecilia Keiper, later Cecilia Palbykin, was born in 1900. She was the third of four daughters. Martha was the oldest, then Agnes, Cecilia, and the youngest, Mildred. Grandpa never did get a boy to help with the farm. My mother had to be the disciplinarian as far as I was concerned because I was such a little devil and Grandpa was always looking over her shoulder to make sure that I was properly disciplined. So, she was pretty hard on me but nothing out of the ordinary. I think she did a good job of trying to make me do what was right.

I always referred to my Mother as "The Doctor." She was something else when it came to taking care of me. When I was a child she gave me worm medicine. I had a red paper with powder to take in the morning and a white paper full of powder to take at noon and a blue paper of powder to take in the evening. This was to get rid of the worms. I wiggled a lot and she was sure I had worms. She also gave me cod liver oil pills that I would burp at school until mid-day. This was a terrible thing to do to a person. If you had an ache or pain she would go into the pantry, and pull down a cardboard box. All of the medicines used were kept in that box. There was something for Grandpa's aching back and Grandma's sore toe and someone's heartburn. If you had any of those symptoms you were going to get that medication. Strangely enough she was not very concerned about other things. One time I jumped into a pigpen that was full of pig manure and landed on a board with a rusty nail sticking up. The nail came clear through my Keds (a canvas shoe) and out the top of my foot. I pulled the board off and it was a puncture wound. It wasn't bleeding badly so she had me soak it in Epson Salts. Today they would rush you to the doctor's office for a tetanus shot, but it "worked." I'm still here.

I was subjected to a lot of things that were not so good. I remember that she used to keep track of my bowel habits. Mom would ask, "Well, did you DO anything today." I got to be an excellent liar because if I didn't she would treat me with Milk of Magnesia. I hated the stuff because it would make me sick. One day she sneaked some into my milk, and in a short time I vomited. After that I could no longer drink milk. Remember we lived on a dairy farm. I was also a skinny, puny little kid who didn't weigh very much. Mom was always trying to get me to eat so I would put on some weight. I used to be a picky eater. I didn't like eggs, asparagus or spinach or any of those things that were good for you. I ate meat and potatoes and anything sweet. This worried my Mother to no end. I remember setting at the table for an hour or so after dinner with a plate full of food in front of me that I was required to finish in order to leave the table. Sitting still that long was torture for me.

When I was really sick she hovered over me like Florence Nightingale. She rubbed Vicks Vapor Rub all over my chest and put a hairy wool cloth on my chest under my pajamas. I also got hay fever regularly. I would wheeze and she would say, "My, he has bronchitis." Then she would "doctor" me until I was over it. This is probably why in later life I had such an aversion to hospitals and doctors. Some of my best friends are doctors and I am afraid I caused them much aggravation. When I was working at Skystream I was put in the hospital for observation. A nurse's aid met me at the door with a wheelchair and in a childish voice said, "Were going to take a ride" and in the same tone I said, "Where are you going to sit?" As soon as I got in the room a nurse told me she was going to give me a bath. I said "I just took a shower but what ever turns you on honey." She left in a hurry and never came back. I had some work to do back at the airport so I let myself out the side door and put a piece of cardboard in the lock so I could get back in. When the nurse told my friend Dr. Coursey I was gone he said "don't worry he'll be back." I came back and nothing was ever said until years later. They put me in the room for people who were possibly suicidal because of a lack of space, or so they said. I had polished chrome for a mirror and other protective devices. It was just like my office, with the hand held radio with which I could talk to each of the airports, and the phone. I even sold a new airplane while in the hospital.

As I said, I was a very scrawny child and one summer when my cousin Bob came down from Chicago my Mother talked to him about teaching me how to fight. He worked with me a little bit to see if he could make a boxer out of me but it was futile. It wasn't in my nature to be physically aggressive. I would fight if provoked but I didn't start fights.

Mother was anxious about losing me in a swimming accident. The Bock boys would go back to Wilmas's to go swimming and I quite often wasn't allowed to go unless an adult would go along. She was so afraid I would drown or get polio, (My cousin Dave Harris did get polio and recovered fully). I learned to swim when someone threw me off of the end of the pier where the water was over my head and your choice was to sink or swim. I refined my swimming abilities by playing in the shallow water at the beach by Wilmas's and eventually learned to swim quite well. I remember having a lot of resentment at watching the cousins going back there to swim and not being allowed to go. Some of the aunts tried to stick up for me asking Mom to allow me to go; but she wouldn't budge. There must have been too much German in her from her father.

I remember Grandma and Mom conspiring to hide the egg money from Grandpa. They hid it in a vase in the china closet, but I knew where it was. I don't think Grandpa was concerned about it since Grandma got the egg money and he got the milk check, but they seemed awful secretive about it. Maybe they had accumulated more than he realized.

Since I was alone and the only child on the farm it was quite lonely for me because there was no one my age to associate with. Whenever my cousins the Bocks came down from Chicago I was thrilled to have someone to play with. Tom was less than a year older than I was and Bob was four or five years older than Tom was. Herb Jr. was even older so he didn't have much to do with me. I remember times when they were all there and we always had great times.

One time Bob and Herb were going to build a shelter in the woods to stay overnight. Tom and I were recruited to help so we went back with them and tried to help. They would send either Tom or me to the house, which was at least a third of a mile from where we were building the lean-to. I would go get the axe and run into Tom who was sent to get the binder twine. When he was coming back with the binder twine I was running for nails. So, we were the gophers for the older boys. When Bob and Herb got the lean-to done they weren't too enthused about letting us in it. But I do have a lot of fond memories about the camp. I recall how we put stones in a circle around the fire to keep it from spreading. We roasted hot dogs and marshmallows and attempted to sleep on the ground. Of course, in the evening you were constantly fighting the mosquitoes, which made a meal of me.

One day I persuaded Mom to let me go into town to the movies with George Emenaker. We met in town, he didn't live too far from town but I was about five miles out. When we came out of the movies my bicycle had a flat tire. I walked it over to my Aunt Mildred's and she called Mom on the phone and she said, "Let the boy stay here, he has a flat tire." Mom was adamant and said, "No, he's coming home." I worked on the tire down at the gas station and when I put air in it the tire exploded, so I went back to Aunt Mildred's. She telephoned Mom again and said, "Well, now he can't come home his tire is shot." Mom said, "then he can walk the bike home." By that time it was about 11:00 o'clock at night when I started walking my bicycle home. There were no lights in the country. No yard lights, no lights in houses and I was walking down the road. It was so dark that I couldn't tell whether I was on the road or not. I could only tell if I started hitting the weeds. It took me a long time to get home since it was five miles. I found out that if I was going to go somewhere I had to be prepared to get home early enough because there was no way in the world that she was going to let me stay over anywhere.

Mom always dressed me like little Lord Fauntleroy. They were very nice clothes but many of them were not what I wanted to wear. For example, I was never too happy with knickers. They made me look like a "nut" but Mom thought they looked good. By that age the other boys were wearing long pants, and I was still wearing "knickers." When I finally persuaded her to buy me some long pants she bought me corduroy. If you've ever had corduroy pants you know that as you walked that went "whiz, whiz, whiz." So I was not happy with those either. I persuaded her one time to get me high top shoes with a neat little pocket on the side that you could put your pocketknife in. I was really proud of those. Dad would also bring clothes down for me, like sailor suits, which I wasn't keen on either. Later on when we moved to Chicago she used all my savings to buy me clothing. She bought a long overcoat and a felt hat that was very stylish. My parents felt that at that age I should learn to start taking care of myself. It was a good thing because I was on my own at seventeen.

Mom was an excellent cook. Both Herb and Bob Bock my cousins rave about her Salvation Army baking power donuts that were made with lard and had powered sugar on the outside (It doesn't sound good but both Bob and Herb remembered them). Not only had she learned what my Grandmother knew but she also learned to make many of the meals that Dad was fond of. She made the greatest chop suey I've ever eaten. She made lemon squares that my children make to this day with her recipe. She was not only an excellent cook, but she was a great baker. She made an orange chiffon cake that stood six inches high.

Mom worked at McCord's radiator factory in Plymouth during the war. It was hard work and much like Rosy the riveter, it was work not common to women at that time. She did real well at it and stayed till the end of the war when I was about fifteen.

After the war was over on VE day a couple of us boys went to a man we knew would sell us some wine. We got the wine and went to the Plymouth downtown area and started down the street with our bottle when someone asked for a drink, it got passed around and it was gone. We spent the rest of the evening wandering around downtown. It was so exciting that we didn't want to go home. Finally I decided to go home and face the music. I approached the house and it was dark, I peered in the window and saw Mom pacing around the living room waiting for me to show up. I was able to get in the house through a cellar window and sneak past Mom and up the stairs to my upstairs room and go to bed without her catching me.

When Dad came back from the service we moved back to Chicago and set up housekeeping at 844 W. Windsor and settled into a routine, Dad went to work every morning, I went to school and Mom took care of the apartment, did the wash and shopped. She soon became bored with the inactivity. She took a job with Kemper Insurance company and seemed to thrive on the office activity and soon had a very good position. There was constant tension when Mom and Dad were together. And as soon as I graduated from high school and left, they separated. Mom returned to Plymouth, and Dad got a place in Chicago and they later divorced.

After Mom came back to Plymouth she lived with Grandmother in an upstairs apartment over Aunt Mildred's. When Mom came to live with Grandma it helped both of them since Mom got a job with Schlosser

Brothers and was able to share the expenses. About six months or so later I came back to Plymouth. There was a concern that I would move in with both of them and put a further burden on them. I remember my Aunt Mildred talking to me and saying "Well, you can stay here tonight, but I want you out of here tomorrow morning." I didn't even stay the first night and I think it relieved everybody's mind. At that time I was seventeen and should have been out on my own and taking care of myself. So, it was a good thing for them to do. I got a sleeping room at 310 N. Plum Street.

I remember Mom and Grandma taking trips in the 1941 Ford that they enjoyed so much. They would load up the car on Sunday after church and drive up into Michigan and stop at one of the roadside tables and eat a picnic lunch they had prepared. Then they would go on and get peaches, cherries, or pears, or whatever was in season and bring them back for canning. It was a great adventure for them because in those days it was a large trip if you drove from Plymouth to South Bend. People looked forward to those outings like we now look forward to going to Europe.

As the children were growing up we would always stop at Grandma and Mother's place after church. We all looked forward to Grandma's little treat on Sunday morning and in later life, even after Grandma had passed away, we still stopped to see Grandma Cee Cee every Sunday morning. The girls would occasionally stay overnight and they would spend quite a little bit of time, baking, talking, or watching TV. They really looked forward to their times with Grandma Cee Cee. They thought she was an angel. She was just an older woman trying to get into heaven.

I remember flying Aunt Agnes and Mother to Florida to our place at Cabana Point and they just loved it. They had a wonderful time. I left them there and Mom became very friendly with the woman who took care of the apartments, they wrote each other after her visit. I did this a couple of times. One time we dropped them off in Tampa on a Lear Jet trip and Tom came up from Miami and took them on to Cabana Point. He returned later to pick them up and delivered them back to Tampa and I took them home in the Lear Jet. They had never experienced this type of thing in their lives and they really seemed to enjoy the trips.

Mom worked for Schlosser Brothers until they closed the plant. She later went to work as an accountant at Price's Abattoir. She had a small income for the majority of her life and yet constantly saved money. I use to say to her, "What are you saving it for? I'm your only child and I'm doing fine, so what are you saving for?" I wanted her to have fun with it. (My children say the same thing to me). One time she was planning on visiting Mildred who moved to Tucson, Arizona but didn't want to spend the $200 for the train ticket. I finally talked her into it and she had a great time. Mom also constantly had the lights off in her home. Just to tease her when I entered the house I would put fifty cents on the television set which was just inside the front door. I then turned on all the lights in the house because she kept it so dark. Of course, her eyesight was beginning to fail at this point and she probably didn't need the bright lights or the glare.

I remember one day Mom was downtown and Susie who was about six was with my Father. Susie ran over to her Grandmother and said, "Cee Cee, have you ever met my Grandfather?" They just looked at each other and smiled. There never was anything wrong with their marriage other than they just didn't get along. There was no third party interfering; they just antagonized each other. In later years they both came for all the holidays and were very cordial. When Dad died, Mom was pretty shaken by it so I knew there was a bond between them.

Mom and Grandma were living in an upstairs apartment at Mildred's building in Plymouth. We were always concerned about Grandma going up and down those stairs. One time we found her on the roof cleaning the windows and she was ninety years old. We located a corner lot right across the street from the church. It wasn't as large as we needed but I went to the zoning board and I was able to persuade them to let me build a house there. We constructed a brand new house at 700 Walnut Street. It was designed in such a way that it could easily be converted into two apartments. I even put the plumbing in for the future modification. Mom had saved some money for the down payment and I offered to make the payments. It was very well constructed with hardwood floors and a nice kitchen with a large dining area, a big living room and two bedrooms. Mom and Grandma were delighted with their new home.

When Grandma passed away we split the house by putting a bathroom in what was the hall and built a kitchen in the south end of the living room under the short window provided for it. That is all we had to do. That made a nice apartment in the back and one in the front, each with a private entrance. This way Mom was able to retain the income from one apartment and live in the other. It turned out to be good plan. I know Mom was extremely depressed when Grandma died and at one time was hospitalized with depression in South Bend. I went to visit her and said, "look at these people around you. They have troubles you don't. You have a place to live and people around you who love you and money coming in." In a very short time she came home. Betty and I went over and redecorated her home for her and she was so delighted.

Mom was a very beautiful woman. She was tall with a great figure and had blue eyes. In looking at her early pictures she had dark auburn hair. She went with my Father for about seven or eight years before marrying. In her diaries, which I still have, she wrote of her feelings about Dad. She would be up one time and down the next. I loved both of them very much. I at least had the money in Mom's later years to help her out. On Sundays we would huddle around the table and have some of Mom's delicious desserts and I would see her from time to time through the week. She kept me busy with any squawk she had at the house. I think the girls enjoyed the visits with their grandma more than the boys, who were older but we all enjoyed going over there Sunday mornings for breakfast.

Mom called me early one morning and said that she was bleeding and wanted me to take her to the hospital. I rushed over and took her to the hospital and checked her in. She thought "Doctors were Gods" and she was on a lot of over the counter medication that she had been taking for years. I wondered if it was doing any good! I talked to the doctor about it and he took her off all medication. The next day I went in and Mom was really mad at me. She said, "You've been talking to the doctor haven't you?" I told her that I had talked to him. She said, "Well, he took all of my medicine away." The next day I went out to see her she was so happy. She said, "Don, I feel so wonderful. I'm so glad that you talked to the doctor." She started to feel much better. She did say that she didn't want to go back to the house and that she wanted to go to the nursing home. So, she went to Miller's Merry Manor in Plymouth. Most elderly people don't feel this way but she thought it was best. She gained weight because she was off of her stomach medicine and ate better. Mom looked good and seamed to thrive in the nursing home. She couldn't see much and couldn't hear very well, but she became quite content. She loved visiting with the other people in the dining room and each other's rooms and there she found a lot of companionship.

We often went to the library and get talking books for her. Every year we went on a buying spree for Mom, and Betty would pick out her dresses. She was always so pleased at what ever we did for her. She grew very protective of the people that shared the room with her and made sure they were covered when visitors came.

The last few months of her life she went downhill quite fast. She would want to go to bed and they would keep her tied in a wheelchair. I finally talked to the doctor and asked them to let her lie down. They ran some tests and decided that she was not going to live very much longer. Her arms were bruised from all of the tests and after that they let her lie down. A few weeks after that she passed away. It wasn't too hard to keep track of Mom's age because she was born in 1900 and she died in 1986. I talked to her shortly before she died and she said, "Don, I don't want you to feel bad about what will happen." She then said, "Soon I will be with Al." At first I thought of my son Alan and then realized that she meant my Dad, Al.

Her funeral was almost as well attended as Dad's. All of the church people and various organizations that she belonged to attended. I remember looking at her in the casket and thinking that she looked so young. She was still beautiful with no wrinkles in her face. The undertaker did quite a good job and she looked twenty years younger than she was.

I still meet people in the church that remark at how wonderful Mom was. Several took communion to her at the nursing home and mentioned that she was a very devout and faithful person. She was always concerned about religion and I think that this was to her benefit. She lived right across the street from the church so it was easy for her to go to mass almost every day.

In her later years Aunt Agnes had moved into a house just across the street and down one house. Aunt Agnes was so good to me when I lived alone in Chicago; she helped me with my laundry and fed me quite often. She was a wonderful lady and lived to the age of ninety-seven. Mom would get her car out and pick up Agnes and they would go off to the market or get their hair done. The two of them had a lot in common and got along quite well and many times took vacations together. I often wondered why they didn't live together but I knew it wasn't meant to be; because they both wanted to be the queen of their own home and valued their privacy and independence.

Cecilia,14 and Martha Keiper 18.

Mother beside an early aircr

Mother and me at the farm.

Mother, and me on my bike.

'randma, and Mother in front
'f the apartment at Mildred's.

Ruth and Martha O'Neill with
me. (They wanted to adopt me)

'randma and Mom cooking
Bock's cottage on Myers lake.

Mother at our wedding. I
was always proud of her looks.

Mom all decked out for church.

Mother and Lillian at our hou.

Me with Steve and Mother holding Alan, Betty glowing.

Steve, Mother, Marty, Alar at the apartment at Mildred

Agnes, Cecilia, Mildred, in front of Agnes's home.

Agnes, and Mother ready to go out on the town.

Agnes and Mother in Florida on a shopping adventure.

Agnes 80th birthday at Bob's both enjoying lunch. 7/8/78

Children

Betty and I often discuss the fact that we were married so young with other people. In fact, I keep referring to it as pre-puberty. But that's not really true. We were 18 years old at the time we got married and very much in love and we still are today.

Our first son Stephen, was born about 15 months after we were married August the 25th 1949. I was concerned about the shape of his head since it kind of came to a peak. We had saved the money to pay the doctor; (I canceled our insurance at Studebaker since it would not pay for the birth). I made an appointment the day after he was born to pay him the $50 delivery fee. While I was there I asked about his head and wondered if he could do something to round it out. The doctor laughed out loud and said that it was quite normal. By the next week he was just fine. He turned into a very beautiful active child with red hair and blue eyes and he was a great joy to both of us. Stephen lives in Tempe, Arizona in a large ranch home with a big swimming pool. He has a beautiful wife, Kristine (Ferguson), and three daughters, Lindsay, (champion swimmer) Brittany, (basketball player) and Danielle, (her dad's helper). They are wonderful children, and fun to be around.

A couple of years later Alan was born September 14th 1951. He was the most beautiful child you ever laid eyes on. He had blond hair that looked like duck down which we later cut in a crew cut. He had a big engaging smile and a sweet disposition. We put a picture of Stephen and Alan together on a Christmas card we sent one year. Stephen used to call him "mine own brudder." Alan, the only one that lives in the Plymouth area, lives on Nataka Trail in a nice community on the south edge of Lawrence Lake. He has an excellent home overlooking the lake and he and his lovely wife Donna (Hillman) have a large family. Amy Rose their eldest and her husband Ken, have three sons Kody, Kyle, and Wade, which are our great grand children. Shanda Stevens, their second daughter, and her husband Shanon have a girl Madison, which gives us our fourth great grandchild. Mark Alan, their son, is a wonderful young man, not only good looking in body (he is a champion wrestler) but in personality.

Martin arrived June 21st 1954. He was curious about everything mechanical and very precocious. He always had a screwdriver in his back pocket taking the doorknobs off and the chairs apart. He was a real delight to have around except for the loose doorknobs and seat backs. He was the one that did most of the lawn mowing because he loved driving the tractor. Our neighbors told us that he could sell iceboxes to Eskimos, since he was quite a talker. Martin lives in the Grand Rapids area in a very nice home on a wooded lot with his wonderful wife, Mary (Theobald), and their daughter, Mary Lamb. Mary Lamb seems to be doing really well in her studies and is well on her way to becoming an automotive engineer.

The whole family is in to drag racing (Marty is a certified driver and just recently reached 198.7 mph.) and the two Marys act as the pit crew. The family spends most of their spare time pursuing this hobby

Our first daughter was born January 4th 1958, a few years after the boys, and we named her Julie. I remember there was no question in my mind when Stephen was born that he would be a boy, I didn't even ask. But this time, I was at the old Parkview Hospital which had tissue paper walls sitting in the hall and I heard the doctor say, "Why it is a girl." So when they came out to tell me I already knew, and she was a little dark haired beauty. Julie Hicks MD, our oldest daughter, lives in Thomson, Georgia with her husband, James Hicks Jr. They have two children. Their daughter, Lillian Perry, was named after Betty's mother, Lillian Perry, and their son, Alexander, named for one of Jim's early ancestors, They live in a nice home on a small ranch with the back of their property bordering a lake. They have a Great Dane dog named Stoney and a black and white cat named Budley. They have several horses and breed them and raise some excellent animals. They also belong to a large hunt club where Jim is a "whipper in" and a staff member and they love to ride in foxhunts.

Then Debra was born December 13th 1959, another beautiful blond girl that always has a sunny disposition and is a delight to be around. We once had some pictures taken of her and they called our house trying to get her to pose for advertising. Debra Jones lives in Spartanburg, South Carolina in a cute two-story home. She is always an achiever and is extremely well organized. Everything she does is done well. She was named "Proprietor of the Year" when she was a managing partner of an Outback Restaurant. She recently was named "Big Sister of the Year" and is now a licensed real estate agent selling lake properties in the Spartanburg area. She has a couple of pets one of which is a dog named Lucky. He had been run over by a car and Debi rescued him. She calls him "The million dollar dog" because of all the money she has spent on him. She also has a black and white cat named T-bone that reminds us of Tuffy each time we see him.

Susan was born February 9th 1962; Susan was my father's sidekick. She is a real classy girl with silky straight black hair and flashing eyes. She was another terrific addition to our family. She was always watching, and always ahead of us, you couldn't put anything over on her. Some of the children said she could hold her own in a cage full of lions. Susan Tarsitano and her husband, Rick Tarsitano, live in a very stylish home decorated by Susan in Gilbert, Arizona. They live about four miles from Stephen. They have two children, Jena and Camille; both of them are live wires just like their mother. Susan and her girls are also in to horses, both riding, and breeding and they have some very good Arabian mounts. She and her daughters spend most of their spare time training her show horses. She also combines business with pleasure by making all kinds of custom riding apparel that she sells to the upscale people that show horses.

Almost eight years after Susan was born, Ann Marie arrived December 29th 1969 with curly red hair (when it finally came in). Both Betty and I were forty years old. I always said we were the only senior citizens in the PTA. Ann says she was the tiebreaker. Three boys and three girls and then there was Ann breaking the tie. She looks more like Betty than any of the other girls. Ann Marie Dickey and her husband, Michael Dickey, have two children, Lauren, a beautiful blond girl with a will of her own, and their precocious son, Logan. Both of them are fun to be with. They have a pet rabbit named Tubby that is litter box trained. They have a nice home in Brooklyn Park, Minnesota a suburb of Minneapolis, with a swimming pool and a large lawn that Michael manicures like a plaid carpet that is the talk of the neighborhood. They have their hands full taking care of the two children. Ann once asked me "How did we ever take care of seven children"? I told her your children take all of your time and ours took all of our time.

This comprises our family as of the year 2000. Some times people ask us facetiously if that's all the children we have. I always say, "Sometimes we didn't get anything." They have all done very well and I'm proud of each and every one of them. I have to be careful in my bragging because I do it so often that people get sick of hearing it. I remember one time we had a man visiting our house that met all the girls, he said "what did you do drown the ugly ones?" Betty said, "wait till you see my sons."

Betty's sister Gloria Nelson and her husband Reynold (Rey) Nelson have built a large printing business in California. They also have an accomplished family, with four children. Their daughter Jamie and Jim Baumann have two children Jeffery and Chelsea. Another daughter Terese and Stephen Dickerson have two children Matthew and Michelle. The third daughter Sandra Andersen has three children Casey, Morgan, and Daniel. And a son Eric Nelson MD and his wife Heather complete their family.

It's difficult to express my feelings about my family. I feel that the reason they have all done so well is the fact that we had so little to give them in the early days that they learned how to make it on their own. When we did have the ability to give the later children more we felt it would be unfair to do so. We always tried very hard to treat each of the children the same even going so far as to be sure we spent exactly the same for each at Christmas time. We still feel this way and are adamant about dividing all of our belongings equally among our children. I really feel that we would turn over in our graves if any of our children were to lose the close relationship they have with each other because of our possessions.

Betty and I always talk about the fact that if we were marooned on a desert island, we would certainly want to be marooned with "our" children. They have proven to be excellent providers, conscientious parents as well as good citizens time and time again. It's extremely difficult to gift anything to them because they are all so independent and they are doing so well by themselves. They are all proud of the fact that they did it without anyone's help. A few years ago we set up a Limited Liability Company that we feel will be a very effective tool in transferring what Betty and I have been able to accumulate over our lifetime to our children. We feel very fortunate to have accomplished this because if we didn't make this provision the government would take our money and squander it as they always do. We feel that the children will use the money and assets in a very responsible and thoughtful way and pass what they have accumulated at the end of their life on to their children, our grandchildren.

Stephen as a child, and with his family today.

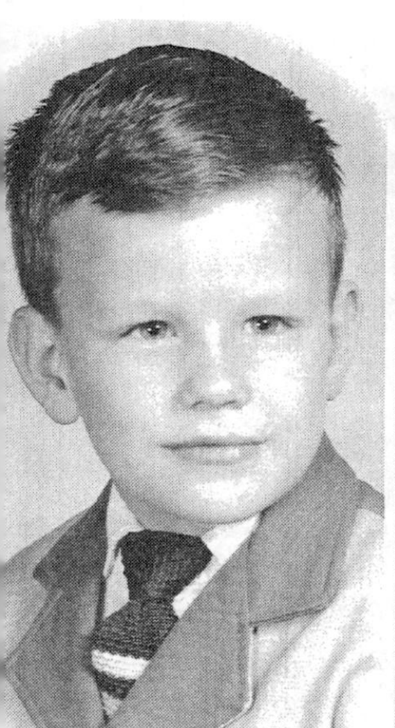

Alan as a child and with his family today.

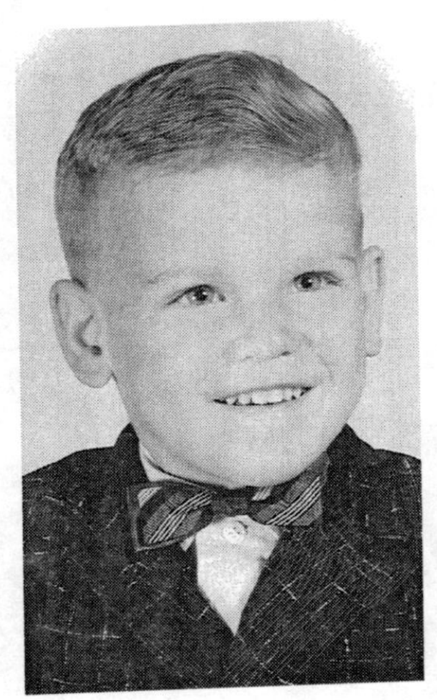

Martin as a child and with his family today.

Julie as a child and with her family today.

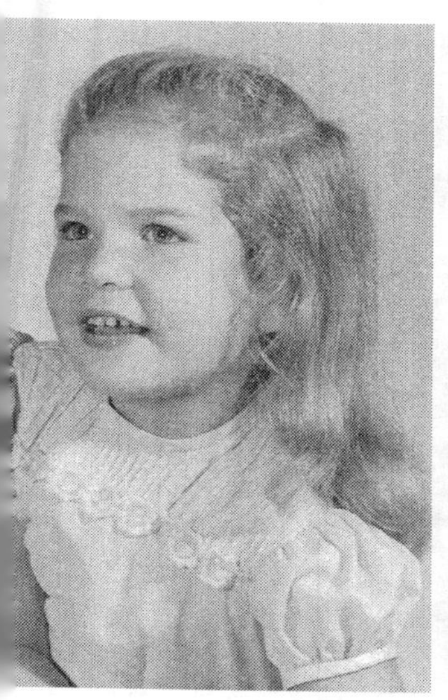

Debra as a child and with her nieces and nephews today.

Susan as a child and with her family today.

Ann Marie as a child and with her family today.

Betty and me with the three boys.

The four girls in a group.

Philosophy

Not too long ago I observed an incident in church that says it all about today's discipline. There was a young lady with a baby in the pew in front of us. The baby was probably about seven or eight months old and had a rattle in it's hand. The baby dropped the rattle; the mother bent over picked it up, wiped it off and gave it back to the baby. Within a short time, the baby dropped it again. The mother again retrieved the rattle and gave it back to the baby, who promptly dropped it. The mother then took the rattle; put it in her purse, the baby screamed the mother opened the purse and gave the rattle back to the baby. This is a perfect illustration of how you lose complete control of children by not taking a firm stand early on. At eight months of age, the baby who cannot speak, and cannot walk is in charge and knows that it can get anything it wants by screaming. That's the way discipline in our country is going today.

People are very reluctant to discipline their children. They take the easy way out by allowing the child to do whatever it wants to do rationalizing that its only a baby. Then they are horrified later on by some of the atrocities committed by children. It doesn't make much sense. Some day, someone in that child's life is going to have to tell it that there are certain rules and regulations that must be complied with to live in this world. I don't recall having problems like that with my children because if they dropped the rattle the second or third time and it was taken away from them, there was no way in hell they were ever going to get it back again. So, they never had a chance to win that battle and therefore we didn't have an out of control child. We took the child out of church until it stopped screaming.

I don't believe "It takes a village to raise a child" It takes parents (Preferably two) who care about the child and who are prepared to give some of their time to raising it. Some liberal people believe that children should be allowed to sue their parents! Some people feel that the government should have a more active role in the raising of our children so they won't have to. These people have usually spent very little time even thinking about the care of their children and are more concerned with their career, possessions, and having fun.

Liberals are always great talkers about helping but when you get down to it they rarely help. They try to get other people to do their work for them. They are also for every governmental program they can think of as long as they can get someone else to pay for it. Their little spiel is the government owes them a living. They are for everything except the free enterprise system, which made this country great. Liberal politicians want you to become dependent on the government so that they will have power over you. This started with liberal programs the last four decades or so when they were in power in congress. We begin to pay people for not working. We now have established several generations of people who have never worked, including our current president, who has lived off taxpayers his entire life. I believe that people who cannot work should be provided with assistance for food and shelter. However, that is an extremely small percentage and I believe that anyone capable of work should not be given any money.

I have always tried to be an independent thinking voter and I always vote for the person I feel is best for the job and for the country. Starting with Truman I voted for every President that was elected except Eisenhower (I voted for Stevenson, a Democrat) until our current President. Ask any liberal how many times they voted against a Democrat and you will find out that they would vote for the devil if he were a Democrat. The current President divided the country into factions and by lying and preying on their fears was able to get a plurality of the voting public, which represents less than 25% of the people in America that, could vote. Those who don't vote or those who vote for a candidate that has no chance, elect people like we have today. They have no one to blame but themselves for our loss of freedom and the loss of prestige for our country worldwide.

The government today is full of non-participating experts. This is particularly true in aviation. People who have no real knowledge about the system and try to regulate the people who know. Liberals feel that any giveaway policy that they can dream up should be good for the country. It should be the opposite. The more we pay people for doing nothing the more of them that show up for a hand out. Thank heavens that the recent changes from a more conservative congress are beginning to make a change in the welfare system. Perhaps we've turned the corner and can hope for some reasonable sanity with regard to these programs in the future.

Another thing liberals are always for is more taxes so they can spend more of the working peoples money, buying votes from the non-working and welfare population. They are always trying to think of another tax they can impose so that they can take your money and spend it because after all you're not smart enough to spend your own money. You need a father figure, such as government bureaucrats to tell you what to do with your money.

When you hear uninformed people talking about taxing the large companies you know that you are listening to a person who has never thought the situation through. "THE END USER PAYS ALL TAXES" Therefore, if the automobile manufacturer is charged taxes, he simply passes is on in the form of higher car prices. When you buy those cars, you pay for the extra taxes. When the gasoline companies are charged higher taxes, they simply add it into the cost of their product and pass it along in the form of higher gasoline prices. When the tobacco companies are charged higher taxes, they simply add it into the cost of their product and pass it along in the form of higher prices. The end user, the person who uses the products, pays all taxes. When a person says tax the gasoline, cigarettes or auto manufacturers, they are really saying tax me because I use these products. There are many people who are totally uninformed and yet speak with great authority.

When I worked at Wheel Horse, several of the executives decided to take a class at Notre Dame with regard to business practices. There were about four or five of us that arrived at Notre Dame to sit in on these business courses. The first professor that lectured us about business obviously never worked outside the academic world and was totally uninformed about the subject he was talking about. We would question him and he would say, "well, that's what is in the book." Never having worked in the real world, he didn't realize that "The book" was dead wrong. There again, were non-participating experts teaching the people of this country what the liberal establishment wants them to teach. We never went back for the second session because we realized that there was nothing they could impart to us that would be of any practical value.

My friend, Conrad Lesh, "Tiz" use to say that the aviation business was full of non-participating experts. He was right too. You could stand by the fence at the airport and listen to them go on by the hour about airplanes. Of course, in most cases, they didn't have anything to do with an airplane and therefore knew little or nothing about the operation or the expertise involved in the flying business.

We have heads of government involved in the every day business of running a city or country that are totally uninformed. We have building inspectors who have never built a building, yet they are making the rules for us to live by. It is any wonder that many of the knowledgeable business people, who have operated a business for years, have given up in disgust! They have sold their business and walked away from the company with all of their knowledge and ability, to let someone come in that really doesn't know what they are doing. Eventually those companies fail!

In looking at my 1954 tax return I see that there were five of us, Betty and me, Stephen, Alan, and Martin. My total income was $2,137.86. I made $1,212.07 at Studebaker. A little bit selling Electrolux sweepers, $835.00 at the Marshall County R.E.M.C. and $40.00 working at a gas station. We were able to survive on such a small income because we didn't allow ourselves to have everything that we wanted. We would never have made it if we had done so. In 1954 we used to feed our family on six or seven dollars a week and yet have wholesome meals. We didn't buy prepared food, cookies, candy, potato chips, or soda pop. We bought cheap cuts of meat, chicken, eggs, cheese and macaroni, potatoes, vegetables, fruit, bread and all the staples. We made our own cookies, our own breakfast coffee cakes with home made frosting drizzled on top and the best French fries in the world to go with the best hamburgers. Betty canned a lot of locally grown food in the summer so we would have it all year long. I didn't feel that we were underprivileged, or poor and I certainly would never have entertained the thought of going on the dole. Remember its not how much money you make it's what you do with that money and in the end it's what you get to legally keep.

Betty didn't feel that she was somehow deprived and she continued to work diligently to keep our house looking nice and to save every penny that she could. In those days, everybody used regular diapers. We washed them, dried them and used them again. In order to keep them from leaking. We used plastic pants over the diapers, which cost twenty-five cents each. Betty repaired the plastic pants by sewing them and using airplane glue to seal the seams. She made clothes. She took old clothes of mine turned them inside out and made them into clothes for the children and they looked terrific, better than the clothes that most kids went to school in. One time she took an old horsehide leather jacket of mine, turned it inside out, and used the rough side out to make a suede jacket for the boys. I remember her buying cloth and making suit coats for the children so that at Easter they had coats that were perfectly made with better tailoring than store bought clothing. Would anyone attempt to do that in this day and age? I doubt it.

When people get married today they feel that they should have a new house and a new car. They should have cable TV and everything immediately, instant gratification. That's what they expect today. Or for that matter why get married? Most women will sleep with you anyway and if she gets pregnant, just "Kill it" by aborting it so it won't interfere with your life. After all our laws say you cannot destroy an endangered bird egg or you will go to jail but you can kill unborn humans any time you want to! As long as they can get the people to believe the country is benefiting by such policies the liberals will continue to advocate them. Some day the bubble will burst.

In the late 1960's I became an aircraft dealer and was selling two particular aircraft that were good values. The Cessna Skyhawk model 172 which sold for $11,995 with a radio and a Cessna Skylane, model 182, which sold for $17,995 with a couple of radios in it. I just priced a new Cessna Skyhawk, model 172, and the price of it is $186,000. I priced the new Skylane, model 182, and the price was $237,000. In a large part, these prices are because of governmental intervention and new regulations of the lives of people as well as liberal courts. Therefore, the private aircraft business is less than a tenth of what it was in years gone by. There are expensive Jet aircraft owned by large corporations or rich individuals, but private flying (General aviation) is practically gone unless you buy an old worn out aircraft.

Most lawyers are honest hard working people and play a necessary part in our way of life. They perform a very important function in the operation of our society from preparing wills and contracts to defending the innocent. They do not deserve the ridicule and scorn they receive from the general public. The reason they have this reputation is because of a few bad apples who have no sense of right or wrong and who will do anything to gain more power, prestige, and money. You know who they are; you see them on the TV talk shows and in the forefront of all liberal causes. They always defend the crooks and the celebrities with the most money. My father had a name for them "shyster lawyers."

Government, in its infinite wisdom seems to feel that they should allow shyster lawyers to pursue every avenue they can to collect money. Beechcraft made an aircraft called the Bonanza, which was delivered in 1946 for around $5,995. That same aircraft today costs a half a million dollars. One of the reasons for that is the original Bonanzas were built with a wing that had counter-sunk rivets. The airplane was clean and very efficient and could get away from an inexperienced pilot and they would come diving out of the bottom of a cloud after loosing it, pull back on the wheel too hard and tear the wings off. So, Beechcraft decided they would make a modification to the aircraft by changing the rivet heads to button head rivets to make it a little stronger. That didn't mean that the first aircraft was poorly built. It only meant that when you put a fool at the controls they can destroy anything. The new rivets just made it a little less likely to come apart in the hands of an idiot. It was a simple product improvement. Every time one of the original Bonanzas goes down, the shyster lawyers get the scent of this and talk to the survivors to get them to sue Beechcraft. Of course, when the Courts upheld these suits the Bonanza went from a $5,995 to a $500,000 airplane because a large part of this increase is due to higher manufacturers insurance and the cost of these foolish verdicts. Very few people can afford to own a Bonanza today. The shyster lawyers get a big part of the settlement money so they are going to do everything they can to secure a conviction. The public pays for all of these settlements in the form of higher priced airplanes, higher insurance and less freedom. The courts pay all this money to somebody who shouldn't have been flying, and didn't know how to fly, and to the shyster lawyers who tried the case.

Our recent more conservative congress enacted the General Aviation Revitalization Act August 17, 1994 which included an 18-year limit on manufactures liability for general aviation aircraft. In the five years since enactment of this Act GA aircraft production has doubled and more than 25,000 new jobs have been created and a doubling of exports of GA aircraft helping our balance of trade problem. I wonder who will redress the wrongs perpetrated on the many victims of the liberal court decisions over the past years.

Even with this Act the May 1974 Cessna Marketing News shows they built 787 units that month! In talking to a Cessna representative recently he told me that they completed less than a thousand units for the entire year! Therefore Cessna went from making approximately ten thousand aircraft per year to less than one thousand per year. That's the kind of damage that non-participating experts achieve when they begin to try to manipulate the market and take away the freedom of the people of our country. A few years back Congress, in its infinite wisdom, decided to put a large tax on aircraft and boats. They closed down ninety percent of both industries. Now, they don't even get the smaller tax they use to get.

Most of our schools don't teach the simple process of keeping a checkbook and being able to reconcile it at the end of the month. I recall one of our daughters going to school and having this process taught to her. When she came home Betty was so thrilled that she had learned something worthwhile that she wrote a letter to the teacher complimenting her and thanking her. My daughter came back and said, "What did you put in that letter?" The teacher broke down and cried when she read it." That teacher had probably been told all the time that it was more important to teach the politically correct way to speak to a person or the proper name for a manhole (people hole) or the sex life of crickets. It's almost against policy to teach anything that is useful such as reading, writing and arithmetic. When I first started school there was a one-room schoolhouse on our bus route, with a stove for heat and an outhouse where we dropped some of the farm students off. I firmly believe those students got a better education in the basics than is given in today's fancy schools.

I believe all people should be treated equally, and judged by their own ability and their personal history; Certainly not given special treatment because of their skin color whether it's yellow, black, white, red, or any other color. Did you ever wonder why it is politically correct to have a Miss Black America yet not acceptable to have a Miss White America? Why is it politically correct to have a National Association for the Advancement of Colored People, yet not OK to have a National Association for the Advancement of White People? Why do people like O. J. Simpson get away with murder when no white man would have a chance of escaping punishment, if confronted with the same evidence? Why did Rodney King drive through a neighborhood on drugs at excessive speeds and when stopped by the police, resist arrest and then sue and collect a multi-million dollar award? Why did Mike Tyson the boxer get accepted back into the boxing community after his rape conviction? I believe it's all because of our liberal media, and their politically correct agenda. They don't want to recognize the fact that a minority could do anything wrong. Criminals are criminals no mater what their color.

In September 1999 Bill Gates gave a huge gift of subsidized education to nonwhite students the so-called minorities (In the global world they are actually huge majorities.) There is no doubt that had this gift been for the exclusive use of whites instead of minorities Bill Gates would have been denounced as a racist. The media would have made the gift front page news pillorying him in bold headlines. This reverse discrimination will lead the public to assume that blacks can't make it on there own and will eat away at their ego until even they won't like themselves, and in the end hurt them more than help.

The liberal media that dominate the TV and is common in the press would like you to believe all the spin they put out. They promote an image of America constantly bending over backwards to please an exploding nonwhite population so they can garner more votes for the liberal politicians. They feel that they must tell you what a person just said in a press conference or interview and put their spin on it because you are not smart enough to understand. They treat us like sheep that must be led to a liberal conclusion constantly avoiding the conservative side and as "the" authority on what we should do and how we should think.

"Dateline July, 16th 1999 John Kennedy Jr. dies in airplane accident" John Kennedy Jr. was responsible for the death of two innocent women by his reckless behavior and the following week the liberal media tried to make it look like he was a fallen hero because he was a Kennedy. (That is nothing new, his Uncle, Teddy Kennedy was responsible for the death of Mary Joe Kopechne a few years earlier with no consequences and there are still some who question the death of Marilyn Monroe when she was involved with President John Kennedy). The TV coverage was overwhelming; and it was impossible to find any other news on TV for over a week. It was obviously pilot error and lack of experience that caused the accident. If that had been you or me it would have been on the back page of the local paper. This happened because it was a Kennedy, and because the media and the liberal administration want to portray all Kennedy's as gods. The administration ordered an extraordinary search by the U.S. Coast Guard, the National Oceanic and Atmospheric Administration as well as the Navy and the Air Force. Experts estimate that the cost of the search /rescue and recovery will be at least one million dollars. What about the burial at sea supported by a U. S. Naval warship? A retired Navy LCDR in Annapolis felt that the President committed an affront of the worst order in honoring a civilian who had never served in the armed forces with a burial at sea supported by a U.S. Naval warship. A decorated Navy veteran, who was a combat flyer with rows of medals, also called upon the president to apologize to the millions of veterans and armed service members who were insulted by this special treatment at their expense

Contrast that with the Michigan woman whose sister drowned in a lake at about the same time and whose body had still not been recovered at the time this was written. She spoke on TV that week wondering how they could find three bodies in an ocean and not find one woman in a lake..

I recall in the later days of Skystream when Paul Meyers was an examiner and was giving a flight test to a student for his private pilot's license. Paul had asked him to do a simple weight and balance problem. Paul came in looked over his shoulder and said, "That's right, you've got it but, what is such and such multiplication problem?" The student said, "I don't know. I can't figure it out without my computer." Paul asked how he got past the written test in South Bend at the FAA office.

The student replied, "Well, they let me use my computer." Paul really didn't believe him and called the FAA and sure enough they had let him use the computer. Paul was told that he would have to let the student use the computer to do the weight and balance prior to his flight. If his batteries go dead, this man will probably kill himself because he no longer has basic knowledge.

We now have cash registers in fast food restaurants that have symbols on the cash register keys. A symbol for a hamburger, for French fries, and Coke or Orange. The people at the register only have to push a symbol to get the price on the screen. If the price happens to come up $2.38, and you hand them a five-dollar bill and they enter it in their cash register and you say, "Just a moment, here's the three cents." This completely throws them because they can't figure out what the change would be since the machine does that for them also. We are developing a generation of people who no longer think and can no longer work these problems out in their head. This is called the "Dumbing down of America" They must have a machine to tell them what to do.

The dumbing down of America seams to go hand in hand with sloppy dressing. When I was a child we dressed for church each Sunday like we were going to see the "Most Important Person" in the world. Mother had a dress and hat and I had a suit coat and a tie and the other people in church dressed the same way. If you look today you will see every conceivable kind of get-up including shorts on men and T-shirts on women. In 1972 the Supreme Court of the United States came down with their verdict that schools could not enforce dress codes. "You can't tell kids what to wear." the judges said in all their mighty wisdom. "It's unconstitutional." The bars at that time were lowered on manners and morals. Those kids are now the parents of the young people of today that are in high school.

An article by Ida Chipman in the Plymouth Pilot said, "What about the Jr. High. The word is out that oral sex is hot at Lincoln Jr. High." They call it getting connected. I have no way to find out if this sex act is occurring on the school grounds or not. I don't even know if it is true, although I've been assured that it is. My information came from two psychotherapists and another knowledgeable person. Pretty good sources, don't you think? An Indiana State Police Officer said, "It's all over the country."

We have a president who indulges in oral sex in the Oval Office even when he is on the phone with other high officials supposedly taking care of the affairs of state. We have a president who is a draft dodger. We have a president who is not a bit bashful about lying to the American public. We have a president who is not ashamed about perjuring himself and not sorry about the "Monica affair" and the cost to this country and to our standing in the world. He is not a bit sorry for having attacked many women over his life span. As long as we have a president committing such acts, why would anyone feel bad about the complete demise of morality in schools and in the United States of America? Just think if his wife can't trust him why should we?

Betty's sister, Gloria Nelson, use to teach in the schools in California. She said that you have to be extremely careful what you even say to a student. If you said something that was too harsh the parents would show up and threaten to sue you or worse. What has this country descended to?

Last year marked the twenty third-year that we have given the Palbykin Award at the Plymouth High School and at the Junior High School. This is an industrial arts award and is given to the student that exhibits exceptional ability in the technical field. All children will not become doctors, bankers, and business people. Some of them will build our houses, some will install our heating and air-conditioning, and some will fix our plumbing. These are important people in our society. We should see them for what they are every bit as necessary as the college graduates and in many cases more so. I recall the joke about the plumber that was called to fix the toilet. After fixing it he presented his bill. The man was shocked by the cost of the repair. He said I am a doctor and even I don't charge that much. The plumber said, "Yes I know I used to be a doctor."

The right of law-biding citizens to purchase and own guns is even being threatened. Regardless of the fact that the second amendment says that this is the law. We are loosing freedoms each day to power hungry politicians and to money hungry shyster lawyers, who work together to take our money and our rights. We have people who are trying to equate the gun with the actions of irresponsible children who were not properly trained by the generation ahead of us many of whom have no morals and don't know the difference between right and wrong. Guns don't kill; people who use guns kill and they should be effectively disposed of by our judicial system. They often just get a slap on the wrist. Using this logic we should ban automobiles since many more people are killed by cars than guns. When the courts start making people responsible for their actions, they won't get in trouble as much. It's that simple. If they are taught the difference between right and wrong as a child, they will be less likely to take the easy way out and do whatever they feel like at the moment and therefore get in trouble.

Please don't take the easy way out; teach your children right from wrong and the advantages of doing things properly. The hard way is often the easy way in the long run. If children are taught that there are consequences to their actions they are far less likely to get in trouble. Be sure and pat them on the back when they do well, and tell them how pleased you are with them.

Many times people ask me "How are you" and I always say "I'm not as good as I once was but I'm as good once as I ever was." I guess I'm still pretty good until about 11:00 p.m. but I don't care to go out on the town like I used to. I certainly don't want to fly all night like I did in times gone by. Friends come to visit and we ask if they want a drink and many times they decline. It's not like the parties we had at 2111 or at the penthouse years ago but it is a time for reflection. In looking back I have been extremely lucky to have almost always worked with good and talented people. I have for the most part worked at jobs that I enjoyed. We have been blessed with many good and long term friends. I have a very limited education except the school of the real world and yet we have been able to have a very productive life. We realized many years ago that our children were the only treasures of real value we would leave in this world. We have had very little money at times in our life and have at times had more than we knew how to enjoy. Later we finally realized that money was only paper and we started to gift some of it to worthy causes, pass it on to our children, and to live a less ostentatious life. Betty and I were just as happy with our life in the garage house on Ferndale as we have been in the penthouse.

People always tell me how lucky I am in my business dealings. Most luck is made by stepping up to the table and risking your money. The time to make your good luck is to purchase a quality item or property at the right price. Many times I wait until a deal or a property matures. If you buy a quality property at the right price you will win in the long run. Selling anything is a matter of taking the right approach to maximize the gain. This will mean proper advertising of one type or the other to bring the item or property to the buyer's attention. There are people who "want to sell" and others that "will sell" and some who "must sell." We always try to buy from those who "want to sell" or "must sell." We have always been the "will sell" owners therefore we will wait for the right buyer not rush to take the first offer.

I have been an extremely fortunate person in my life. I have a wonderful wife; Betty and we have been married for almost fifty-two years at the writing of this book. I have been lucky enough to have seven great children, all of whom I am extremely proud. The family has enjoyed remarkable health. We have managed to maintain good relations with our children and to help them if and when they will accept it. We feel that we have imparted good common sense to them and we are happy with the way their lives have turned out. It has not always been easy but we have usually been pleased with the course of action we have taken. We were not always right but we tried to do the best we could and to correct our mistakes if at all possible. If I die tomorrow I can truthfully say I have had a "wonderful life" and there is not much I would change if I had it to live over again.

Genealogy

For those of you who want to know more about where we came from I have enclosed abbreviated versions of our family trees and some of the more interesting pictures from our past. It's always facinating to me to get a glimpse of people and how they lived in years gone by. With today's technology and the advanced standard of living that we enjoy it's hard to understand how people survived even a hundred years ago, much less several hundred ago.

Betty's genealogy would fill another book and I am trying to talk her into writing one. It would be more interesting than "Palbykin" and would give a real look at her ancestors over the hundred's of years of their existence. Betty has however documented some of her more celebrated relatives and you can only imagine what could be related in the many stories about their lives. I have also left a page in the back for notes.

William S. & Elizabeth Perry Family

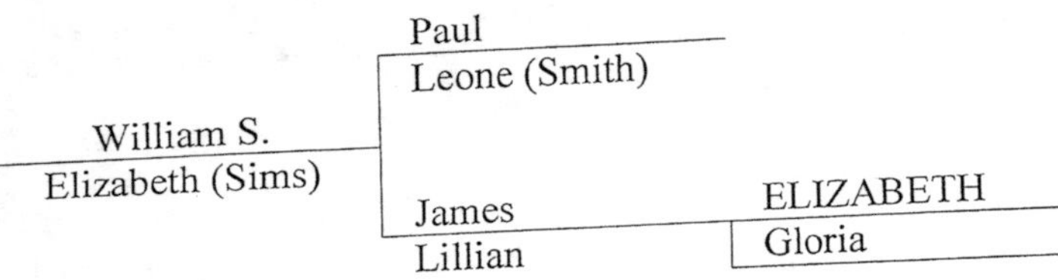

William S. and Elizabeth Perry

George & Jennie Kertson Family

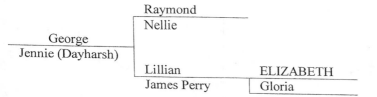

George
Jennie (Dayharsh)

- Raymond
  Nellie
- Lillian
  James Perry
  - ELIZABETH
    Gloria

Jennie Kertson

John V. & Anna Keiper Family

- John V. / Anna C. (Donnelly)
  - Martha / John O'Neill
    - Ruth
  - Agnes / Herbert Bock
    - Herbert
    - Robert
    - Thomas
  - Cecilia / Albert Palbykin
    - DONALD
  - Mildred / James Fox
    - David
    - Ronald

John V. and Anna Keiper

Simon & Elizabeth Palabykian Family

- Simon
  Elizabeth (Kirikonan)
  - Francois (Pope)
    Antoinette
    - Frank Jr.
    - Robert
  - Robert
  - Albert (Palbykin)
    Cecilia
    - DONALD
  - Lucie
    Arther Albright
    - Arther Jr.
    - Madelaine
  - Antoinette
  - Leon (Paul)
    Edna
    - Susan
    - Judith
  - Madelaine (Pal)
  - Annette (Pal)

Simon and Elizabeth Palabykian

Donald J. & Elizabeth Palbykin Family

- Donald / Elizabeth (Perry)
  - Stephen / Kristine
    - Lindsay
    - Brittany
    - Danielle
  - Alan / Donna
    - Amy / Ken Rose
      - Kody
      - Kyle
      - Wade
    - Shanda / Shannon Stevens
      - Madis[illegible]
    - Mark
  - Martin / Mary
    - Mary Lamb
  - Julie / Jim Hicks
    - L. Perry
    - Alexander
  - Debra
  - Susan / Rick Tarsitano
    - Jena
    - Camille
  - Ann Marie / Michael Dickey
    - Lauren
    - Logan

Donald J. and Elizabeth M. Palbykin
50 th Wedding Anniversary

For those of you interested in our genealogy,
My paternal Grandmother Elizabeth Sims Perry
can trace her lineage in this manner:

On her Mother's side she was the Granddaughter of Samuel Strong, who was the son of Mina Chandler Kimball who was the daughter of Lt. Moses Kimball, son of Ebenezer Kimball, son of Benjamin Kimball, the son of Ursula Scott, the founder of our line in America.

Through Ursula we can trace our ancestors to six
Barons of Runnemede and then to the
"Charlemagne Pedigree" 747-814
and then to Alfred the Great
see the pages 9, 12, 13
from the Kimball book
that follows:

Elizabeth M. Palbykin

LT. MOSES. AND JEMIMA (CLEMENT) KIMBALL

LT. MOSES KIMBALL5 (Richard1, Benjamin2, Ebenezers3, Abner4) was a direct descendant of Richard and Ursula (Scott) Kimball who came to America in the "Elizabeth" 1634. Ursula Scott's descent from Charlemagne, from Hugh the Great, leader of the first 'Crusade and from the six Barons of Runnemede will be found in the next section of the book. These charts were made from the data compiled by James Morton.

MILITARY RECORD. When Moses Kimball was commissioned Lieutenant is not a matter of record. He was probably commissioned after the Revolution. He was known as Lt. Kimball for his tombstone in the cemetery at Warrenton, O. reads "To the memory of Lt. Moses Kimball, a soldier in the Revolution. Died November 9, 1828 in the 82nd year of his age."

Moses is credited with having served in the Battle of Lexington, April 19, 1775 Ref. Vet. Ad. Washington, D.C. Four days after this battle, he was back in New Hampshire where he signed up in Capt. Baldwin's 'Co., Col. Stark's Regt. as a Sergeant. This Co. fought at Bunker Hill where Moses "received a wound in the thumb of his left hand." Jemima's pension papers contain this information: "During the battle of Bunker Hill, Capt. Baldwin was killed and died in my husband's arms". Further on she says "Moses became crippled with rheumatism and was not able to go about his farm the last 19 years of his life." Moses' name appears on the roll of the "Capt. Henry Dearborn's 'Co., 'Col. Arnold's detachment"; "on the pay roll of the Co. that marched from 'Cambridge to Quebec 1775; "on the roll of the men from Hopkinton to join the northern continental army at Saratoga, John Hale's 'Co. Ref. N. H. State papers, Revolution Vol I, p. 50, 185, 216; Vol. II, p. 408.

Moses Kimball never applied for a pension but his wife, Jemima was "allowed a pension on her application executed Oct. 4, 1838 at which time she was living in Warren twp, Jefferson 'Co. O'. and was 85 years old."

LIFE OF-- Moses Kimball was born in Haverhill, Mass., Nov. 8, 1747, the son of Abner and Dinah (Barnard) Kimball. Not very much is known of his early years. He was left an orphan when five years old; his grandfather, Ebenezer Kimball died young; his mother, Dinah probably had a difficult time rearing 10 children. Very early, we find Moses in N. Hopkinton, N. H. where he met and married Jemima Clement, a second cousin once removed on Oct. 16, 1771, Rev. James Scales officiating at the ceremony. All of the ten children except Charles, the youngest, was born in N. Hopkinton. Rev. Charles Marcus Kimball says that his father, Charles, was born at Portsmouth, N. H.

Hopkinton, N. H. is a small hilly town interposed with small valleys and well watered. There are two ponds west of town. From one of these, a branch of the Concord River springs. Another pond gives forth a branch of the Providence River and a branch of the Charles River also comes from this vicinity. The mineral spring containing carbonic acid; carbonate of lime and iron is much visited. The town was purchased of the natives by Mr. Leverett, president of Harvard College to perpetuate a legacy left the College by Edward Hopkins. The town was named in his honor. For several years, the College leased their ground to the early settlers.

THE ROYAL 'CONNECTIONS OF URSULA. (SCOTT) KIMBALL.

"'CHARLEMAGNE PEDIGREE" OF URSULA SCOTT KIMBALL

Charles Martel (6887741), m Rotrude (d. 724);
Pepin the Short (714-768), m Bertrada, dau of Charibert, Count of Laon;
Charlemagne, Emperor of Franks and Romans (Apr 2, 747--Jan 28, 814) m. about 771 Hildegarde of Saubia (755--Apt. 30, 783);
Louis I, le Debonnaire, King of France and Roman Emperor (778~June 20, 840), .m. about 798 Judith of Bavaria;
Louis I 'Germanicus, King of Germany (806-878) m Emma, dau Count of Bavaria;
Charles II, the Bald (823-878) m (second wife) Richildis;
Princess Judith, m. Baldwin I, Bras .de Fer, Count of Flanders;
Baldwin II, the Bald (d 918) m. 889 Elfrida, dau of Alfred the Great, King of England;
Arnolph I Magnus, m. Alisa, dau of Herbert I, ·Count of Vermandois;
Baldwin III, Count of Handers (d. 982), m. Matilda, dau of Herman Billing, Duke of Saxony;
Arnolph II, Count of Flanders (d. 988), m. Susanna, dau. of Berengarius II, King of Italy;
Baldwin IV, Barbatus, 'Count of Valenciennes, m. Eleanora, dau of Richard III the good, Duke of Normandy; .
Baldwin V, the Pious, 7th 'Count of Flanders (d. 1017), m. Princess Adela, dau of Robert II, the Pious, King of France;
Lady Matilda, m. William the Conqueror, Duke of Normandy, King of England (d. 1085);
Henry I, Beauderc, King of England (1068-1135), m. Princess Matilda of Scotland, dau of Malcolm III, 'Canmore, King of Scotland;
Matilda (or Maud) (1104-1167), m. (second husband) 'Geoffrey Plantagenet Count of Anjou;
Henry II, King of England 1133-1189, m. Eleanor of Aquitaine (d. 1202);
John, King of England_(1160-1216), m. (second wife) Isabel, dau of Aymer de Taillefer, Count of Angoulesme;
Henry III, King of England (1206-1272), m. Eleanor, dau. of Raymond Berenger, Count of Provence;
Edward I, King of England (1239-1307), m. Princess Eleanor, dau of Ferdinand III, King of 'Castile;
Princess Joan plantagenet, m. Gilbert de 'Clare, 9th Earl of Clare;
Allanore de Clare,_m. Hugh le Despencer .(d. 1326);
Isabelle le .Despencer, m. Richard Fitz-Alan, Earl of Arundel (d. Jan 24, 1375);
Philippa Fitz-Alan m Sir Richard Sergeaux, Knt (d Sept 30, 1393);
Philippa Sergeaux (b. 1381), m. Robert Pashley;
John Pashley, m. Lowys Gower;
Elizabeth Pashley, m. Reginald Pympe;
Anne Pympe, m. Sir John Scott;
Sir Reginald Scott (1538-1599) m (second wife), Mary Tuke;
Henry Scott d 1624, m. Martha Whatlock;
Ursula Scott,_m. Richard Kimball, founder of Kimball line in America;

URSULA SCOTT

Ref. Lineage Book, Barons of Runnemede p 318

Ursula Scott was the dau of Henry Scott of Rattlesden, County, Sussex, England, who died there Dec 24, 1624. She married Richard Kimball, probably born at Lawford, England circa 1590 and died June 22, 1676, at Ipswich, Mass. He was of the Parish of Rattlesden, .County Sussex, at the time he left for the New World, with his wife, six children and a servant, John Laverick. They embarked at Ipswich, County of Suffolk, England, April 10, 1634, in the ship "Elizabeth", William Andrews, Master and arrived in Boston Harbor. They later removed to Watertown, Mass to make their home. He was made a freeman, May 6, 1635, and a Proprietor, 1636/7. The family made another move to Ipswich. After the death of Ursula, Richard Kimball married, Oct 23, 1661 the widow of Henry Dow of Hampton, N. Hampshire

Surety Barons (1) Hugh Bigod (2) Roger Bigod (3) Gilbert de Clare (4) Richard de Clare (5) John de Lacie (6) Saire de Quincey

Hugh *Bigod,* Earl of Norfolk and Suffolk, was the eldest son of Roger Bigod, Earl of Norfolk and Isabel, dau of Hamelyn Plantagenet, Earl of Surrey. He succeeded to his father's estates, but enjoyed them for a short time only, for he died 1224. He m. Maud, dau of William le Mareschall, Earl of Pembroke, Protector of England.

Saire de Quincey, Lord of Groby, son of Robert de Quincey was created Earl of Winchester by King John in the 8th year of his reign. He was one of the Barons to whom the ,City and Tower of London were resigned. He went to the Holy Lands and assisted at the seige of Damietta. He married Margaret, dau of Robert Blanchmains de Beaumont and Petronell de Grentemaisnil. He died 1219

Gilbert de Clare, Earl of Gloucester and Herrford, was the son of Richard de Clare, by Amicia, dau and at length sole heir of William, Earl of Gloucester. He married Isabel le Mareschal, dau of William, Earl of Pembroke, Protector of England. He died 1229 and was buried in the .Choir of Tewkesbury Abbey.

John de Lacie, Constable of .Chester and Lord of Halton Castle, was the son of Roger de Lacie and Alice de Mandeville. In 1217, he paid an immense sum for livery of his lands. It was for his good services at the seige of Damietta that he was rewarded by a second marriage with Margaret de Quincey through whom he received the Earldom of Lincoln. He died 1240

Martha Jane Monaghan m. Patrick Donnelly b. 1836 Manchester England Mother of 10 children including Anna Donnelly Keiper, my Grandmother.

DONNELLY FAMILY
Girls: left to right Polly Ropp, Martha Butler, Anna Keiper, Lucy Walters, Etta Beck.
Boys left to right: Will, Jim, Alf, Frank, Ralph.

John and Anna Keiper Wedding Feb 19, 1895

Notes